NATIVE PLANTS
FOR SOUTHWESTERN LANDSCAPES

# Native Plants for
# Southwestern Landscapes

BY JUDY MIELKE  UNIVERSITY OF TEXAS PRESS
AUSTIN

Copyright © 1993
by the University of Texas Press
All rights reserved

Printed in Hong Kong
Fifth paperback printing, 2002

Requests for permission to reproduce
material from this work should be sent to
Permissions, University of Texas Press,
Box 7819, Austin, TX 78713-7819.

⊗ The paper used in this publication meets
the minimum requirements of American
National Standard for Information
Sciences—Permanence of Paper for Printed
Library Materials, ANSI Z39.48-1984.

LIBRARY OF CONGRESS
CATALOGING-IN-PUBLICATION DATA

Mielke, Judy, 1959–
    Native plants for southwestern
landscapes / Judy Mielke. — 1st ed.
        p.      cm.
    Includes bibliographical references and index.
    ISBN 0-292-75553-8 (alk. paper)
    ISBN 0-292-75147-8 (pbk.)
    1. Desert plants—Southwest, New. 2. Native
    plants for cultivation—Southwest, New.
    3. Desert gardening—Southwest, New.
    4. Native plant gardenting—Southwest, New.
    5. Landscape gardening—Southwest, New.
    I. Title.
    SB427.5.M53      1993
    635.9'51'0979—dc20          93-12092

All photographs are by Judy Mielke except
where indicated with initials at bottom of
photograph or beside caption.

WDB   W. D. Bransford
RG    Ron Gass
CM    Charles Mann
SP    Steve Priebe
BS    Benny Simpson

# Contents

TO MY PARENTS,
CARL AND DOROTHY MIELKE

**Acknowledgments** A number of people played an important role in the development of this book. Steve Priebe's horticultural knowledge and finesse in editing made the text much more understandable. The keen proofreading of Bill Ehrler caught many an error I would have overlooked. Jane Cole, librarian at the Desert Botanical Garden, was most helpful in tracking down information.

I am indebted to many botanists, horticulturists, and other landscape professionals throughout the Southwest for sharing with me their vast knowledge of native plants. Thank you to Bill Bourbon, Laura Bowden, Wally Camp, Mark Dimmitt, Ron Gass, Wendy Hodgson, John Hogan, Dan James, Matt Johnson, Joe McAuliffe, Sarah McCombs, Bill Murphy, Kent Newland, Donald Pinkava, Greg Starr, Jon Stewart, Jimmy Tipton, Tom Wilson, and Allan Zimmerman.

Rita Jo Anthony, W. D. Bransford, Norman G. Flaigg, Ron Gass, Charles Mann, the National Wildflower Research Center, Steve Priebe, and Benny Simpson generously provided photographs.

I owe a special thank you to Art Pizzo. In addition to using his artistic ability in creating the sketches, he helped me in so many other ways—making trips to photograph plants, doing research, and reviewing the text—but perhaps most important, always being there with encouragement and support.

## Introduction

Native plants have gained in popularity over the past decade, but the amount of information available about growing them hasn't kept pace. This book will help close the gap. It is written in a style easily understood by beginning gardeners, yet it contains enough information to satisfy the needs of landscape professionals, including landscape architects, installation contractors, and maintenance personnel.

The first chapter will introduce you to the world of native desert plants. It describes the Mojave, Sonoran, and Chihuahuan deserts, which cover much of the Southwestern United States and Northern Mexico. Emphasis is placed on the plant life, climate, and topographic characteristics of these three deserts. A weather chart presents a detailed picture of the averages and extremes for cities throughout the desert region.

In the chapter on growing native plants, you will learn not only such basics as how large to dig the planting hole and how to get rid of weeds, but also more complicated matters such as developing an irrigation schedule. Sketches of planting, tree staking, and pruning technique accompany the text.

Everything you need to know about growing beautiful wildflowers is explained simply in Chapter 3. For those who have an area scarred by construction that they'd like to bring back to its original appearance, the chapter on revegetation will be enlightening.

Descriptions of 280 trees, shrubs, vines, grasses, groundcovers, herbaceous perennials, cacti, and other succulents make up the balance of this book. In addition to information on each plant's foliage, flowers, fruits, and mature size, you can learn where the plant comes from—geographic origin, elevation, and specific habitat type. Details of a plant's origin, supplemented by the cultural information given for each species, can give you some clues about how to grow it. Irrigation, soil, light, temperature, and pruning requirements are included in the culture sections.

The challenge of putting plants together into a pleasing design is made a little easier by the suggestions for landscape use. Aesthetics are considered, as are functional needs such as visual screening and erosion control. Many of the native plants described have value for attracting wildlife, another aspect of landscape design.

Finding a plant for a specific use such as shade or fragrance is a simple task with the lists provided in the first appendix. Because there's no substitute for observing plants "in real life," the second appendix provides a list of gardens that have native plants on display.

Whatever your level of knowledge—whether you're a landscape professional or someone who can't tell a cactus from a Creosote Bush—*Native Plants for Southwestern Landscapes* can be a valuable tool. You'll want to read the first few chapters to gain a general understanding of growing native plants, then refer to the individual plant descriptions as necessary while you explore further the fascinating world of native desert plants.

NATIVE PLANTS
FOR SOUTHWESTERN LANDSCAPES

# 1.
## *Why Natives?*

The Southwestern deserts contain some of the most unique natural landscapes in the world. Rugged mountain ranges, gentle plains, and sandy arroyos support a great diversity of plants, from the gnarled Ironwood tree to the delicate Mexican Gold-poppy. The vegetation may be complex, with an intermingling of trees, shrubs, cacti, other succulents, and groundcovers, or a more simple composition of two to three dominant plant species. Sometimes the plainest landscape becomes breathtakingly beautiful, such as when abundant rainfall coupled with mild temperatures coax forth a tapestry of wildflowers.

You can look to the desert for inspiration and incorporate some of that natural beauty into your own planned landscape. Plants native to the Southwestern deserts can fulfill both aesthetic and functional needs in exchange for very little attention. These plants have adapted to the desert's harsh conditions over thousands of years, so they're used to the temperature extremes, intense sunlight, low humidity, drying winds, and poor soils.

An important benefit of incorporating native plants into planned landscapes is that of replacing some of the natural vegetation that was displaced by development. While it is not possible to replicate nature, you can restore a small part of the desert ecosystem. Wildlife will be attracted to a landscape with native plants, which can provide shelter, nesting material, and food.

Nowhere else in this country can planned landscapes so reflect the natural beauty of the desert. Southwestern gardeners have a unique opportunity to develop a landscape with regional character by choosing from the wonderful variety of native plants.

DESERT PROFILES

The three warm deserts that cover much of the Southwestern United States and Northern Mexico are the Mojave, Sonoran, and Chihuahuan. Although they share the characteristics of low rainfall, high temperatures, and in some cases common plant species, each desert has a distinct character.

## MOJAVE DESERT

The Mojave Desert is dominated by low, widely spaced shrubs. Creosote Bush (*Larrea tridentata*) and White Bursage (*Ambrosia dumosa*) are two of the most common species. The cacti are mostly low-growing Prickly-pear and Cholla (*Opuntia* species). Short-lived annual wildflowers brighten the Mojave Desert in late March, April, and May, when prompted by winter rains. Trees are limited, although the distinctive Joshua Tree (*Yucca brevifolia*) occurs in the higher elevations, and its distribution essentially delineates the boundaries of this desert. Much of the Mojave Desert lies in southern California, with smaller portions in southern Nevada, southwestern Utah, and northwestern Arizona.

The Mojave Desert receives most of its rainfall as gentle showers in the winter, between November and March. The moisture comes from the Pacific Ocean and decreases across the desert from west to east. Occasional summer thunderstorms occur in the eastern portion. Cold winters are the norm for this desert, although it also holds the record high temperature for North America: 134° F in Death Valley. Sections of the Mojave Desert lie below sea level, while the highest elevations are around 5,000 feet. About three-fourths of the desert lies between 2,000 and 4,000 feet in elevation.

SONORAN DESERT

The most noticeable feature of the Sonoran Desert is its variety of plant forms: large cacti such as Saguaro, many types of smaller cacti, leaf succulents, trees, shrubs, herbaceous perennials, and annual wildflowers. There are also many different species of plants. This diversity of life forms and species can be credited to the Sonoran's mild winters (some areas never experience freezing temperatures) and the moisture received throughout two rainy seasons. Gentle, widespread winter rains come from the Pacific Ocean, while summer thunderstorms that originate in the Gulfs of Mexico and California can dump large amounts of rain in a short period of time, but are often very localized.

The Sonoran Desert is shaped somewhat like a horseshoe that wraps around the Gulf of California. More than two-thirds of its total area lies in Mexico, on the Baja California peninsula, and in the mainland state of Sonora. In the United States, this desert occupies extreme southeastern California and southwestern and south-central Arizona. Elevations in the Sonoran Desert range from below sea level to 3,450 feet, with the majority of the region lying below 2,000 feet.

## CHIHUAHUAN DESERT

The Chihuahuan Desert occurs primarily in the Mexican states of Chihuahua and Coahuila, with smaller portions in Durango, Zacatecas, Nuevo León, and Sonora. Western Texas and southern New Mexico contain significant areas of Chihuahuan Desert vegetation. The Chihuahuan Desert enters extreme southeastern Arizona in three relatively small sections. Some areas in this desert exceed 6,500 feet in elevation, while the lowest portion is along the Rio Grande, at 1,000 feet. Much of the desert lies between 3,500 and 4,200 feet in elevation.

Shrubs are the dominant plant form in the Chihuahuan Desert. Trees are mostly confined to waterways or rocky hills. Leaf succulents, most notably Lechuguilla (*Agave lechuguilla*), are common, and a variety of small cacti also occur. The Chihuahuan Desert is characterized by hot summers and cold winters, with periods of up to seventy-two hours below freezing. Summer precipitation originating in the Gulf of Mexico accounts for 70–80 percent of the annual rainfall.

## Table 1: Weather of Desert Cities

### CHIHUAHUAN DESERT

Alamogordo, NM
Carlsbad, NM
Clifton, AZ
Deming, NM
Douglas, AZ

El Paso, TX
Las Cruces, NM
Lordsburg, NM
Pecos, TX
Socorro, NM

Truth or Consequences, NM
Van Horn, TX

### MOJAVE DESERT

Barstow, CA
Beatty, NV
Caliente, NV
Death Valley, CA
Kingman, AZ

Las Vegas, NV
Palmdale, CA
St. George, UT
Twentynine Palms, CA

### SONORAN DESERT

Ajo, AZ
Blythe, CA
Casa Grande, AZ
El Centro, CA
Imperial, CA

Needles, CA
Palm Springs, CA
Parker, AZ
Phoenix, AZ
Tucson, AZ

Wickenburg, AZ
Yuma, AZ

| Elevation (Feet) | Avg. Yearly Rainfall (Inches) | Mean of Daily Max. Temp.—July (Degrees F) | Mean of Daily Min. Temp.—Jan. (Degrees F) | Record High (Degrees F) | Record Low (Degrees F) |
|---|---|---|---|---|---|
| 4,350 | 10.62 | 95.3 | 27.5 | 110 | − 14 |
| 3,232 | 11.94 | 95.6 | 29.2 | 111 | − 18 |
| 3,460 | 12.26 | 101.2 | 31.0 | 113 | 4 |
| 4,331 | 8.6 | 94.9 | 25.7 | 109 | − 12 |
| 4,098 | 12.16 | 92.8 | 28.9 | 107 | 9 |
| 3,918 | 8.5 | 94.6 | 30.2 | 111 | − 8 |
| 3,881 | 8.57 | 93.8 | 25.7 | 109 | − 10 |
| 4,250 | 10.52 | 96.8 | 25.7 | 110 | − 14 |
| 2,610 | 9.57 | 99.7 | 27.4 | 118 | − 9 |
| 4,585 | 8.87 | 93.6 | 22.3 | 107 | − 14 |
| 4,820 | 8.51 | 92.4 | 26.9 | 105 | − 5 |
| 4,030 | 10.23 | 94.5 | 29.9 | 112 | − 7 |
| 2,162 | 4.14 | 102.6 | 31.7 | 116 | 3 |
| 3,314 | 4.71 | 99.7 | 27.7 | 115 | 7 |
| 4,402 | 8.44 | 95.9 | 17.4 | 109 | − 13 |
| − 152 | 2.17 | 115.6 | 40.1 | 126 | 19 |
| 3,539 | 9.65 | 97.1 | 31.6 | | |
| 2,162 | 4.06 | 103.9 | 32.6 | 116 | 8 |
| 2,596 | 7.38 | 97.7 | 32.2 | 113 | 6 |
| 2,760 | 7.47 | 101.9 | 26.6 | 115 | 1 |
| 1,975 | 3.34 | 105.2 | 34.9 | 118 | 13 |
| 1,763 | 8.62 | 103.2 | 42.0 | 115 | 18 |
| 395 | 3.1 | 108.6 | 40.5 | 122 | 20 |
| 1,405 | 8.58 | 106.4 | 35.8 | 120 | 14 |
| − 37 | 2.81 | 109.2 | 37.8 | 122 | 16 |
| − 64 | 2.07 | 106.4 | 41.1 | 119 | 23 |
| 913 | 3.97 | 108.6 | 40.7 | 122 | 23 |
| 411 | 5.2 | 109.1 | 40.8 | 123 | 22 |
| 425 | 4.08 | 109.1 | 38.4 | 121 | 17 |
| 1,117 | 7.11 | 105 | 39.4 | 122 | 17 |
| 2,444 | 11.35 | 101.3 | 38.2 | 111 | 16 |
| 2,095 | 11.25 | 104.9 | 31.0 | 118 | 12 |
| 194 | 2.65 | 106.8 | 43.2 | 119 | 24 |

# 2.
# *Growing*
# *Native Plants*

Before you can enjoy the rewards of planting and nurturing native plants, you must first acquire them. Sometimes locating a particular plant requires a bit of sleuthing, but native plants on the whole are becoming more and more available. There are even some native plants that have become such an accepted element of planned landscapes that people may not think of them as natives, for example, Texas Ranger (*Leucophyllum frutescens*) and Desert-fern (*Lysiloma microphylla* variety *thornberi*).

Your local nursery is a good place to begin your search for native plants. If you don't find the plant you're looking for, ask someone at the nursery if it can be ordered. Even if the answer is no, you will have helped communicate an interest in native plants. Nurseries are part of the "Catch-22" of native plant availability. If a nursery doesn't perceive a demand for the plants, it won't stock them. Nurseries have to stay profitable, after all, and they can't afford to have inventory that doesn't sell. But when native plants aren't available, landscape architects don't specify them on plans, and home gardeners choose something else at the nursery as a substitute. So speak up at your local nursery and let them know you'll buy native plants when they become available. Meanwhile, continue your search.

A reliable, if not constant, source of native plants is botanical garden and arboretum plant sales. These events may be held only once a year, so be sure not to miss them. You should find a nice variety of plants, including some kinds not available anywhere else. Knowledgeable staff can assist you in making selections and offer advice on cultural requirements. An added benefit of shopping at botanical garden and arboretum plant sales is that you can often see mature specimens of the plants you're thinking of buying.

PLANT SELECTION

Selecting a healthy plant involves some careful inspection. First, look for healthy, undamaged foliage. The plant should be free of pests and diseases. Be sure to check the undersides of leaves. Avoid rootbound plants, which have roots growing above the surface of the soil or growing out of the drainage hole. A general look at the size of the plant in relation to the size of the pot can also reveal whether or not the plant is overdue for repotting. Sometimes the opposite is true; the plant has been recently potted up, and the roots haven't become established in the new container. You don't get your money's worth in this scenario, and you risk damage to the roots if the soil crumbles away when you unpot the plant.

Look for indications that the plant will develop the form you desire. A shrub with many branches when young should develop into a full, attractive plant with age. If you want a single-stemmed plant, look for one with a dominant central branch. Trees should have strong trunks that won't require staking for support.

Although it's tempting to purchase a plant in bloom, you may be trading vigor for beauty. When a plant blooms, it directs its energy toward reproduction, or making seed, so less energy may be available for establishing a good root system. Another temptation may be to buy the biggest plant available. You do get more of an instant landscape that way, but often a younger plant has more vigor and becomes established more quickly. A 1-gallon-size plant can usually catch up to a 5-gallon plant in one or two years. The monetary savings can be considerable, particularly if you're buying a lot of plants. And small holes are easier to dig than big ones!

## PLANTING TIME

The best time for planting most desert native plants is fall, from late September to early December. Cooler temperatures throughout fall and winter allow roots to become established before the plants must endure summer's stress. Gardeners in the coldest desert areas should do most of their planting in the spring, after the danger of severe frost is past. Even in the warmer areas, tender plants such as Elephant Tree (*Bursera microphylla*) should only be planted in the spring. You can plant during the summer, but the heat is hard on new transplants, and you'll have to water more often than during cooler times.

## PLANTING TECHNIQUE

Planting can be hard work, but it can be very satisfying too. Digging an adequate hole is one of the keys to success. A good rule of thumb for determining the size of the plant-

Rootball
Backfill
Undisturbed
Soil

**Planting**

ing hole is that it should be three times as wide and about the same depth as the container. The task will be easier if you moisten the soil a few days before digging. Once the hole is dug, fill it with water. This does two things: creates a moist environment for the new plant and indicates any problems with drainage. If the water hasn't soaked in after an hour or two, bail it out and dig deeper to check for caliche. Solidified calcium carbonate is the technical name for caliche; it looks like buried concrete. Caliche can occur in layers from an inch to several feet thick, and it may be buried well below the soil surface or exposed. Water and roots won't penetrate caliche, so you must break through it before planting. An iron digging bar or a pick is helpful. If the caliche layer is too thick to break through, you can select another planting site or go ahead and plant, realizing that you'll have to be very careful not to over-water and that large plants might be stunted.

Adding organic material such as compost or forest mulch to the backfill soil has long been an accepted practice in planting desert plants, but recent research suggests that this may not be necessary. Only the worst soils or most delicate plants benefit from amending the soil. In such cases, use about 25 percent organic matter by volume.

You may need to return some of the backfill to the hole so the new transplant will be situated at the same level as it was growing in the pot, not planted too deeply or too shallowly. Carefully unpot the plant, untangle any matted roots, position the plant properly in the hole, and add soil around the rootball. Firm the soil gently with your hands or the shovel handle to eliminate any air pockets.

You may need to stake newly planted trees that aren't strong enough to stand on their own. Ideally, you should purchase sturdy plants, but sometimes staking is unavoidable. Another purpose of staking is to anchor the rootball

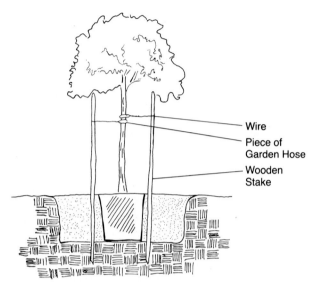

Wire
Piece of
Garden Hose
Wooden
Stake

**Staking**

to keep the plant from swaying too much, which could cause breakage of newly forming roots. Set two stakes firmly in the ground, about a foot on either side of the tree, or further away if necessary to avoid driving the stakes through the rootball. Remove any stakes used by the nursery. Loops of wire (either plastic-coated or seven-strand twisted) attached to the stakes can be used to support the trunk. A short section of garden hose slipped over each wire will cushion the trunk. Allow the trunk a little room for movement back and forth. You should check the ties occasionally to be sure they're not binding the plant. As soon as the tree can support itself, remove the staking.

An essential step in the planting process is to water the new transplant. You can make a basin around the plant with extra backfill soil and fill it with water, or you can simply lay a hose near the base of the plant, turn the water on to a trickle, and leave it for several hours. The entire rootball needs to be moistened.

*Planting Cacti*

A somewhat different planting technique is used for cacti. A week or two before planting, unpot the cactus and gently remove the soil from the roots. Lay the plant in a dry, shaded location so any damaged roots can callus over. After digging a hole slightly larger than the rootball, examine the soil. A heavy soil should be amended by mixing one part sand with two parts backfill. Coarse-textured soils won't require amendment. Put enough backfill in the hole so the cactus will be planted at the level at which it was growing previously. Small cacti can be handled using sturdy tongs and gloves. Don't pick up Prickly-pear or Cholla plants (*Opuntia* species) with gloves, however, because the tiny glochids (hairlike spines) and larger barbed spines will make the gloves useless for future wear. Larger cacti may require more than one person to help with planting. A piece of old garden hose makes an ideal sling that can be used to carry and position the cactus in the planting hole. Rather than watering after planting, wait about two weeks, then provide a deep soaking.

IRRIGATION

Some people think that native plants don't need irrigation. Once the plants are established, many can survive on rainfall alone, but the key words are *established* and *survive*. Like any new transplants fresh from being pampered in the nursery, native plants will require supplemental irrigation, at least through their first summer. After that, they probably can survive without irrigation, but in a landscape situation some extra water through the summer months will keep them looking better, with lusher foliage and more flowers.

Many variables influence a plant's need for irrigation, including the age of the plant, type of plant (tree, shrub, cactus, etc.), soil type, time of year, and whether the plant is growing in shade or sun.

There is no set formula for irrigation frequency, but to determine amount, a good rule of thumb is *water deeply*. Thorough soakings will encourage the roots to extend into the lower layers of soil, where they are less subject to variations in moisture and to the extremely high summertime temperatures experienced by the surface soil layer.

Shallow, rocky soils require a somewhat different approach to watering. Decrease the amount of water applied with each irrigation by about half, but increase the frequency to nearly twice as often as with other soils.

The following recommendations should be considered as general guidelines. Tailoring a water regime to your specific needs will require some effort on your part. Take note of the soil and how fast it drains, and get to know your plants. Regular observations will be necessary in the beginning.

After a fall planting, a new plant should be watered deeply about once a week; through the winter, irrigation every two to three weeks should be enough. With the onset of warmer temperatures in spring, the frequency of irrigation can be increased to weekly, and when the daytime high temperatures near 100° F, water every three to four days. As fall and cooler weather approach, reduce the irrigation so new, frost-sensitive growth is not encouraged. In the plant's second and third year of establishment, gradually increase the interval between irrigations, but continue to water deeply. Once established, many desert native plants can be grown successfully with some supplemental irrigation through the summer and during prolonged drought in the other seasons. Be sure to reduce your watering schedule when it rains a significant amount: $\frac{1}{2}$ inch or more.

Cacti don't need as much irrigation as other types of plants. You can water them once a month through the first summer of establishment; after that rainfall alone should be sufficient.

Several methods of irrigation are available. The simplest utilizes a garden hose with the water set at a slow trickle and laid near the base of the plant. Each plant should be watered for at least an hour. A long screwdriver or metal rod is helpful for checking the depth of water penetration. Ideally, the wetted zone should extend beyond the rootball to encourage deep root growth. You can create a shallow basin around the plant and fill that with water. A more thorough soaking could be accomplished by filling the basin twice.

If you have a number of plants, drip irrigation might be the most practical method. Plastic tubing and emitters deliver water at a slow rate directly to the root zone of each plant. Normally the tubing is buried a few inches below the surface to conceal it and to prevent deterioration due to the sun. Plants can be placed on different irrigation lines according to their requirements, and the entire system can be run by an automated timer.

## FERTILIZATION

Native desert plants have evolved in soils with very little nitrogen content, so it is not critical to provide fertilizer to the plants in your landscape. If you want to speed the growth rate, nitrogen can be applied to young plants at the beginning of the growing season, and again in mid- to late summer. Keep in mind, though, that the new growth encouraged by fertilizer requires additional moisture to sustain. Never fertilize late in the season, or you risk winter cold damage to the tender new growth that fertilizer helps produce.

## PRUNING

Like fertilizer, pruning is optional for native plants. The ones growing wild in the desert don't get pruned, yet they continue to prosper. There *are* some health-related reasons for pruning, but for the most part aesthetics is the motivation. For example, some plants become straggly with age, and cutting them back severely encourages fuller growth. Dead branches can be removed to improve the plant's appearance; witches'-broom and infestations of mistletoe should be cut out to prevent their spread. (See the description of Blue Palo Verde, *Cercidium floridum*, in Chapter 5 for further information). The scarring that often occurs when tree branches rub against each other can be prevented by selective pruning. Safety concerns may necessitate pruning, as when a tree shading a patio or play area has low-growing branches that people might bump into.

Much of the beauty of native plants lies in their natural form and character. All too often, unnecessary pruning compromises that beauty. The common practice of shaping (torturing) native plants into balls or cubes is not only time-consuming but may reduce the flower display if buds are cut off along with the foliage. And formally pruned plants are inappropriate for most planned landscapes in the Southwest. Certain native plants will accept being pruned into hedges, but aesthetically this practice is appropriate only for a landscape that is designed to complement traditional, formal architecture.

Major pruning of trees should be done from late winter to early spring. Occasional removal of small branches may

**Shearing the plant will encourage
unnaturally dense growth at the ends of branches**

**Cutting back branches to varying lengths
will result in a more natural-looking plant**

be done anytime throughout the year. Extensive summer-time pruning is not recommended because of the potential for sunburn to branches exposed by the removal of foliage. Tree species such as Mesquite (*Prosopis*) that tend to bleed sap from wounds should be pruned in the fall and early winter. Bleeding can be minimized by making only small cuts, less than 3 inches in diameter. Some bleeding is usually not harmful to plants, but heavy bleeding can cause bark damage below the wound and can retard callusing of the wound. Pruning sprays or paints are not necessary in the desert Southwest's warm, dry climate. The wound should be allowed to dry naturally.

All branches to be removed should be cut back to the next major limb. Leave a short stub, which stimulates thickening and strengthening of the trunk. The stubs can be cut off when the trunk is strong enough. In addition to aesthetic reasons, there are health-related reasons to re-

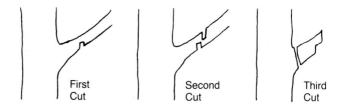

First Cut     Second Cut     Third Cut

**A three-step technique for pruning a large limb**

move pruning stubs. Eventually the tissue in the stubs will die, creating entry points for insect pests or disease. Care should be taken to make a clean cut with no jagged edges, which heal more slowly than clean cuts. Always use sharp tools sterilized with bleach.

Branches smaller than 1 inch in diameter can be cut with hand pruning shears or loppers. Large branches should be cut with a pruning saw, using a three-step method. If just one cut is made, the weight of the branch may cause splitting or tearing before the cut is finished. The first cut should be made on the underside of the branch to be removed, several inches out from the main branch and about halfway through the branch. Make the second cut just beyond the first, all the way through the branch from top to bottom. The third cut is made near the main branch to remove the stub created by the second cut. This final cut should be made outside the collar, the slight swelling at the base of the limb to be removed. The tissue of the collar produces a chemical barrier to the spread of decay organisms. If the final cut is made flush with the main branch, it may cut into the chemical barrier, creating a wound more susceptible to decay. This type of cut also results in a larger wound, which may take longer to heal. Some desert trees such as Palo Verde (*Cercidium* species) lack a branch collar, and pruning wounds heal poorly. It is preferable not to prune major branches of such species.

When pruning shrubs, make the cuts at a fork in the branch rather than at a random place along the branch. Simply "shearing" the shrub will stimulate growth near the outer edge, which looks unnatural and doesn't allow sufficient light to penetrate to the inner foliage. If pruning for size control or to encourage denser growth, cut the branches back to varying lengths. Pruning for a drastic reduction in size should be spread over several months' time to avoid excess shock and to minimize the visual impact.

Some of the plant descriptions in Chapter 5 have specific instructions for pruning.

### COLD PROTECTION

Newly planted or frost-tender plants may require some protection during cold nights. The means of protection can be as simple as a large cardboard box (upended) or an old blanket. The main objective is to keep warm air trapped around the plant rather than letting it escape into the atmosphere. You may want to pound stakes into the ground to keep the weight of the covering from harming the plant. Avoid using plastic tarps for protection; plastic's ability to conduct cold causes any foliage touching the plastic to be damaged.

### PESTS

Native plants generally have few pest problems, and for the most part the pests are seasonal and can be controlled by non-chemical means.

Aphids are tiny, soft-bodied insects that can be green, brown, black, red, or orange. They use piercing-sucking mouthparts to extract a plant's juices, causing stunted and distorted growth. Aphids prefer tender young foliage or flower buds. A forceful spray of water from a garden hose is often effective for controlling these pests, and so is an application of insecticidal soap. The process may need to be repeated several times for effective control.

Cicadas arrive with the summer monsoons. The males are more noticeable, as they make a buzzing sound when trying to attract a mate, but the females actually cause the damage to plants. Female cicadas deposit their eggs under the tender skin of new growth, usually causing the branch tips to die. There is no practical control for cicadas. You can prune the damaged branches for a better appearance.

Other insect pests that affect particular plants are described in the appropriate plant descriptions in Chapter 5.

The four-legged, furry pests may be your biggest problem. If you live near open desert, ground squirrels, rabbits, and even javelinas (peccaries) may discover your plants. A round "cage" made of chicken wire or welded wire mesh can deter jackrabbits and cottontails. A more substantial fence will be necessary to keep javelinas from destroying plants. Ground squirrels are nearly impossible to keep away from new transplants, since they'll crawl through or over or dig under fencing. Fortunately, they do not cause a great deal of damage.

WEED CONTROL

One classic definition of a weed is "an unwanted plant." Another is "a plant out of place." An example of the latter definition would be a volunteer Mesquite tree seedling growing too close to the house. "Weeds" such as these can be transplanted to a more suitable location or potted and given to a friend. The more bothersome weeds are typically annuals, often originally from other parts of the world. They can be effectively controlled with a pre-emergent herbicide, which is sprayed on the ground before the rainy season(s). This type of herbicide prevents weed seedlings from developing but does not affect established plants. You should not use a pre-emergent herbicide in any area where you plan to sow wildflower seed. Weeding by hand or with a tool can be as effective as an herbicide, although it requires more work and probably is not practical for a large-scale landscape.

# 3.
# *Wildflowers*

When the desert erupts with color from the rainbow hues of wildflowers, it's an unforgettable sight. The individual flowers may not be large, but the cumulative effect of thousands—maybe even millions—of them is stunning. It's a good thing that these fickle flowers make such a lasting impression, because some botanists estimate that a really good bloom may occur only once a decade.

Abundant, evenly spaced rainfall is one of the key factors in a good wildflower year. A rain of at least 1 inch is generally required to trigger germination of the seeds. Continued moisture is also critical, or the seedlings will grow very little and may ultimately produce only one flower for each plant or dry up altogether.

Warm-season wildflowers usually won't germinate during the cool season, and the same is true for cool-season species during warm weather. The type of soil in which the wildflower seed germinates affects its growth, primarily due to the soil's water-holding capacity. Clayey or loamy soil retains more moisture than sandy soil. Extreme heat or a severe frost anytime during the wildflower seedling's development can reduce the bloom.

Just as wildflowers in nature require a certain combination of temperature, moisture, and soil conditions to bloom, so do cultivated wildflowers.

## PLANTING SEASON

Your timetable for planting will be determined by the species of wildflower. Generally, spring-blooming wildflowers germinate in the preceding fall, and summer-bloomers germinate in early summer. Because you can provide supplemental irrigation for your wildflowers, you have more leeway in planting time, but in general it's best to follow nature's timetable.

## SITE SELECTION

Most desert wildflowers prefer a sunny, well-drained location. Six to eight hours of sunlight each day will encourage robust plants and an abundance of flowers. Insufficient light usually results in spindly growth and few blossoms. If your site has limited sunlight, you can choose wildflower species that naturally occur in low-light situations, such as under trees or shrubs or in a northern exposure.

SOIL PREPARATION

Wildflowers are often touted as a carefree way to a colorful yard. Sometimes it is implied that you simply toss some wildflower seed on the ground then wait for the flowers to appear. Wildflowers *are* simple to grow; however, some soil preparation is necessary. The seed must find its way into niches within the soil layer, or your future wildflower garden may end up as bird food.

To start, loosen the soil of the planting area to a depth of 3–4 inches. A rotary tiller set to cultivate shallowly will make preparing a large area less work, or a rake can be used to roughen the soil surface. The technique is not as critical as the end result: a loose, crumbly layer of soil. Severely compacted soil (for example, areas that automobiles have driven over) may require more extensive preparation. Use a rotary tiller or other equipment that penetrates to a depth of at least 1 foot. Breaking up the compacted soil not only encourages better root growth but also allows proper drainage. Weed seeds will be brought to the surface by cultivating, so disturb the soil only as much as is necessary to prepare the seedbed. Soils are easier to cultivate when slightly moist. Time your work to follow a rain, or water the area several days prior to cultivation. Soggy soil should not be tilled, as it is very prone to compaction from foot traffic and equipment.

What if your site happens to be rocky? *Some* rocks may be beneficial. A scattering of small rocks helps create niches favorable for wildflower seedling establishment. The rocks not only provide some concealment for seed and seedlings from predators but also act as a mulch, retaining soil moisture. Seedlings that grow among rocks may also benefit from extra warmth absorbed from the sun and reradiated by the rocks at night.

Since native wildflowers are adapted to desert soils that are typically alkaline and low in organic matter, many soils need nothing further than cultivation prior to planting. Particularly barren soils may benefit from incorporation of compost or some other type of organic material. A 2-inch-deep layer of compost worked into the planting area will contribute nutrients as well as improve the water-holding capacity of sandy soil and improve aeration of clayey soil.

Ask wildflower experts about using fertilizer and you'll get answers ranging from "Don't even think about it" to

"Sure—it makes bigger, healthier wildflowers." There's probably a happy medium somewhere. It makes sense to let wildflowers fend for themselves nutritionally, unless they seem stunted. On the other hand, you may be planting wildflowers in an environment different from their natural habitat, so some soil amendment might be in order. Perhaps you want to plant Arroyo Lupine (*Lupinus succulentus*), a species that prefers soils typical of a desert wash: loose, well-drained, and often containing organic matter deposited by occasional flooding. But your site has dense, heavily compacted soil. You could create a better environment for the Arroyo Lupine by incorporating organic matter and coarse sand into the soil. A more practical solution, though, would be to select wildflower species that naturally occur in situations similar to yours.

Another factor in growing wildflowers that may dictate the use of supplemental fertilizer is planting density. In cultivation wildflowers are often planted more densely than they would occur in the wild, and competition for both moisture and nutrients is increased. A general-purpose fertilizer, applied at about half the rate recommended for vegetable or traditional flower gardens, should compensate for the increased competition for nutrients in a densely planted wildflower garden. In any scenario, use fertilizer with restraint. Heavy applications of nitrogen will encourage foliage at the expense of flowers.

GERMINATION PRE-TREATMENT

Some wildflower seeds contain chemical or physical barriers to germination that must be overcome for germination to occur. This reluctance to germinate keeps seeds from sprouting when conditions are not favorable. Chemical inhibitors in the seed coats of certain species must be leached away by substantial rainfall before the seeds will sprout. The seeds won't germinate in response to a light rain that would not provide adequate moisture for survival. Other seeds have a hard seed coat that must be worn away, perhaps by a rough-and-tumble ride down a desert wash swollen by rain. Soaking such seeds in water or wearing away the seed coat with a solution of household bleach and water at a 1:10 ratio can be used to encourage germination. Many wildflowers will germinate readily without any pre-treatment, provided they are planted during the proper growing season. Despite your best attempts to provide the correct pre-germination treatment, the seedlings may refuse to appear. The good news is that a year's exposure to natural processes may prompt germination the following season. Refer to the table at the end of the chapter for information on pre-treatments for specific wildflowers.

## PLANTING

Wildflowers look most natural when the seed is hand broadcast over the planting area. Small seed, or small quantities of seed, can be mixed with sand for increased bulk and easier sowing. Wildflower mixes containing different-sized seeds should be stirred frequently to assure an even distribution of species. To avoid running out of seed before you've covered the entire area, sow it sparingly. You can always go over the area again with the remaining seed. After sowing, rake the area to cover the seed lightly with soil.

## WATERING

Unless you are fortunate enough to plant with a rainstorm approaching, you'll need to water the seedbed. A sprinkler with a fine spray is suitable; you can also use a garden hose with a mist nozzle. The top $\frac{1}{2}$ inch of soil should be thoroughly wetted. Keep the seedbed moist until seedlings appear, after which time the frequency of watering can be decreased as the plants mature. Once established, desert wildflowers can dry out somewhat between waterings without suffering. Thorough yet infrequent irrigation that encourages deep root growth is far better than daily, light waterings.

## PROTECTION AGAINST PREDATORS

Wildflower seed and young seedlings are vulnerable to predation from birds and other animals. Fencing the seeded area will discourage rabbits, though birds are often the most serious threat to your wildflowers. Small areas may be covered with bird netting (the type used on fruit trees or strawberries), but this method is not practical for large areas. You might try various scare tactics to keep the birds away, such as setting out strips of shiny mylar or inflatable snakes, or even placing Tabby on guard, but you'll probably have to resign yourself to some loss of seed and seedlings. Once the seedlings reach a certain stage of maturity (usually 2–3 inches tall, with several sets of leaves), they don't seem as enticing to birds.

## THINNING

In contrast to running short on seed while planting, another common problem is overseeding. Crowded plants will fail to thrive because of competition for moisture, nutrients, light, and space. Thinning may be necessary to achieve a healthy stand of wildflowers. Pulling out seedlings is a trying task for the soft-hearted, but in the long run thinning is beneficial to the remaining wildflowers. One method of thinning involves pulling an iron rake through the too-thick seedlings, uprooting some of them. Hand-thinning is a more time-consuming technique, but it is less disturbing to the seedlings that remain. Thin as soon as the seedlings are large enough to handle, before their root systems become entwined with those of neighboring seedlings. The optimal amount of space to allow each seedling depends on the species. Envision the plant when mature and allow enough room for each seedling to develop fully. The table at the end of this chapter gives the mature size of forty native annual wildflower species.

## SEED COLLECTING

As your wildflowers bloom, enjoy their beauty, but don't forget to continue watering. Adequate moisture will prolong flowering and encourage abundant seed production. Collecting seed to sow again is rewarding and easy to do. Watch the maturing blossoms for seed formation, then gather the seedheads when a majority of the seed is ripe. Waiting until all the seed is mature usually means losing some of the seed which ripened earlier and fell to the ground. A paper grocery bag works well for collecting and drying the seedheads. After the seed has cured for several weeks in a cool, dry place, separate and discard the chaff and store the seed in a sealed container. Annual wildflow-

## Table 2: Annual Wildflowers

| Scientific Name | Common Name | Family |
|---|---|---|
| Abronia villosa | Sand-verbena | Nyctaginaceae |
| Allionia incarnata | Trailing Four O'Clock | Nyctaginaceae |
| Chaenactis stevioides | Esteve's Pincushion | Asteraceae |
| Coreopsis bigelovii | Desert Coreopsis | Asteraceae |
| Dyssodia micropoides | Woolly Dogweed | Asteraceae |
| Erigeron divergens | Spreading Fleabane | Asteraceae |
| Eriophyllum lanosum | Woolly Daisy | Asteraceae |
| Eschscholtzia mexicana | Mexican Gold-poppy | Papaveraceae |
| Geraea canescens | Desert Sunflower | Asteraceae |
| Helianthus annuus | Sunflower | Asteraceae |
| Ipomopsis longiflora | Pale Blue Trumpets | Polemoniaceae |
| Kallstroemia grandiflora | Arizona-poppy | Zygophyllaceae |
| Lasthenia chrysostoma | Goldfields | Asteraceae |
| Layia glandulosa | White Tidy Tips | Asteraceae |
| Layia platyglossa | Tidy Tips | Asteraceae |
| Lesquerella gordonii | Gordon's Bladderpod | Brassicaceae |
| Lupinus arizonicus* | Arizona Lupine | Fabaceae |
| Lupinus havardii* | Big Bend Lupine | Fabaceae |
| Lupinus sparsiflorus* | Desert Lupine | Fabaceae |
| Lupinus succulentus* | Arroyo Lupine | Fabaceae |
| Machaeranthera bigelovii | Purple Aster | Asteraceae |
| Machaeranthera gracilis | Slender Goldenweed | Asteraceae |
| Malacothrix glabrata | Desert-dandelion | Asteraceae |
| Mimulus bigelovii | Monkeyflower | Scrophulariaceae |
| Monoptilon bellioides | Mojave Desert Star | Asteraceae |
| Nama demissum | Purple Mat | Hydrophyllaceae |
| Oenothera deltoides | Birdcage Primrose | Onagraceae |
| Oenothera primiveris | Evening Primrose | Onagraceae |
| Orthocarpus purpurascens | Owl-clover | Scrophulariaceae |
| Pectis angustifolia | Lemonweed | Asteraceae |
| Pectis papposa | Chinchweed | Asteraceae |
| Perityle emoryi | Rock Daisy | Asteraceae |
| Phacelia crenulata* | Scalloped Phacelia | Hydrophyllaceae |
| Phacelia distans | Wild Heliotrope | Hydrophyllaceae |
| Phacelia integrifolia | Baby Curls | Hydrophyllaceae |
| Platystemon californicus | Cream Cups | Papaveraceae |
| Rafinesquia neomexicana | Desert-chicory | Asteraceae |
| Salvia columbariae | Chia | Lamiaceae |
| Sphaeralcea coulteri | Coulter Globe-mallow | Malvaceae |
| Verbesina encelioides | Golden Crownbeard | Asteraceae |

* Pre-treatment:
12-hour hot-water soak

| Origin | Flower Color | Blooming Season | Ht. × Wdth. | Sowing Season | Light | Soil |
|---|---|---|---|---|---|---|
| AZ,CA,Mex. | Pink-purple | Sp,Su | 10″ × 3′ | F | ○ | Sa |
| AZ,CA,CO,NM,TX,UT,Mex. | Violet | Sp,Su,F | 6″ × 3′ | F,Sp | ○ | Sa,Gr |
| Western North America | White | Sp | 1′ × 8″ | F | ○ | Gr |
| CA | Yellow | Sp | 8″ × 1′ | F | ○ | Gr |
| TX,Mex. | Yellow | Sp,Su | 4″ × 6″ | F | ○ | Gr |
| Western North America | Lav. to white | Sp,Su | 1′ × 1½′ | F | ○/◗ | Sa,Gr |
| AZ,CA,UT,Mex. | White | Sp | 4″ × 6″ | F | ○ | Gr |
| AZ,NM,TX,UT,Mex. | Orange | Sp | 8″ × 1′ | F | ○ | Gr |
| AZ,CA,UT | Yellow | Sp | 2′ × 1′ | F | ○ | Sa |
| Most of North America | Yellow | Sp,Su,F | 6′ × 4′ | Sp,Su | ○ | any |
| AZ,CA,NE,NM,TX,UT,Mex. | Pale blue | Sp,Su,F | 1½′ × 1′ | F,Sp | ○ | Sa |
| AZ,CA,NM,TX,Mex. | Orange | Su,F | 1½′ × 2′ | Su | ○ | Sa |
| AZ,CA,OR,Mex. | Yellow | Sp | 4″ × 4″ | F | ○ | any |
| AZ,CA,ID,NM,UT,WA,Mex. | White | Sp | 1′ × 1½′ | F | ○ | Sa |
| CA | Yellow & white | Sp | 1′ × 1½′ | F | ○ | Sa |
| AZ,CA,NM,OK,TX,UT,Mex. | Yellow | Sp | 6″ × 10″ | F | ○ | Sa |
| AZ,CA,NV,Mex. | Violet | Sp | 2′ × 1½′ | F | ○ | Sa |
| TX | Blue | Sp | 2′ × 3′ | F | ○ | Gr |
| AZ,CA,NV,NM,Mex. | Blue | Sp | 1′ × 1½′ | F | ○ | Sa |
| AZ,CA,Mex. | Blue | Sp | 2′ × 3′ | F | ○ | Sa,Gr |
| AZ,CO,NM,NV | Lavender | Sp,Su,F | 3′ × 2′ | F | ○ | any |
| CA,TX | Yellow | Sp,Su,F | 1′ × 1′ | F | ○ | Gr |
| AZ,CA,ID,NV,OR,Mex. | Pale yellow | Sp | 8″ × 1′ | F | ○ | Sa,Gr |
| AZ,CA | Pink | Sp | 6″ × 6″ | F | ○ | Sa,Gr |
| AZ,CA,Mex. | White | Sp | 2″ × 3″ | F | ○ | Sa,Gr |
| AZ,CA,UT,Mex. | Purple | Sp | 3″ × 10″ | F | ○ | Sa |
| AZ,CA,NV,OR,UT,Mex. | White | Sp | 10″ × 1½′ | F | ○ | Sa |
| AZ,CA,CO,NM,TX,UT,Mex. | Yellow | Sp | 6″ × 1′ | F | ○ | Sa,Gr |
| AZ,CA,Mex. | Pink | Sp | 6″ × 6″ | F | ○ | Sa,Gr |
| AZ,NM,TX,Mex. | Yellow | Su,F | 6″ × 1′ | Su | ○ | Sa,Gr |
| AZ,CA,NM,TX, UT,Mex. | Yellow | Su | 6″ × 10″ | Su | ○ | Sa,Gr |
| AZ,CA,Mex. | White | Sp,Su | 8″ × 1′ | F | ○ | Rocky |
| AZ,CA,NM,UT,Mex. | Violet | Sp | 1′ × 8″ | F | ○ | Gr |
| AZ,CA,NV,Mex. | Lavender | Sp | 8″ × 1′ | F | ○/◗ | Sa,Gr |
| AZ,CO,KS,NM,OK,TX,UT,Mex. | Purple | Sp,Su | 1′ × 10″ | F | ○ | Sa,Gr |
| AZ,CA,UT,Mex. | Cream | Sp | 6″ × 6″ | F | ○ | Gr |
| AZ,CA,NM,TX,UT,Mex. | White | Sp | 1′ × 1′ | F | ○/◗ | Sa,Gr |
| AZ,CA,NM,UT,Mex. | Blue | Sp | 1′ × 1′ | F | ○ | Gr |
| AZ,CA,Mex. | Orange | Sp | 1½′ × 1′ | F | ○ | Sa |
| W & SE US, Mex. | Yellow | Sp,Su,F | 2′ × 1′ | F,Su | ○ | Sa,Gr |

Sp = Spring  ○ = Full sun  Sa = Sandy
Su = Summer  ◗ = Partial shade  Gr = Gravelly
F = Fall

ers can look weedy while the seed is maturing. Understanding that this stage is necessary for the perpetuation of the wildflowers may make the unkempt appearance easier to accept.

## CLEAN-UP

After most of the seed has ripened and been harvested, you can pull the plants, shaking them to scatter any remaining seed. You may wish to run a lawn mower over the plants to shred the dried foliage, creating a mulch that returns some of the plant's nutrients to the soil.

## RE-ESTABLISHMENT IN SUBSEQUENT YEARS

Some wildflower species reseed readily, providing color year after year. Others need some assistance each year. Observing the wildflowers at your particular site over time will help you learn which species reseed by themselves and which ones need annual sowing. You may wish to provide supplemental water as the time for germination nears, particularly if there has been little natural rainfall. Periodic irrigation as the seedlings mature will also help ensure a vigorous stand of wildflowers.

## WILDFLOWER MIXES

The commercial wildflower mixes that have become readily available can be a convenient way to get a nice variety of species. Be aware, however, that a mix titled "Southwestern" may not necessarily be comprised of all native species. Oftentimes species from other parts of the country or even other parts of the world are included in the mix. Typically these exotic species are fast to establish and provide a lot of color. That vigor can be a potential problem if the plants reseed too aggressively and become weeds. Most mixes list the species contained, so you can determine whether or not they are native.

# 4.
# *Revegetation*

Desert areas that have been degraded by building construction, road work, utility-line trenching, or some other negative impact can be repaired. An exact restoration is difficult, if not impossible, to achieve; however, revegetation can capture the essence of natural desert.

## SITE ANALYSIS

The first step in a revegetation project is to survey a portion of undisturbed desert that represents the former condition of the disturbed area. Take note of the plant species present, their relative density, and any particular plant associations, such as cacti growing in the shelter of shrubs. Also notice the contours of the land and the texture of the surface. Sketches or photographs may be helpful supplements to your notes.

## SOIL PREPARATION

Back at the revegetation project site, examine the soil. Look for compaction caused by heavy equipment or contamination from dumping of construction debris. If sowing seed is part of the revegetation plan, the soil should be prepared to a minimum depth of 4 inches; the optimum is 8 inches. A rotary tiller or tractor is most practical for large areas, but a small site could be cultivated by hand. The soil should be loose and crumbly but not pulverized. Gravel and larger rocks can remain, particularly if they were a component of the original surface texture.

Fertilizer, if used, should be incorporated into the soil at this stage. The additional nutrients can give seedlings a boost. Ammonium phosphate (16-20-0), a good starter fertilizer, can be applied at a rate of 1 pound per 100 square feet in sandy soil, and about half that amount for heavier soil.

## IRRIGATION

Before you do any planting, you need to decide on a method of irrigation. One option is to rely on natural rainfall. Certainly it involves the least money and effort. This method can only be used for seeded projects; plants will need supplemental irrigation after transplanting. With rainfall as the only source of water, seed germination may be unreliable and seedling establishment slow. Other alternatives are temporary sprinkler or drip systems, a quick coupler system with hoses for hand watering, or, for sites without access to water, a truck with a water tank and pump.

PLANTING

Disturbed desert areas can be revegetated with seed, plants, or a combination of the two. Seeding is the technique to use for areas that won't receive supplemental irrigation. The seeds will germinate when moisture conditions are favorable. An advantage of using seed is the greater variety of species available as compared to plants. The seed mix should be developed based not only on the particular species of trees, shrubs, succulents, and herbaceous plants that you want to establish on your site, but also on their relative abundance. Other variables affecting the composition of the mix are time of sowing, soil type, slope, and whether or not irrigation will be used. Developing a good seed mix is as much an art as a science; you may want to enlist the help of a commercial seed supplier.

The ideal time for sowing seed is just prior to the rainy season. In the Mojave Desert and western portions of the Sonoran Desert, the fall is best. The central and eastern Sonoran Desert receives rain in summer and fall, so either time would be good for planting seed in those locations. Most of the moisture received by the Chihuahuan Desert comes in the summer; seed-sowing should be planned accordingly.

Hand broadcasting is usually the most practical method of sowing seed. Stir the mix often to assure even distribution of large and small seeds. Lightly rake the planting area to just cover the seed with soil.

Revegetation with plants provides an immediate visual effect. You can use nursery-grown or desert-salvaged plants. Using salvaged plants, either purchased from a reputable source or transplanted from an area slated for clearing, provides several advantages. First, certain species may not be readily available as nursery stock. Second, desert-salvaged plants have more character, due to age and individual variations, than the mass-produced nursery plants.

Last, nursery-grown plants may have more trouble adapting to the harsh reality of desert conditions at the revegetation site. On the other hand, nursery-grown plants may have a better-established root system than desert-salvaged plants.

Successfully transplanting trees and shrubs from the desert depends primarily on water. If possible, moisten the ground prior to digging. With a spade, dig around the rootball and lift it out of the ground, retaining as much soil as possible. You can put the transplant in a pot or directly into a planting hole. Ample water after the move will help the plant survive. Ideally, the transplants should be kept moist for the first few weeks, then gradually weaned from irrigation. Large shrubs and trees are usually boxed for transplanting. Professional plant movers have developed techniques for successfully transplanting even mature desert trees.

Whether you use nursery-grown or salvaged plants, one of the keys to a natural-looking revegetation is the spacing of plants. Refer to your site analysis notes, sketches, or photographs to establish planting densities and associations. Desert vegetation doesn't grow evenly spaced. Plants are often clumped together, with large bare spaces in between.

When a combination of plants and seed is used for revegetation, the plants are usually put in first, then the seed is sown.

POST-ESTABLISHMENT CARE

Irrigation is necessary for new transplants. Small plants should be watered through one growing season, large shrubs given extra water for one to two years, and trees for three to five years. Cacti can manage on natural rainfall. Other activities that will contribute to the success of your revegetation are weeding, thinning, and providing protection from animals. Of course, the size of your project will determine the feasibility of doing any of these things.

A well-planned revegetation project will improve in appearance each year, and the area should eventually look like it was never disturbed.

# 5.
# *Plant Descriptions*

You should think of this chapter as an encyclopedia of native plants for landscape use. Refer to it for descriptions of the plants, their geographic distribution, cultural requirements, and suggestions for using them in the landscape. The text is written in plain language, so you shouldn't need a botanical dictionary nearby as you read. Each entry lists the common name first, although the entries are alphabetized by scientific name. Sometimes several common names are given. The first one listed is the most commonly used, and it will be repeated throughout the text. When a scientific name has been changed, the former name, or synonym, is given in parentheses. In the headings, "synonym" has been abbreviated to "syn.," "variety" to "var.," and "subspecies" to "ssp." The family name is given, accompanied by its common name. Some of the family names may not be the same ones you're familiar with; for example, Leguminosae has been changed to Fabaceae. This change reflects the *International Code of Botanical Nomenclature* decision to have all family names end in "aceae." Other changes include Labiatae to Lamiaceae, Gramineae to Poaceae, and Compositae to Asteraceae.

## DESCRIPTION

Each description gives the plant's growth form and typical mature size. The foliage, flowers, and fruits, if significant, are described. Whether the foliage is deciduous or evergreen is noted. The flowering period indicates the range of time over which the species as a whole blooms; an individual plant may or may not flower for the entire period indicated. Any special features such as fragrant foliage or flowers are mentioned. Whenever a plant has a potentially negative feature, such as spines or allergenic pollen, that too is noted.

## NATIVE DISTRIBUTION

This section describes the plant's natural habitat, elevational range (if known), and geographic distribution. You can use this information to determine whether or not a native plant is likely to do well in your situation. Table 1 (Weather of Desert Cities) in Chapter 1 gives the elevations of cities throughout the Southwest. The exact elevation of your site can be determined with an altimeter or by checking a topographic map.

## CULTURE

Recommendations regarding irrigation, soil type, and light exposure are made for each plant. When the comment is made that a species can survive on rainfall, that means when the plant is mature and receiving a quantity of rainfall similar to where it is found naturally. The cold hardiness is also given. A variety of factors influence a plant's ability to withstand cold, including the age of the plant, whether it is actively growing or dormant, and the duration of the cold period. Special notes on pruning, pests, or diseases may be added to the discussion.

## LANDSCAPE USE

General suggestions are given for utilizing the plant in a landscape setting. You certainly should not be limited to the possibilities listed. A book on landscape design could give you additional ideas for utilizing plants as aesthetic and functional elements in a landscape.

## Guajillo, Berlandier Acacia
### *Acacia berlandieri*
FABACEAE [PEA FAMILY]

*Description* Lush, fernlike foliage covers the spreading branches of Guajillo. The rounded shrub grows to 10 feet high and 12 feet wide. Light green, 4-inch-long leaves are divided into seven to ten pairs of 1½-inch-long delicate leaflets. In mild-winter areas the foliage is evergreen. Guajillo does have thorns, but they are small and flexible—hardly a menace. Spring brings fragrant, cream-colored puffballs, which develop into pods 4–5 inches long and 1 inch wide.

*Native Distribution* Dry limestone hills in the south-central and near-west portions of Texas and south and east to Querétaro and Veracruz, Mexico, are the habitat of Guajillo. The plant grows between 1,000 and 3,000 feet in elevation.

*Culture* Guajillo's cold hardiness extends to 20° F. It grows best in full sun and requires little water after establishment; most soil types are acceptable, provided they are well drained.

*Landscape Use* Poolside plantings are one possible application of Guajillo. The feathery foliage is also welcome around patios. Cluster several plants of Guajillo to screen an unattractive view.

## Whitethorn Acacia, Mescat Acacia
### *Acacia constricta*
FABACEAE [PEA FAMILY]

*Description* Whitethorn Acacia is a graceful, spreading shrub with medium green, lacy foliage and conspicuous, ½-inch white spines. Occasionally some of the branches or even the entire plant may be spineless. At maturity it can reach 10 feet high and 15 feet wide. The compound deciduous leaves are usually 1 inch long and half as wide. In late spring, and sometimes in summer and fall, yellow-orange, fragrant ball-shaped flowers dot the foliage. The pods of Whitethorn Acacia are reddish brown, curved, about 4 inches long, and constricted between the seeds.

*Native Distribution* Whitethorn Acacia's range extends from Arizona to western Texas, and southward from Baja California and Sonora to Tamaulipas and San Luis Potosí, Mexico. Its habitat includes washes, gravelly plains, and rocky hillsides, between 1,500 and 6,500 feet in elevation.

*Culture* Find a sunny location in well-drained soil for Whitethorn Acacia. Shallow alkaline soils or caliche are okay. This shrub is very drought tolerant; once established, it can get by on rainfall alone, or you can provide supplemental irrigation once a month in summer for faster, lusher growth. Plants are cold hardy to 5° F. The seeds germinate easily; you'll need to pull the volunteers unless you want a grove of Whitethorn Acacia.

*Landscape Use* Whitethorn Acacia looks best when combined with other plants so that its winter bareness isn't too noticeable. You might use it near a patio where the flowers can perfume the air, but keep in mind that the branches are armed with spines. The spininess can be used to advantage as a security barrier. Quail eat the seeds and bees use the flowers to make honey.

## Sweet Acacia
### *Acacia farnesiana* (syn., *Acacia smallii*)
FABACEAE [PEA FAMILY]

*Description* So named for its ½-inch, yellow, ball-shaped fragrant flowers, Sweet Acacia blooms in spring and occasionally in fall. Plump, woody pods are 2 inches long and dark brown to black at maturity. The vase-shaped large shrub or multistemmed

*Acacia constricta* Whitethorn Acacia

*Acacia berlandieri* Guajillo; detail above left

*Acacia constricta* Whitethorn Acacia

*Acacia farnesiana* Sweet Acacia

tree reaches 15–20 feet in height with a similar spread. Lacy, fernlike leaves 2 inches long by 1 inch wide are twice-divided into tiny oval leaflets. Sweet Acacia's straight white spines, ¾ inch long, occur in pairs. The plant is evergreen in mild winters.

***Native Distribution*** Sweet Acacia occurs in disjunct populations in southern California and Arizona, south-central and western Texas, Florida, and throughout Mexico to South America. Its habitat includes arroyos, plains, and hillsides, between 2,500 and 5,000 feet in elevation.

***Culture*** Temperatures below 15° F can damage flower buds, twigs, or even the entire plant, which will freeze to the ground in severe cold. Although Sweet Acacia is drought tolerant, deep soakings periodically through the summer will encourage a faster growth rate. Sweet Acacia can be grown in all types of soil, even poorly drained. Provide full sun for the plant. Moderate pruning is required to develop a tree form with multiple stems. A single-stemmed tree is possible with early and regular training. Branches often sprout from the base or along main branches of young Sweet Acacias. Remove these before they become large in order to maintain a tree form. Without any pruning, Sweet Acacia is an attractive, moderately dense shrub.

***Landscape Use*** Sweet Acacia's medium size is suitable for courtyards, patios, small yards, streetside plantings, parking medians, and other areas where a larger tree would be overwhelming. Sweet Acacia can become the focal point of a landscape, particularly when in bloom. The plant's dense branching pattern and spines could be utilized for a security planting. Sweet Acacia could also be incorporated into a naturalistic desert landscape.

## Catclaw Acacia
### *Acacia greggii*
FABACEAE [PEA FAMILY]

***Description*** Fuzzy, pale yellow flower spikes about 2 inches long perfume the air around Catclaw Acacia in spring. Rust-colored pods are flat to twisted, usually 3 inches long by ¾ inch wide. The feathery, gray-green foliage of Catclaw Acacia is winter-deciduous and can also drop during extreme drought. Scattered along the gray branches, partially hidden by the leaves, are the short, curved spines that give this large shrub its common name. At maturity Catclaw Acacia can be 10 feet high and 15 feet wide.

***Native Distribution*** Catclaw Acacia often forms thickets along washes, but it also occurs on rocky hillsides and desert flats below 5,000 feet in elevation. It is found in southeastern California, southern Nevada, southeastern Utah, Arizona, New Mexico, and western Texas, and also in Chihuahua, Sonora, and Baja California, Mexico.

***Culture*** This plant's northerly distribution is an indication of its cold tolerance—to 0° F. Yet it also grows in the hottest desert areas and is very drought tolerant. After new plants become established, they can be left on their own or given a deep soaking once a month in the summer. Plant Catclaw Acacia in full sun where the soil is well drained. The growth rate is moderate. Without pruning, Catclaw Acacia will grow as a large shrub with branches to the ground. You can remove the lower foliage to expose the picturesque, often gnarled trunk. Catclaw Acacia's canopy rarely gets large enough for people to stand upright beneath, even with extensive pruning.

***Landscape Use*** Catclaw Acacia's pleasing, mounded shape can add interest to naturalistic desert plantings. The attractive foliage and flowers and interesting trunk warrant the shrub's use as an accent plant, but you'll probably want to include some evergreen plants nearby to lessen the visual impact of Catclaw Acacia's winter bareness. Be sure to keep the branches clear of walkways, patios, or play areas. The spines don't just poke—they grab and hang on. No intruder would want to tangle with a security planting of Catclaw Acacia. Desert animals take advantage of the plant's protectiveness by seeking shelter and making nests among the branches. The seeds are eaten by quail; the flowers are an important source of nectar for bees.

## Santa Rita Acacia, Fernleaf Acacia
### *Acacia millefolia*
FABACEAE [PEA FAMILY]

**Description**  The foliage of this rounded deciduous shrub is light green and very delicately textured. The plant can grow to 12 feet high and 15 feet wide. Six-inch-long leaves are divided into five to ten pairs of primary leaflets each 1 inch long. The primary leaflets have twenty to thirty pairs of tiny secondary leaflets about 1/16 inch long. The airy leaves tend to droop, lending a graceful air to the plant. Cream-colored flower spikes 2 inches long and 1/2 inch wide are arranged in clusters among the leaves. They bloom in July and August with a sweet, musky fragrance. The fruit is a reddish brown, papery pod 4 inches long by 1/2 inch wide.

**Native Distribution**  Santa Rita Acacia grows in southeastern Arizona and also in Sonora, Sinaloa, and Chihuahua, Mexico, between 3,500 and 5,500 feet in elevation. Typical habitat includes rocky canyons and hillsides, particularly limestone ridges.

**Culture**  Provide supplemental water once or twice a month in summer for lusher foliage and better flower production. Santa Rita Acacia prefers well-drained soil and full sun, though it tolerates partial shade.

Plants are hardy to at least 25° F. Limit pruning to the removal of dead wood so the plant's natural character can be preserved.

**Landscape Use**  Santa Rita Acacia's fernlike foliage adds a lush feeling to patio or courtyard plantings. The slightest breeze sets the leaves to swaying. Coarse-textured plants nearby might overpower Santa Rita Acacia; plants with a similar texture but darker color, such as Velvet Mesquite (*Prosopis velutina*), could complement the shrub. If your landscape includes a lawn area, Santa Rita Acacia would certainly be appropriate for planting nearby.

## Viscid Acacia
### *Acacia neovernicosa*
FABACEAE [PEA FAMILY]

**Description**  Viscid Acacia's few branches grow mostly upright to 10 feet, spreading to 8 feet. This shrub is deciduous. The entire plant, including the leaves, stems, and pods, is sticky from the secretions of glands. Fernlike, 1-inch leaves are divided into one or two pairs of primary leaflets, and there are six to ten pairs of tiny secondary leaflets. Pairs of 1/2-inch spines occur along the branches. Fragrant yellow puffball flowers 1/3 inch in diameter are sprinkled throughout the shrub from April to July. The fruits that follow are 2½ inches long and 1/4 inch broad and noticeably constricted between the seeds.

**Native Distribution**  Viscid Acacia is a common plant of the Chihuahuan Desert, occurring in southeastern Arizona, southern New Mexico, and western Texas, and also in Sonora and Chihuahua to Zacatecas and Querétaro, Mexico. The plant grows on rocky hillsides and mesas, particularly those of limestone origin, from 3,500 to 5,000 feet in elevation.

*Acacia greggii* Catclaw Acacia

*Acacia millefolia* Santa Rita Acacia

*Acacia greggii* detail

*Acacia millefolia* detail

Above and below: *Acacia neovernicosa*
Viscid Acacia

*Culture* Select a sunny location with well-drained soil for Viscid Acacia. It tolerates drought once established, and it is cold hardy to 0° F. Much of Viscid Acacia's character is due to the open branch structure; don't compromise that by pruning—remove only dead material.

*Landscape Use* Viscid Acacia could get lost in most landscapes unless silhouetted against a plain background or isolated from other plants so that its sparse branches are more noticeable. Because of its spines, Viscid Acacia should be kept away from pedestrian areas. It could be used in median and roadside plantings. Viscid Acacia would also be useful for revegetation purposes.

## Blackbrush Acacia
### *Acacia rigidula*
FABACEAE [PEA FAMILY]

*Description* Blackbrush Acacia's rigid, thorny branches form a large shrub or small tree to 12 feet high and about as wide. Its harshness is softened by rich, dark green foliage and light gray bark. The 1-inch-long deciduous leaves are divided into a pair of leaflets, with ⅓-inch-long oval secondary leaflets. Yellow flower spikes, 2–3 inches long and ½ inch in diameter, appear from March to June. Slender woody pods to 3 inches long develop from the flowers.

*Native Distribution* This shrub is found in southern and western Texas, as well as in Coahuila, Nuevo León, Tamaulipas, San Luis Potosí, Jalisco, and Veracruz, Mexico, at 1,100–1,800 feet in elevation. Blackbrush Acacia grows on limestone hillsides and in canyons.

*Culture* This plant will accept a wide range of soils, from sandy to loamy, even caliche. Good drainage is preferred. Plant Blackbrush Acacia in full sun, and water it

until establishment, then provide supplemental irrigation only in prolonged drought. It is hardy to about 20° F. Blackbrush Acacia grows slowly, yet it can be trained into a tree form by pruning away the lower branches. Its natural shrubby form is equally attractive.

*Landscape Use* You could use Blackbrush Acacia as a specimen plant, with some evergreen plants nearby to provide interest in winter. The deep green foliage would make a fine background for light-colored plants. Blackbrush Acacia could serve a utilitarian purpose as a physical barrier or screen.

## Roemer Acacia, Catclaw
### *Acacia roemeriana*
FABACEAE [PEA FAMILY]

*Description* Creamy white puffball flowers ½ inch in diameter dot the rounded form of Roemer Acacia in April and May. This deciduous shrub has deep green, 3-inch-long compound leaves twice-divided into about forty ¼-inch oval leaflets, giving the foliage a delicate texture. Roemer Acacia's young stems and curved thorns are deep red. The 3-inch-long, 1-inch-wide flat or twisted pods are light green with a red margin when young, becoming entirely reddish brown with maturity. A typical size of Roemer Acacia is 8 feet high and 10 feet wide.

*Native Distribution* Roemer Acacia occurs on dry plains, in canyons, and in brushlands, from 1,050 to 4,600 feet in elevation, in western and central Texas and southern New Mexico, and in Chihuahua, Coahuila, and Nuevo León, Mexico.

*Culture* For best growth, provide Roemer Acacia with full sun, although it will tolerate light shade. It prefers irrigation once or twice a month through the summer, with well-drained soil. This shrub tolerates cold to 15° F.

***Landscape Use*** The deep green, lacy foliage of Roemer Acacia would make a good backdrop for plants with light-colored, coarse-textured foliage. A few possibilities include Guayule (*Parthenium argentatum*), Jojoba (*Simmondsia chinensis*), and Banana Yucca (*Yucca baccata*). An excellent informal screen could be developed by planting Roemer Acacia in an irregular line.

## Twisted Acacia, Schaffner's Acacia
### *Acacia schaffneri*
FABACEAE [PEA FAMILY]

***Description*** Deep green, feathery foliage is closely set along Twisted Acacia's angular branches. The large shrub or small tree can reach 15 feet high and 20 feet wide. Its 1½-inch-long, 1-inch-wide, finely divided leaves drop in late fall, revealing short thorns along the branches. Yellow, ball-shaped flowers ½ inch in diameter appear in spring with the new foliage. The 4-inch-long seed pods are light green and velvety when young, becoming dark brown and woody with age.

***Native Distribution*** This plant is found on rocky hillsides and grasslands in Chihuahua, Coahuila, Durango, San Luis Potosí, and Zacatecas, Mexico.

***Culture*** Twisted Acacia will tolerate a wide range of soils, if they are well drained. After establishment, plants require no supplemental irrigation unless faster growth than the normally moderate rate is desired. This plant drops its leaves with the onset of cold weather, but it is hardy to at least 17° F. Give Twisted Acacia a site in full sun with plenty of room to develop. The branches naturally grow low to the ground; you'll need to do some pruning to achieve a tree form.

***Landscape Use*** This picturesque plant deserves a prominent place in the landscape. Its twisted branches are best displayed against a plain background such as a stucco wall. Nearby plants should be low-growing so they don't detract from Twisted Acacia's interesting form. Twisted Acacia can provide summer shade for southern or western exposures yet allow the warmth of winter sunlight through. Another potential use for Twisted Acacia is as a security barrier. For the maximum effect, allow the lower branches to remain.

## Schott Acacia
### *Acacia schottii*
FABACEAE [PEA FAMILY]

***Description*** The ¼-inch-long, ⅛-inch-wide leaflets (usually six to ten) are widely spaced along the midrib of Schott Acacia's 1½-inch-long leaves, giving the entire shrub a lacy appearance. Among the deciduous, compound leaves are ¾-inch-long white spines. Schott Acacia normally reaches a height of 4 feet, with a 5-foot spread. The ½-inch, yellow ball-shaped flowers can appear anytime from May to September. Brown or black glands dot 2- to 3-inch-long pods, which are ¼ inch wide and constricted between the seeds.

***Native Distribution*** Schott Acacia grows between 2,300 and 4,000 feet in elevation, on desert flats and rocky limestone slopes in western Texas and in adjacent Chihuahua, Mexico.

***Culture*** Plant Schott Acacia where it will receive full sun. It is quite drought tolerant, as well as cold tolerant to around 10° F. A well-drained soil is ideal.

***Landscape Use*** The contrast of delicate foliage and sharp white spines makes Schott Acacia an interesting accent plant. Keep it a safe distance from pedestrian

*Acacia rigidula* Blackbrush Acacia

*Acacia roemeriana* Roemer Acacia

*Acacia schaffneri* Twisted Acacia

*Acacia schottii* Schott Acacia

areas, but not so far that its beauty is hidden. Schott Acacia could also play a less visible role as part of a natural-ized desert landscape. Planting Schott Acacia near a bold-foliaged plant would emphasize the difference in foliage texture.

Its graceful form will be shown to best advantage against a plain wall or the skyline. This tree doesn't get too large; use it in entry courtyards, patios, or other small spaces. Keep the ornamental trunk unobstructed by other plants' growth.

## White Bark Acacia, Palo Blanco
### *Acacia willardiana*
FABACEAE [PEA FAMILY]

**Description** Pale cream to silver papery bark distinguishes White Bark Acacia from other desert trees. Graceful, weeping branches are sparsely foliated with 5-inch-long leaves. The leaves have 4-inch midribs, which split at the end into a pair of primary leaflets 1 inch long, each with about ten tiny secondary leaflets. The foliage takes on a wispy appearance when the leaflets drop in spring or early summer, leaving only each leaf's needle-like midrib. Cream-colored flower spikes 2 inches long appear in spring, followed by dark brown, papery pods 3 inches long by ¾ inch wide. White Bark Acacia's slender form can measure 20 feet high and 10 feet wide at maturity.

**Native Distribution** White Bark Acacia grows on rocky hillsides in Sonora, Mexico.

**Culture** A warm, sheltered microclimate is necessary for growing White Bark Acacia. Temperatures below the mid-20s F will cause foliage damage. Culture otherwise is fairly simple: White Bark Acacia likes full sun and doesn't need much water—unless you want to push its growth rate—and it tolerates poor soil. The tree needs no pruning, and if you let the bark flake off naturally, you'll get some interesting mottled patterns.

**Landscape Use** White Bark Acacia is an outstanding accent plant in the landscape.

## Wright Acacia
### *Acacia wrightii*
FABACEAE [PEA FAMILY]

**Description** Wright Acacia is a semi-evergreen shrub to small tree that can reach 10 feet in height and width. Short, catclaw-like spines occur on the gray branches. The gray-green compound leaves are ¾ inch long and occur in pairs, with four to twelve ¼-inch oval leaflets. Creamy white flower spikes 2 inches long and ½ inch wide appear from March through June and sometimes later following rains. The fruit of Wright Acacia is a flat, reddish brown pod 2–3 inches long by ¾ inch wide.

**Native Distribution** Arroyos, canyons, and rocky hillsides of central, southern, and western Texas, to Tamaulipas, Nuevo León, Coahuila, Chihuahua, Sonora, and Baja California, Mexico, are home to Wright Acacia.

**Culture** This *Acacia* is hardy to at least 5° F. Full sun is preferred, as is well-drained soil, though clay or caliche is tolerated. Wright Acacia is very drought tolerant after it becomes established. Irrigation once or twice a month in summer will maintain a moderate growth rate. The amount of pruning necessary will depend on the desired effect. A tree form can be attained by removing the lower branches as the plant matures, or Wright Acacia can be allowed to grow naturally into a large shrub.

**Landscape Use** Wright Acacia could play one of several roles: screen and security barrier, wildlife shelter, or backdrop for accent plants. Because of the curved spines, situate the plant well away from pedestrian or play areas. The flowers are favored by bees for making honey.

## *Agave* species
AGAVACEAE [AGAVE FAMILY]

One of the most ornamental succulents you could choose for the landscape is *Agave*. Among the more than 130 species there is considerable variation in plant size, form, leaf shape, color, and flower.

Agaves are so effective as accent plants because their bold form contrasts dramatically with the fine texture of most desert trees and shrubs. Cacti and Agaves complement each other nicely when used in a succulent garden. The fascinating symmetry of Agave's leaves can best be appreciated near a walkway or patio—just be aware of the plant's mature size and allow it enough room to develop. Plants that do encroach upon pedestrian areas can be made less menacing by clipping about ½ inch from the leaf tips, thereby removing the terminal spines. Agaves typically grow slowly, making them ideal for pots.

You should provide Agaves with well-drained soil, whether they are grown in pots or in the ground. Full sunlight is preferred. Partial shade usually causes weak, spindly growth. Agaves are very drought tolerant. Water them deeply but infrequently until they become established (usually within several months), then water only in summer if prolonged drought occurs. Severely drought-stressed leaves will shrivel at first, then go a little bit limp. Some people cut away the lower leaves as they become dry through the natural process of aging. This results in neater-looking plants, but when taken to the extreme it makes them resemble pineapples. There is no health-related reason to prune the leaves.

Agaves bloom only at maturity, which can be from five to fifty years of age, depending on the species. The plants expend all their energy in producing the flower, then die. Many types of Agave produce offsets, which can be allowed to mature to replace the parent plant. At first, the flowering stalk looks like a giant asparagus spear, then it branches into either a candelabra form or a spike. The stalk is usually at least 5 feet high; the larger the plant, the bigger the stalk.

An insect pest, the agave snout weevil (*Scyphophorus acupunctatus*) can affect *Agave* species. The large, broad-leaved plants seem to be the preferred targets of this small, black, hard-bodied insect. The adult is ¾ inch long, with a long snout. In the spring, it tunnels into the center of the plant and lays its eggs, which hatch and develop into cream-colored grubs an inch long. A fungus introduced into the Agave by the weevil causes the plant to rot, providing food for the larvae. In the case of a severe infestation, you can even hear chewing sounds from inside the plant! Sometimes you can see the adult's entry hole, which is about the diameter of a pencil. The most visible symptom of agave snout weevil infestation is wrinkling, then wilting, of the leaves. Eventually the plant collapses; by that time it usually has a foul smell. The plant should be removed and destroyed, and any adults or grubs should be killed. Birds such as curve-billed thrashers or cactus wrens may scratch around in the loosened soil and find snout weevil adults or larvae you missed. The most effective way to avoid infestations is to plant only the smaller-leaved *Agave* species, which seem to be less desirable to the weevils. During May and June, when the adults are most active, you can sprinkle about a teaspoon of granular Diazinon on the ground at the base of each plant or spray the liquid form of Diazinon on the leaf bases. Since Diazinon is a relatively short-lived insecticide, you may want to reapply it every two weeks.

Above and below: *Acacia wrightii*　　BS
Wright Acacia

*Acacia willardiana* White Bark Acacia

## Golden-flowered Agave
### *Agave chrysantha*

Blue-gray leaves form a rosette about 2 feet high and 3–4 feet wide. Golden-flowered Agave rarely forms offsets. In June and July yellow flowers cluster on the upper third of a candelabra-type flower stalk. Golden-flowered Agave occurs only in central Arizona, on foothills and mountain slopes between 3,000 and 6,000 feet in elevation. It is cold hardy to at least 15° F.

Above and below: *Agave chrysantha*
Golden-flowered Agave

## Desert Agave
### *Agave deserti*

*Agave deserti* subspecies *deserti* grows on gravelly slopes in southern California and northern Baja California, Mexico, between 1,300 and 4,000 feet in elevation. The 1½-foot-high by 2-foot-wide gray-green plants form colonies that may reach 10 feet in diameter. Yellow flowers bloom on a candelabra-type flowering stalk 12 feet high from May to July.

*Agave deserti* subspecies *simplex* looks a lot like the typical species, but it usually doesn't form colonies. This subspecies is found in southeastern California, southwestern Arizona, and Sonora, Mexico, at elevations from 800 to 5,000 feet. Desert Agave is probably hardy to at least the low 20s F.

## Havard Agave
### *Agave havardiana*

Havard Agave is a handsome plant 1½ feet high and twice as wide, with stout gray leaves. The flower stalk is candelabra-like with large clusters of yellow flowers in summertime. The plant occurs from 4,000 to 6,500 feet in elevation, in the desert and on rocky grassland slopes of the mountains. Its geographic range includes southwestern Texas and Chihuahua and Coahuila, Mexico. Havard Agave can tolerate temperatures to 15° F without damage.

## Lechuguilla
### *Agave lechuguilla*

Lechuguilla is considered an indicator plant of the Chihuahuan Desert, meaning its presence indicates the limits of the desert. It has one of the most extensive ranges of the Agaves, from southern New Mexico and western Texas to much of Mexico, including the states of Chihuahua, Coahuila, Durango, Zacatecas, Nuevo León, Tamaulipas, San Luis Potosí, Mexico State, and Hidalgo. Lechuguilla grows on rocky limestone slopes from 2,000 to 6,500 feet in elevation.

The mostly upright leaves of Lechuguilla are long and slender, with downward-slanting teeth along the margins. Leaf color is light green to yellow-green. Individual plants grow to 10 inches high by 8 inches wide and produce many offsets. In late spring, Lechuguilla sends up a slender spike with purplish or yellowish flowers. It is cold hardy to 15° F or below.

## New Mexico Agave
### *Agave neomexicana*

As the common name suggests, New Mexico Agave occurs primarily in New Mexico, also reaching just south of the state border into Texas. Its habitat ranges from rocky limestone slopes to grasslands, between 1,400 and 7,000 feet in elevation. New Mexico Agave's medium-sized gray to light green rosettes sucker freely. At maturity the parent plant can reach 16 inches high with a spread of 2 feet. The flowers appearing in spring on the candelabra-type stalk are reddish in bud and yellow in bloom. Very cold hardy, New Mexico Agave can withstand temperatures to 0° F.

*Agave deserti* ssp. *deserti* Desert Agave

*Agave havardiana* Havard Agave

Above and below: *Agave neomexicana* New Mexico Agave

Left: *Agave lechuguilla* Lechuguilla

## Agave ocahui

Dark green, unarmed leaves 1½ feet long by 1 inch wide curve upward into a very symmetrical and striking rosette measuring 1½ feet high and nearly 3 feet wide at maturity. The flower stalk of *Agave ocahui* is a slender spike covered with yellow flowers from April through June. The natural distribution is limited to northeastern Sonora, Mexico, on rocky hillsides between 1,500 and 4,500 feet in elevation. *Agave ocahui* is cold hardy to 15° F.

## Palmer Agave
### *Agave palmeri*

Bluish green leaves with numerous spines on the margins form a rosette 3 feet high and 4 feet wide that usually doesn't form offsets. A candelabra-type flower stalk, up to 15 feet tall, produces greenish yellow flowers in June and July. Palmer Agave occurs at the upper edges of the Sonoran Desert on rocky hillsides, into the grassland and oak woodland communities in southeastern Arizona and southwestern New Mexico and Sonora and northwestern Chihuahua, Mexico. It ranges from altitudes of 3,000 to 6,000 feet. Plants can tolerate temperatures to 15° F.

## Toumey Agave
### *Agave toumeyana*

Toumey Agave grows on rocky hillsides and mesas from 2,000 to 5,000 feet in elevation, in central Arizona only. The light green leaves form a grasslike clump about 1 foot high and 2 feet across. White, threadlike fibers occur along the 9-inch-long, ½-inch-wide leaves, which may be patterned with white lines. Slender flower stalks with greenish yellow flowers emerge from mature plants from May to July, reaching a height of 6 feet. Toumey Agave is hardy to about 20° F.

## Utah Agave
### *Agave utahensis*

Utah Agave develops compact rosettes of light gray-green leaves. The rosettes offset freely; at maturity a plant cluster can be 1 foot high and 2 feet across. Yellow flowers bloom along a slender stalk from May through July. Utah Agave grows on rocky slopes in southwestern Utah, southeastern Nevada, California, and Arizona, between 3,000 and 6,000 feet in elevation. Plants can withstand temperatures to 0° F.

## Queen Victoria Agave
### *Agave victoriae-reginae*

If your space is limited, consider planting Queen Victoria Agave. Stout, dark green leaves with white lines form a tight rosette 8 inches high and about 1 foot across. Some people think it resembles an artichoke. In June and July, pale green flowers crowd along a 4-foot spike. Queen Victoria Agave grows on rocky limestone slopes between 4,000 and 5,000 feet in elevation in Coahuila, Durango, and Nuevo León, Mexico. It can tolerate cold to at least 10° F.

## Whitebrush, Bee Brush
### *Aloysia gratissima* (syn., *Aloysia lycioides*)
VERBENACEAE [VERVAIN FAMILY]

***Description*** Loose spikes of tiny white flowers tinged with purple blanket Whitebrush after heavy rains spring through fall. The flowers are strongly vanilla-scented; the foliage is also fragrant. The deciduous leaves are oblong with a point, ¾ inch long and ¼ inch wide, dull green, rough on top and hairy below. The leaf margins are either smooth or sparsely toothed. Whitebrush is a spreading shrub to 6 feet high and 8 feet wide. Its many branches are usually brittle and slender.

***Native Distribution*** Whitebrush occurs in southeastern Arizona, southern New Mexico, and much of Texas, and also south throughout Mexico to Oaxaca and South America. The shrub grows in various habitats, including desert grass-lands, rocky slopes, arroyos, canyons, and woodlands, at elevations between 1,100 and 5,000 feet.

***Culture*** Whitebrush tolerates partial shade but prefers full sun. Most soil types, even poorly drained, are acceptable. After establishment, some supplemental irrigation during the summer will benefit Whitebrush. It is hardy to at least 15° F.

***Landscape Use*** An informal hedge or screen could be established using White-brush. Another use of the delicately textured shrub is as a background planting for accent plants. Its vanilla-scented flowers would be most appreciated near buildings or walkways. Combined with evergreen plants, Whitebrush's bare branches in winter won't be as noticeable.

## Oreganillo, Wright's Bee Brush
### *Aloysia wrightii*
VERBENACEAE [VERVAIN FAMILY]

***Description*** Oreganillo's ½-inch-long, medium green oval leaves are richly textured. The upper surface is crinkled, the undersides are covered with fine white hairs, and the leaf edges have many rounded teeth. The shrub drops its aromatic foliage in winter, revealing an intricately branched form. Mature size is 5 feet high and equally wide. Fragrant tiny white flowers occur at the ends of branches in slender spikes 1½ inches long. Oreganillo blooms spring through fall.

***Native Distribution*** Arroyos, canyons, rocky slopes, and grasslands at altitudes from 1,500 to 6,500 feet in southern Nevada, southeastern California, New Mexico, western Texas, and northern Mexico to Durango and Zacatecas are home to Oreganillo.

***Culture and Landscape Use*** Cultural requirements and landscape use are the same as for Whitebrush (*Aloysia gratissima*).

## Giant Bur-sage, Canyon Ragweed
### *Ambrosia ambrosioides*
ASTERACEAE [SUNFLOWER FAMILY]

***Description*** Giant Bur-sage is a shrubby perennial, usually woody at least at the base and sometimes throughout. Three feet high and 4 feet wide is a typical mature size. The evergreen, deep green leaves are arrow-shaped, 4 inches long, 1 inch wide at the base, sparsely covered with stiff white hairs, and coarsely toothed along the edges. February through May is the flowering period of Giant Bur-sage, though the light green flower clusters are barely noticeable. The fruits resemble cockleburs. They are about ½ inch long, with slender, hook-tipped spines.

Left: *Agave ocahui*

*Agave palmeri* Palmer Agave

*Agave toumeyana* Toumey Agave

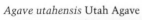

*Agave utahensis* Utah Agave

*Agave victoriae-reginae* Queen Victoria Agave

*Aloysia wrightii* Oreganillo; detail above

BS

Left: *Aloysia gratissima* Whitebrush; detail above left

**Native Distribution** Giant Bur-sage is
typically found in sandy washes and
canyons to 4,500 feet in elevation in
southern Arizona and southern California,
and also in Baja California, Sonora,
Sinaloa, and Durango, Mexico.

**Culture** Temperatures below about 30° F
can damage Giant Bur-sage, and it will
freeze to the ground in the low 20s F;
however, the plant usually recovers and
looks lusher than before. In fact, if it
doesn't freeze back, you may want to
prune it nearly to the ground in spring.
Well-drained soil is important, and either
full sun or partial shade suits Giant Bur-
sage. Supplemental irrigation about every
other week in the summer will keep
plants from looking ratty.

**Landscape Use** This is one of those plants
better suited to a supporting rather than a
starring role, because it has no exceptional
features. The foliage could serve as a
backdrop to flowering perennials or silver-
leaved accent plants. Giant Bur-sage
would be good to include in a naturalistic
wash planting. If you have allergies, think
twice about planting this ragweed relative.

Bur-sage, Triangleleaf Bur-sage
*Ambrosia deltoidea*
ASTERACEAE [SUNFLOWER FAMILY]

**Description** Bur-sage is a rounded shrub to
1½ feet high and 2 feet wide. The slender
gray branches become woody with age.
Bur-sage foliage is gray-green, particularly
on the undersides of the 1-inch-long by ½-
inch-wide, triangular- to lance-shaped
leaves. Sometimes the leaf edges are entire
(smooth-margined), though more commonly they are finely toothed. Bur-sage is
evergreen, but in severe drought it will
shed some leaves. Small yellow-green
flowers bloom from December to April,
followed by fruits about the size of a pea
and densely covered with hooked spines.

**Native Distribution** Bur-sage is a common
plant on flats, gravelly hillsides, and mesas
in south-central Arizona and in Sonora
and Baja California, Mexico. It occurs at
elevations between 1,000 and 3,000 feet.

**Culture** A variety of soils are acceptable to
Bur-sage. It prefers full sun and is hardy to
about 22° F. Although it is very drought
tolerant, periodic irrigation in the summer
will keep it looking better. The growth
rate is moderate, and since the form is
naturally compact, you shouldn't have to
do any pruning.

**Landscape Use** Bur-sage's small size and
unassuming appearance allow it to work
in a variety of landscape situations. It is
tough enough for highway median plantings yet attractive enough to plant around
a home. Use Bur-sage throughout a cactus
garden to soften and unify the planting.
You might try it as a groundcover for
erosion control. A naturalistic Sonoran
Desert landscape would hardly look
complete without some Bur-sage. And
Bur-sage plays a nurturing role to other
desert plants. As a "nurse plant," it
provides shade and physical protection to
help seedlings of Palo Verde (*Cercidium*
species), cacti, and other desert plants
survive until they're big enough to make it
on their own. Despite all its attributes,
Bur-sage should not be a dominant plant
in your landscape if you suffer from
allergies.

White Bur-sage
*Ambrosia dumosa*
ASTERACEAE [SUNFLOWER FAMILY]

**Description** White Bur-sage is an intricately branched evergreen shrub about
2 feet high and 3 feet wide. The common
name refers to the light gray to white
stems and the lacy leaves, which are
½ inch long and ¼ inch wide. The leaves
are light green when young but become

gray with age. At maturity the slender branches become spiny. Small greenish flowers at the ends of stems aren't noticed much by anyone except allergy sufferers, who may be bothered by the wind-blown pollen. White Bur-sage normally has two blooming periods: from February to June and from September to November.

**Native Distribution** Southern Nevada and Utah, eastern California, and western Arizona, as well as Baja California and northern Sonora, Mexico, are home to White Bur-sage. It is a common shrub of the desert, occurring on dry plains, mesas, and slopes and in washes and canyons, generally from 500 to 3,500 feet in elevation.

**Culture** In the desert, White Bur-sage grows in loose, well-drained soil, so you should try to provide the same conditions in your landscape. Full sun is best. The plant is very drought tolerant once established. White Bur-sage is hardy to 10–15° F or lower.

**Landscape Use** White Bur-sage develops a delicate, open appearance with age. An interesting contrast could be achieved by planting it with a coarse-textured plant such as Brittlebush (*Encelia farinosa*) or Quail Brush (*Atriplex lentiformis*). The bold forms of *Agave* and *Yucca* also contrast well with White Bur-sage. Several plants could be massed for a groundcover effect. White Bur-sage also works well in small spaces. It can be incorporated into naturalized desert landscapes, placed in a random manner.

## Cane Beardgrass

**Andropogon barbinodis (syn.,
Bothriochloa barbinodis)**
POACEAE [GRASS FAMILY]

**Description** The seedheads of Cane Beardgrass are about 4 inches long, with several upright, fluffy branches. They appear from April to October. This perennial bunchgrass can reach 3 feet high and 1½ feet or more in diameter. Cane Beardgrass has rough-textured leaf blades to 3 inches long and ¼ inch wide.

**Native Distribution** Cane Beardgrass occurs from Oklahoma and Texas through New Mexico and Arizona to California, as well as south to Mexico. Typical habitat consists of open sandy or gravelly ground and rocky slopes, from 1,000 to 6,000 feet in elevation.

**Culture** Full sun to partial shade is acceptable for this grass, which grows best in well-drained soil. Cane Beardgrass is very drought tolerant once established. More vigorous growth results with irrigation through the warm season. The plant's cold hardiness extends to 10° F. You can cut older, ratty-looking clumps of grass to the ground in early spring to rejuvenate.

**Landscape Use** An attractive meadow effect can be achieved by incorporating Cane Beardgrass and other grasses with annual and perennial wildflowers. Cane Beardgrass can be scattered throughout a naturalistic desert landscape for variation in texture. Used *en masse*, the grass provides erosion control on a slope.

## Flame Anisacanthus, Wright Anisacanthus

**Anisacanthus quadrifidus var. wrightii**
ACANTHACEAE [ACANTHUS FAMILY]

**Description** Brilliant red to orange flowers appear on Flame Anisacanthus from June to November. The 1½-inch-long flowers are narrow and tube-shaped at the base, separating above into four parts that form a cross shape. This deciduous, irregularly branching shrub can reach a height of 3 feet with a 4-foot spread. When young, the branches are dull green and covered with a soft fuzz; older branches have tan,

*Ambrosia ambrosioides*
Giant Bur-sage

*Ambrosia deltoidea*
Bur-sage

*Ambrosia dumosa*
White Bur-sage

Above left and right: *Andropogon barbinodis* Cane Beardgrass

*Anisacanthus quadrifidus* var. *wrightii* Flame Anisacanthus

shredding bark. The leaves are 1½ to 2 inches long and ¾ inch wide at the base, narrowing to a point at the tip.

**Native Distribution** Flame Anisacanthus grows on rocky stream banks and floodplains in southwestern Texas and in Coahuila, Nuevo León, and Tamaulipas, Mexico.

**Culture** Full sun promotes the best flowering, although Flame Anisacanthus will tolerate partial shade. Once established, it is drought tolerant. Supplemental water will encourage heavier flowering. The shrub is cold hardy to 5° F. It will grow in clay, loam, sand, or caliche, but good drainage is preferred. Cut the plant back severely in late winter to promote full growth and more flowers.

**Landscape Use** This long-blooming shrub could be used in a flower garden; place it near the back or along the edges so it has room to spread. Another potential use is in a naturalistic desert landscape. Hummingbirds and butterflies are attracted to the brightly colored flowers of Flame Anisacanthus.

## Desert-honeysuckle
### Anisacanthus thurberi
ACANTHACEAE [ACANTHUS FAMILY]

**Description** Desert-honeysuckle's orange, 1½-inch-long tubular flowers occur most abundantly in spring but also in summer and fall. The light to medium green leaves are 1½ inches long, ½ inch wide, and lance-shaped or oblong. Desert-honeysuckle has an upright form when young, spreading somewhat with age to 3 feet wide. A typical height of this mostly deciduous shrub is 4 feet.

**Native Distribution** Rocky canyons and sandy washes in southern Arizona, southwestern New Mexico, and adjacent Sonora and Chihuahua, Mexico, are habitat for Desert-honeysuckle, which grows at elevations between 2,000 and 5,000 feet.

**Culture** Desert-honeysuckle grows best in full sun but does tolerate partial shade. Well-drained soil is preferable. Once established, Desert-honeysuckle can survive on rainfall alone, though supplemental irrigation about twice a month through the summer keeps the foliage looking lusher. Its cold hardiness extends to at least the mid-20s F. A severe pruning every few years will rejuvenate the foliage and promote more flowers.

**Landscape Use** An informal hedge can be planted using Desert-honeysuckle. Its relatively small size allows it to be used in various situations, including poolside plantings, median strips, near buildings, or in mixed plantings. You could mimic its natural occurrence by planting it along a wash.

## Queen's Wreath, Coral Vine
### Antigonon leptopus
POLYGONACEAE [BUCKWHEAT FAMILY]

**Description** Lush green foliage and large sprays of pink flowers give Queen's Wreath a tropical appearance. The vine is herbaceous from a slightly woody base, and it climbs vigorously by tendrils. The leaves are heart-shaped, about 4 inches long and 3 inches wide. Except in the mildest winters, the foliage dies back to the ground. With the onset of warm weather, it regrows from an underground tuber. With some support, it can grow to 25 feet in height and width. It blooms from midsummer to fall.

**Native Distribution** Queen's Wreath hails from Mexico, on the Baja California peninsula and from Sonora to Chihuahua and Oaxaca. It is found along washes, in canyons, and on slopes, often clambering over trees and shrubs.

*Culture* Queen's Wreath loves heat and sunshine. A protected location that receives plenty of light is ideal. The foliage will brown and drop at temperatures below freezing. In areas where the temperature goes below the mid-20s F you should protect the roots with mulch. The plant is tolerant of different soil types. Growth is rapid with moderate waterings and even faster with ample. Queen's Wreath is drought tolerant once established, but its means of enduring drought (dropping leaves) may not be acceptable in a garden setting.

*Landscape Use* When you need a fast-growing vine to provide shade or screening, choose Queen's Wreath. The foliage is quite attractive and the flowers are an added bonus. Trained on a patio trellis, it can create cooling shade in the summer, yet its deciduous nature allows the sun's warmth to penetrate in winter. The flowers attract bees.

A cultivar (cultivated variety) named 'Baja Red' has deep rose flowers.

---

## Prickly-poppy
### *Argemone platyceras* (syn., *Argemone munita*)
PAPAVERACEAE [POPPY FAMILY]

*Description* Showy white 4-inch flowers with yellow centers bloom almost year-round, though most heavily in spring and summer. The delicate, crepe paper–like petals are an unusual contrast to the prickly foliage. The leaves are gray-green, 6 inches long by 3 inches wide, and deeply lobed. Both the upper and lower leaf surfaces, as well as the stems, are densely covered with ¼-inch yellow spines. Prickly-poppy's sap is also yellow. The plant is a short-lived perennial reaching 3 feet high and 2 feet wide.

*Native Distribution* This distinctive plant is most abundant in dry, sandy soil. It ranges from South Dakota and Wyoming to Texas, California, and northern Mexico, from 1,500 to 8,000 feet in elevation.

*Culture* Prickly-poppy grows best in sandy, well-drained soil, with full sun. It does fine on rainfall alone. The lower limit of its cold tolerance is 15° F.

*Landscape Use* Prickly-poppy's spiny foliage and fragile-looking flowers create a stunning combination that could be the focal point of a flower garden. Because of the unfriendly foliage, be sure to locate plants a safe distance from walkways and patios.

---

## Purple Threeawn
### *Aristida purpurea*
POACEAE [GRASS FAMILY]

*Description* Purple Threeawn is a densely tufted bunchgrass to 1½ feet high and about as wide. Its slender stems and 6-inch, delicate, nodding heads have a purplish cast. The awns, or bristles, are 2 inches long, with three attached to each seed. This grass produces heads from April through October. Purple Threeawn's leaf blades range from 2 to 6 inches long and less than ⅛ inch broad.

*Native Distribution* This grass's distribution includes Arkansas, Kansas, Colorado, Utah, Texas, New Mexico, southern Arizona, and northern Mexico. It grows on sandy or rocky plains and slopes, frequently on roadsides, from 1,000 to 5,000 feet in elevation.

*Culture* A variety of soil types are acceptable for this grass. It grows best in full sun, with rainfall alone or perhaps with a monthly irrigation in summer. It is cold hardy to 10° F or below. Purple Threeawn can be cut to the ground after the seedheads ripen, or the older plants can be pulled to allow volunteer seedlings to mature.

Above left and right: *Anisacanthus thurberi* Desert-honeysuckle

*Antigonon leptopus* Queen's Wreath

*Argemone platyceras* Prickly-poppy;
detail below left

*Aristida purpurea* Purple Threeawn

**Landscape Use** Purple Threeawn lends a graceful feeling to any landscape. It can be scattered with wildflowers to achieve a meadow effect or mass-planted as an accent. Try combining it with a coarse-textured plant such as Prickly-pear (*Opuntia* species) for contrast. The seeds of Purple Threeawn attach readily to socks and other knit clothing, so keep the grass away from sidewalks.

## Sand Sagebrush
### Artemisia filifolia
ASTERACEAE [SUNFLOWER FAMILY]

**Description** The upright branches of Sand Sagebrush appear wispy because of the silvery, threadlike leaves. Strongly aromatic, the three-part evergreen leaves are less than ⅟₁₆ inch wide and 1 inch long. From spring through fall, yellowish white flowers bloom, noticed primarily by people who suffer from allergies. The shrub grows to a height of 4 feet and a width of 5 feet.

**Native Distribution** Sand Sagebrush inhabits sand dunes and other areas with deep, sandy soil, between 2,500 and 6,000 feet in elevation. Its range extends from Nebraska and Wyoming to Nevada, and south to Arizona and Texas. In Mexico it occurs in the state of Chihuahua.

**Culture** If your soil isn't sandy, or at least very well-drained, choose another plant to substitute for Sand Sagebrush. It prefers full sun and is very tolerant of cold and drought. Temperatures to 0° F or lower won't harm this shrub. Once established, Sand Sagebrush will survive on rainfall alone in most desert areas; however, supplemental irrigation once or twice a month in the summer will promote a lusher appearance. You'll ruin the plant's graceful appearance if you shear it. Any stems that need pruning should be taken back to a main branch or the plant's base.

**Landscape Use** Sand Sagebrush can be planted as an informal hedge or as a background plant. Its foliage moves with the slightest breeze, lending a graceful feeling to the landscape. It is useful for soil erosion control.

## Western Mugwort, White-sage
### Artemisia ludoviciana
ASTERACEAE [SUNFLOWER FAMILY]

**Description** The aromatic evergreen foliage of Western Mugwort is silvery green from a fine covering of white hair. The slender 2- to 3-inch-long leaves are variable in shape, from entire (smooth-margined) to toothed or lobed. This herbaceous perennial spreads by rhizomes (creeping underground stems) to form colonies about 2 feet high and 3 feet or more wide. The tiny yellowish white flowers are carried in loose spikes above the foliage from July to October. Western Mugwort's wind-borne pollen is allergenic.

**Native Distribution** Western Mugwort is widespread in temperate North America, at elevations from 2,500 to 8,500 feet. Typical habitat includes dry plains, slopes, and canyons.

**Culture** Western Mugwort can grow in a variety of soil types if they are well drained. Partial shade is acceptable, even preferred in the hottest desert areas, but the most attractive foliage will be produced in full sun. Once established, Western Mugwort needs extra water only during extended drought. Frost damage isn't a concern with this plant—it is cold hardy to 0° F or lower. Because of its way of spreading by underground rhizomes, Western Mugwort can be aggressive, particularly in rich soil. Cutting the plant back or mowing once a year in late summer will promote full, dense growth.

**Landscape Use** Plant Western Mugwort where its vigorous root system will provide soil erosion control but not overtake other plants. A mass planting would be attractive. The silvery foliage could be contrasted with green-foliaged plants or combined with other gray-toned plants for a monochromatic garden. A variety of plant forms and textures would give the planting interest.

## Pineleaf Milkweed
### *Asclepias linaria*
ASCLEPIADACEAE [MILKWEED FAMILY]

**Description** Needlelike leaves about 1½ inches long cover the upright, flexible stems of Pineleaf Milkweed. If you break off or prune a stem, the white sap characteristic of milkweeds oozes out. This evergreen plant can be considered a shrub, because the stems near the base are usually woody. The rounded form typically reaches 2 feet high and 3 feet wide. White flowers in clusters 2 inches across bloom from March through October. Papery, inflated fruits turn from pale green to tan at maturity. They measure 2 inches long and 1 inch wide. The end of the fruit narrows to a point.

**Native Distribution** Rocky slopes, canyons, and arroyos are typical habitats for Pineleaf Milkweed. Its range includes southern Arizona and much of Mexico, at elevations of 1,500–6,000 feet.

**Culture** Pineleaf Milkweed prefers well-drained soil and full sun. Its growth rate is usually moderate, though this can be affected by soil type and the amount of irrigation. Give plants a deep soaking once or twice a month in the summer. Pineleaf Milkweed is cold hardy to at least the mid-20s F.

**Landscape Use** Pineleaf Milkweed's foliage can add interest to the landscape. A plain background such as a stucco wall shows off the foliage best. In an open area, a mass planting of at least three plants would have the greatest impact. The flowers, which bloom over a long period, attract butterflies. You might want to incorporate Pineleaf Milkweed into an entry planting or use it near a patio or pool.

## Desert Milkweed
### *Asclepias subulata*
ASCLEPIADACEAE [MILKWEED FAMILY]

**Description** Desert Milkweed's slender gray-green stems grow vertically to 4 feet from a woody base. The plant's spread can reach 2 feet or more. Leaves 2 inches long by ⅛ inch wide appear on new growth but soon drop. The white milky sap that oozes from cut stems contains rubber. From spring through fall, flat-topped clusters of pale yellow flowers top each stem. The pod is ornamental too: horn-shaped and 3 inches long, it narrows from a ¾-inch-diameter base to a point. The pod splits open when ripe to disperse a silvery fluff of seeds.

**Native Distribution** Desert Milkweed typically grows in sandy washes and less frequently on desert plains or rocky hillsides. It occurs in southern Nevada, western Arizona, and southeastern California, and in Baja California, Sonora, and Sinaloa, Mexico, from near sea level to 2,500 feet.

**Culture** Good drainage is important for Desert Milkweed, as is full sun. It is hardy to at least the low 20s F. After plants are established, they can tolerate long periods of drought. Excessive watering encourages succulent growth favored by aphids. The pests are usually seasonal and don't seriously stunt the plants.

**Landscape Use** This plant's form creates a strong vertical accent in the landscape. You might use it in a courtyard or near a pool. Desert Milkweed lends an authentic note to desert wash plantings, and the flowers attract butterflies.

*Artemisia filifolia* Sand Sagebrush

*Artemisia ludoviciana* Western Mugwort

*Asclepias linaria* Pineleaf Milkweed

Below left and right: *Asclepias subulata* Desert Milkweed

## Fourwing Saltbush, Chamiso
### *Atriplex canescens*
CHENOPODIACEAE [GOOSEFOOT FAMILY]

**Description** Fourwing Saltbush is a densely branched, rounded shrub, to 5 feet high and 8 feet wide. The evergreen leaves are pale gray-green, slender, and 2 inches long. Anytime from March through September, inconspicuous yellow-green clusters of male and female flowers are borne on separate plants. The masses of yellowish tan fruits on the female plants are conspicuous. Each ½-inch fruit has four papery wings.

**Native Distribution** This is the most widely distributed *Atriplex* species in the United States. Its north-south range extends from Alberta, Canada, to San Luis Potosí, Mexico. Within the United States it occurs from South Dakota to eastern Washington and from California to Texas, on alkaline flats, dry slopes, grasslands, and along washes. Fourwing Saltbush grows from sea level to 7,000 feet in elevation.

**Culture** Fourwing Saltbush can grow in a broad range of soil types, including saline soil, and it tolerates alkalinity. The plant is very drought tolerant once established. You can increase its growth rate and ultimate size by providing supplemental water. The additional moisture also encourages lusher foliage. Choose a sunny location for planting. As its occurrence in the northern United States and Canada might suggest, Fourwing Saltbush is tolerant of cold. Tender young growth can be nipped by low temperatures, but the foliage recovers quickly. After most of the fruits have fallen, the fruiting stalks can be removed to improve the shrub's appearance.

**Landscape Use** Various birds, including towhees, sparrows, finches, doves, and quail, and desert mammals eat the seeds of Fourwing Saltbush. Animals also use the shrub for cover and nesting. The plant forms an extensive root system, valuable for erosion control. It establishes easily on disturbed sites. At times its vigor leads to invasiveness, so keep an eye out for unwanted seedlings, particularly in well-watered areas. Fourwing Saltbush can be used for informal or clipped hedges and background plantings. The silvery foliage highlights green plants.

## Tubercled Saltbush
### *Atriplex acanthocarpa*
CHENOPODIACEAE [GOOSEFOOT FAMILY]

**Description** Silvery gray evergreen foliage covers the rounded form of Tubercled Saltbush, which can reach 2–3 feet in height and width. The leaves are lance-shaped to oblong, toothed, to 1 inch long and ½ inch wide. The common name refers to the ¼-inch tubercles, or finger-like projections, on the spongy fruits. Inconspicuous clusters of light greenish gray flowers appear in summer and fall.

**Native Distribution** Tubercled Saltbush grows on alkaline flats from 2,000 to 4,400 feet in elevation in southeastern Arizona, southern New Mexico, and western Texas, and in Chihuahua, Nuevo León, and San Luis Potosí, Mexico.

**Culture** Choose a location with full sun for Tubercled Saltbush. It can grow in silty, alkaline soils or other soil types. The compact form should not require pruning. Tubercled Saltbush is very drought tolerant, although a deep soaking every few weeks through the summer will help maintain a moderate growth rate. The shrub is hardy to the low 20s F or below.

**Landscape Use** Tubercled Saltbush could be used for a low, informal hedge, or as a foundation planting near buildings, to link the structures with the landscape visually. The attractive silvery foliage creates a contrast when interplanted with green-foliaged plants such as Creosote Bush

(*Larrea tridentata*), Ruellia (*Ruellia peninsularis*), or Autumn Sage (*Salvia greggii*). The foliage could also form a neutral backdrop to flowering perennials.

---

## Desert-holly
### *Atriplex hymenelytra*
CHENOPODIACEAE [GOOSEFOOT FAMILY]

**Description** Holly-shaped leaves are responsible for this plant's nickname; however, it is not a holly but is in the same family as Fourwing Saltbush (*Atriplex canescens*). The compact evergreen shrub reaches 2 feet high and 3 feet wide at maturity. Silvery white leaves measure 1½ inches long and nearly as wide. With age, the leaves take on a purplish cast. Inconspicuous gray-green flowers appear from February to April, then develop into disk-shaped papery fruits ¼ inch in diameter.

**Native Distribution** Desert-holly grows in gravelly washes, on alkaline flats, and on slopes, below 2,500 feet in elevation. Its distribution includes southwestern Utah, southern Nevada, southeastern California, southwestern Arizona, Baja California, and Sonora, Mexico.

**Culture** This sometimes finicky plant does best in coarse, well-drained soil, with full sunlight. Be careful not to overwater through the summer. Once established, Desert-holly can survive on rainfall only or with perhaps one irrigation per month during the warm season. Desert-holly is reliably hardy to the upper 20s F. The compact form needs no pruning.

**Landscape Use** Take full advantage of Desert-holly's striking silvery foliage by placing it against a darker background: boulders, a low wall, or deep green plants. The spiny-looking foliage complements cacti and other succulents. The silver-blue Agaves are stunning interplanted with Desert-holly.

## Quail Brush
### *Atriplex lentiformis*
CHENOPODIACEAE [GOOSEFOOT FAMILY]

**Description** The blue-gray leaves of Quail Brush are variable in shape, from oblong to oval to triangular, and 1½ inches long by 1 inch wide. The gray branches are often sharp-tipped. This deciduous, many-branched shrub has a rounded form and measures 8 feet high with a 12-foot spread. Clusters of greenish flowers appear along the branches from February through April, followed by tan, papery fruits about ⅛ inch across.

**Native Distribution** Quail Brush is native to southwestern Utah, southern Nevada, southeastern California, the western half of Arizona, and the Mexican states of Baja California and Sonora. It usually grows on alkali flats and slopes, below 3,000 feet in elevation.

**Culture** Quail Brush will grow in most soil types, including poorly drained ones. Full sun encourages the best growth. It looks better with supplemental irrigation once or twice a month through the summer. Extra water will promote moderate to fast growth. Quail Brush is hardy to 15° F, at least. Removing the old seedheads will make the plant look tidier. Although pruning is not necessary, it can be used to encourage a more compact form.

**Landscape Use** If you have a site with poorly drained alkaline soil where other plants struggle, consider Quail Brush. It can be mass-planted for a screen or background. The silvery foliage contrasts well with green plants such as Desert Broom (*Baccharis sarothroides*). The shrub provides food and cover for a variety of desert wildlife.

*Atriplex acanthocarpa* Tubercled Saltbush

BS

*Atriplex canescens* Fourwing Saltbush

*Atriplex hymenelytra* Desert-holly

*Atriplex lentiformis* Quail Brush

## Obovateleaf Saltbush
### *Atriplex obovata*
CHENOPODIACEAE [GOOSEFOOT FAMILY]

**Description** This low, rounded evergreen shrub is generally woody only at the base. Its mature height is about 1 foot, with a 2-foot spread. The thick silver-gray leaves are oval, to ¾ inch long and ½ inch wide. Both the greenish gray flowers, which occur in loose spikes, and the disclike fruits are inconspicuous.

**Native Distribution** Obovateleaf Saltbush is found in western and south-central Colorado, western Texas, southern New Mexico, and southeastern Arizona. In Mexico, it occurs in Chihuahua, Durango, and Zacatecas. Typical habitat is desert flats in dry, alkaline soil, at altitudes to 5,500 feet.

**Culture** This plant accepts a wide range of soil types, from well-drained to the heavy soil of its native habitat. It prefers full sun. Obovateleaf Saltbush is cold hardy to near 0° F. Once established, only occasional irrigation through the summer is recommended. Excessive water encourages rank growth.

**Landscape Use** Obovateleaf Saltbush makes an excellent groundcover. Its compact size suits it to a variety of landscape situations, including median plantings. The light foliage could be combined with darker plants such as Sugar Sumac (*Rhus ovata*) for a dramatic contrast.

## Desert Saltbush, Cattle-spinach
### *Atriplex polycarpa*
CHENOPODIACEAE [GOOSEFOOT FAMILY]

**Description** The small, ½-inch-long by ¼-inch-wide, silvery leaves of Desert Saltbush drop early in the season, revealing an intricate framework of slender, stiff branches. The shrub averages 4 feet high with a width of 6 feet. From February to October, light greenish gray inconspicuous flowers appear on separate male and female plants. The papery fruits are tan when ripe, and only ⅛-inch long.

**Native Distribution** Desert Saltbush is usually found on alkaline flats below 3,500 feet in elevation. Its range includes southwestern Utah, southern Nevada, southeastern California, and southern and western Arizona. In Mexico, Desert Saltbush occurs in Baja California and Sonora.

**Culture** This shrub can grow in poorly drained alkaline soil as well as in more favorable soil types. It prefers full sun. The rounded shape typically needs no pruning. Desert Saltbush is very drought tolerant, and it can get by on rainfall alone once established. It is hardy to 25° F or below.

**Landscape Use** Desert Saltbush's primary use in the landscape is for soil erosion control. It can be planted in naturalistic desert landscapes, particularly in alkaline spots. The common name Cattle-spinach refers to the fondness of cattle for the shrub. Although your plants won't likely be grazed by livestock, the seeds provide food for desert birds.

## Desert Broom
### *Baccharis sarothroides*
ASTERACEAE [SUNFLOWER FAMILY]

**Description** GREEN! is the first thought many people have when they see Desert Broom, a rounded evergreen shrub to 5 feet high and about as wide. The linear leaves are ¾ inch long by ⅛ inch wide and brighter green than most other desert foliage. In severe drought the leaves will drop, but the greenish color of the stems remains. Desert Broom plants are either male or female, according to flower type. The flowers on both plants are small, white, and inconspicuous. After blooming in the fall, the female flowers develop into seeds, which cover the plant with a fluffy blanket of white. It's a beautiful sight . . . until the seeds start to blow around and make a mess. The seeds germinate easily, creating the added nuisance of unwanted plants. You can avoid the problem by asking the nursery for plants grown from male cuttings.

**Native Distribution** Desert Broom is found from southern California through southern Arizona to southeastern New Mexico, and in the Mexican states of Baja California, Sonora, and Sinaloa. The plants are common along washes, in bottom-lands, and on low hills. Desert Broom is quick to colonize disturbed areas such as roadsides. Its elevational range is from near sea level to 5,500 feet.

**Culture** Any soil is okay for Desert Broom, even poorly drained or alkaline. It isn't fussy about water, either, accepting anything from ample irrigation to rainfall only. The growth rate will be fast with moderate water. You can control rank growth caused by excessive water or rich soil by pruning Desert Broom nearly to the ground. It will regrow with healthy, dense foliage. Desert Broom is cold hardy to at least 15° F. It will grow in full sun or partial shade.

**Landscape Use** If you need a quick hedge or privacy screen, plant Desert Broom and give it a little water. This fast-growing plant has also been utilized for revegetation and erosion control on banks. The fresh green foliage mixes well with silver-foliaged plants such as Brittlebush (*Encelia farinosa*) or Texas Ranger (*Leucophyllum frutescens*). You might use it as a backdrop for flowering plants. Desert Broom tolerates a variety of adverse conditions, a quality that suits it to the inhospitable strips of land beside and between roadways.

# Bahia
## *Bahia absinthifolia*
ASTERACEAE [SUNFLOWER FAMILY]

**Description** Yellow, daisylike flowers 1 inch in diameter bloom above Bahia's silvery foliage in spring and fall. Bahia is a perennial, with many herbaceous branches rising from a woody base. It reaches 1 foot high and a little wider. The leaves are about 2 inches long, and linear (long and narrow) or somewhat wider and three-cleft.

**Native Distribution** Bahia is found on rocky slopes and desert plains, often in caliche soil. Western Texas, southern New Mexico, southeastern Arizona, and Chihuahua and Sonora, Mexico, are included in the plant's geographic range.

**Culture** This perennial can grow in shallow, caliche soil and prefers full sun. Though it is drought tolerant, supplemental irrigation will extend the flowering season. Bahia withstands temperatures to 15° F. The growth rate is fast, and new plants volunteer readily.

**Landscape Use** Attractive foliage and flowers and a neat habit suit Bahia for use in a low border or flower garden. It could be intermingled with other wildflowers and grasses in a meadow-type planting. Bahia, in a mass planting, would serve well as a groundcover.

# Desert-marigold
## *Baileya multiradiata*
ASTERACEAE [SUNFLOWER FAMILY]

**Description** Desert-marigold blooms just about all year, slowing down only in cold weather. The flowers are bright yellow, daisylike, and almost 2 inches in diameter, borne singly on 1-foot-high stems. Soft white hairs cover the lobed gray-green leaves, which are 2 inches long and 1 inch wide. The foliage forms a compact, 6-inch-

*Atriplex obovata* Obovateleaf Saltbush

*Atriplex polycarpa* Desert Saltbush

*Baccharis sarothroides* Desert Broom

*Bahia absinthifolia* Bahia

high, 1-foot-wide mound. Desert-marigold is a short-lived perennial, but it reseeds readily, so there's usually a constant supply of new plants.

**Native Distribution** Desert-marigold graces desert plains, mesas, and rocky slopes from southeastern California, southern Utah and Nevada, Arizona, New Mexico, and western Texas, to Chihuahua, Coahuila, Sonora, and the Baja California peninsula in Mexico. It also seems to like the disturbed soils along roadways, where it benefits from runoff. The plant usually occurs at elevations below 5,000 feet.

**Culture** Give Desert-marigold a sunny location and a little extra water during dry periods, and it will reward you with a profusion of flowers. Don't overdo the irrigation, though, or you'll get a spindly plant with more foliage than flowers. Desert-marigold is very cold hardy. The soil can be sandy, gravelly, or loamy, though good drainage is necessary. You can encourage prolonged bloom by pruning back the dried flower stalks, or you can rejuvenate the entire plant by shearing it about 3 inches above the ground. For a large planting, it might be easier to use a lawn mower.

**Landscape Use** Almost any landscape will look better with some Desert-marigold. It is nice when scattered in a naturalistic landscape, or in a flower bed with other showy perennials such as *Penstemon* species or Globemallow (*Sphaeralcea ambigua*). Since Desert-marigold doesn't grow very large, you can tuck it into a variety of small spaces. Desert-marigold can soften the appearance of and add color to a cactus garden without requiring excessive irrigation that might rot the cacti. The flowers last a long time when cut for bouquets.

# Red Barberry
## *Berberis haematocarpa*
BERBERIDACEAE [BARBERRY FAMILY]

**Description** Red Barberry derives its name from the juicy red berries, which are ¼ inch in diameter. They are relished by birds and various mammals. Reportedly a delicious jelly can be made from the berries. The evergreen shrub has erect, stiff branches that reach a height of 5 feet with an equal spread. Each leaf is divided into five leathery, grayish green, toothed leaflets about 1 inch long by ½ inch wide. The foliage resembles holly. Small clusters of fragrant yellow flowers appear from February to May.

**Native Distribution** Red Barberry grows at the upper edges of the desert and into the chaparral vegetation, on rocky slopes and canyons, and occasionally along washes. It is found in Arizona, New Mexico, western Texas, and northern Sonora, Mexico, between 3,000 and 7,000 feet in elevation.

**Culture** Since Red Barberry normally grows at higher elevations, it will need supplemental irrigation during the summer in low desert areas. A deep soaking every two weeks should be adequate. Full sun to partial shade is acceptable. Red Barberry is cold hardy and adaptable to most well-drained soils.

**Landscape Use** Attractive foliage, pretty flowers, and showy berries make Red Barberry a good candidate for landscape use. As a foundation planting around buildings, it has the added advantage of providing some deterrent to break-ins because of the prickly foliage. Red Barberry can serve as an accent plant or be incorporated into a grouping of desert plants. The gray tones of the foliage complement other gray-leaved plants such as Brittlebush (*Encelia farinosa*) or Woolly Butterfly Bush (*Buddleia marrubifolia*). One or more Red Barberry plants can help attract wildlife to your landscape.

## Agarita
### *Berberis trifoliolata*
BERBERIDACEAE [BARBERRY FAMILY]

***Description*** Beautiful, blue-gray foliage is the most striking feature of this rounded shrub, which can grow to 6 feet high and about as wide. Agarita's evergreen, hollylike leaves are divided into three leaflets, each 2 inches long by ¾ inch wide. Clusters of small fragrant yellow flowers appear from February through April. The show doesn't stop then, because bright red ¼-inch berries ripen into fall. Reportedly, the berries make good jelly.

***Native Distribution*** Agarita occurs on flats and rocky hillsides and in pastures. Its range extends from southern and western Texas, through southern New Mexico and Arizona to northern Mexico, including Chihuahua, Coahuila, Nuevo León, Zacatecas, and San Luis Potosí.

***Culture*** Agarita can grow in various types of well-drained soil. The shrub will tolerate partial shade but prefers full sun. Once established, it requires only occasional summer watering. It is quite cold hardy, to at least 15° F.

***Landscape Use*** Attractive foliage, flowers, and fruits suggest Agarita for use as an accent plant. The prickly foliage combines well with succulents such as *Yucca* and *Agave*. That same feature can be useful in security plantings. Agarita could be planted as an informal hedge. Birds love the red berries, and the dense foliage provides good cover.

## Sideoats Grama
### *Bouteloua curtipendula*
POACEAE [GRASS FAMILY]

***Description*** The common name Sideoats Grama refers to the 2-foot-high seed stalk, which bears its twenty to forty spikes mostly along one side. This perennial bunchgrass blooms from April to October. It can reach a height of 2 feet, with a 1½-foot spread. Its foliage is bluish green, drying to a tan color in fall. A typical leaf blade measures 8 inches long and ⅛ inch wide.

***Native Distribution*** Sideoats Grama's range covers southeastern Canada, all of the United States except the extreme northwestern and southeastern sections, and from Mexico south to Argentina. As you might suppose from its broad distribution, Sideoats Grama occurs in a variety of habitats, including prairies, rocky slopes, mesas, woodlands, and forest openings. The elevational range is 2,500–7,000 feet.

***Culture*** Supplemental irrigation during the summer will keep Sideoats Grama looking good. Once or twice a month should be sufficient. Mowing or cutting back by hand in late winter, before new growth begins, will rejuvenate the grass. Sideoats Grama grows best in full sun; it isn't too particular about soil type, though. Because this grass can survive as far north as Canada, it should have no trouble with cold temperatures anywhere in the Southwest.

***Landscape Use*** The fine texture and graceful form of Sideoats Grama complement flowering perennials such as Desert-marigold (*Baileya multiradiata*) and Paperflower (*Psilostrophe cooperi*). In a large area, a meadow effect could be achieved by using this grass with other grass species among perennial and annual wildflowers. Sideoats Grama could be used to soften the hard edges created by sidewalks and patios or to control soil erosion with a mass planting. An additional benefit of planting this grass is that birds and other desert animals relish its seeds.

*Baileya multiradiata* Desert-marigold

*Berberis trifoliolata* Agarita

*Berberis haematocarpa* Red Barberry;
detail below left

*Bouteloua curtipendula* Sideoats Grama

## Blue Grama
### *Bouteloua gracilis*
POACEAE [GRASS FAMILY]

**Description** Blue Grama produces 1-inch seedheads from July to October that curl into a semicircle when dry. Blue Grama is a low-growing bunchgrass to 1½ feet high and 10 inches wide, which can spread to some extent by rhizomes (creeping underground stems). The leaf blades are as long as 6 inches but only ⅛ inch wide, and bluish green turning to a straw color.

**Native Distribution** This grass is native to the western half of North America, extending east to Manitoba, Canada, and Wisconsin and Missouri. Blue Grama occurs on dry plains, rocky hillsides, and mesas, to mountain meadows and forest openings, mostly between 4,000 and 8,000 feet in elevation.

**Culture** Blue Grama should be planted in full sun. It accepts a broad range of soil types. Once established, it is drought tolerant; in summertime, supplemental irrigation every few weeks will encourage abundant production of the ornamental seedheads. When Blue Grama is used as a bunchgrass, it should be cut back severely in late winter to rejuvenate. Sown from seed at a dense rate, it can serve as a turf grass. It will need periodic mowing to a height of 2–3 inches. Blue Grama is hardy to at least 5° F.

**Landscape Use** The curled seedheads of Blue Grama can add interest to a perennial flower garden. It could also be used on a larger scale in a wildflower meadow, interplanted with annual and perennial wildflowers. Blue Grama can be used as a turf grass, and it provides excellent erosion control. The seeds are eaten by birds and other desert animals.

## Woolly Butterfly Bush
### *Buddleia marrubifolia*
LOGANIACEAE [LOGANIA FAMILY]

**Description** Marble-sized orange flower heads and silver-green foliage make a nice combination in Woolly Butterfly Bush. The rounded evergreen shrub reaches a height and width of 5 feet. A dense covering of hairs makes the 1-inch-long and ¾-inch-wide leaves soft to touch. Woolly Butterfly Bush blooms March through August.

**Native Distribution** Woolly Butterfly Bush's home is southwestern Texas and northern Mexico, including the states of Chihuahua, Coahuila, Zacatecas, and San Luis Potosí. It often grows on limestone, in canyons and arroyos, and on slopes, between elevations of 1,800 and 3,800 feet.

**Culture** Plant Woolly Butterfly Bush on a sunny site with well-drained soil. It is very drought tolerant once established, and cold tolerant to at least 15° F.

**Landscape Use** As the common name suggests, butterflies are attracted to this shrub. Patio or poolside plantings would be enhanced by Woolly Butterfly Bush's pretty flowers, which are slightly fragrant. Its silver foliage could be played off deep green plants such as Texas Mountain-laurel (*Sophora secundiflora*), or the plant could stand alone as an accent. Woolly Butterfly Bush is a good-sized plant for a low, informal hedge. Planted near buildings, it can help blend the structure into the landscape.

## Elephant Tree
### *Bursera microphylla*
BURSERACEAE [TORCH WOOD FAMILY]

**Description** This small tree's massive trunk with papery, peeling bark inspired the common name Elephant Tree. In areas protected from frost, Elephant Tree can reach a height of 18 feet with a 20-foot spread. Elsewhere, it may only be a shrub, with a typical size of 6 feet by 8 feet. The wood, bark, and drought-deciduous foliage are aromatic. Dark green compound leaves measure 2 inches long, with seven to thirty-five 4-inch-long, 1/16-inch-wide leaflets. Elephant Tree blooms in July and August, although the small creamy white flowers are not conspicuous. The 1/4-inch oval fruit has yellowish, leathery skin.

**Native Distribution** Elephant Tree is found on rocky hillsides and flats in south-eastern California and southwestern Arizona, as well as in Baja California and from Sonora to Zacatecas, Mexico. It grows below 2,500 feet in elevation.

**Culture** A frost-free location is necessary for growing Elephant Tree; it can be damaged below 30° F, and it will freeze to the ground at 24° F. The plant prefers full sun and well-drained soil. Elephant Tree is very drought tolerant; however, it will drop its leaves during severe moisture stress. Provide supplemental water once a month through the summer to keep it looking good.

**Landscape Use** Elephant Tree can be a stunning accent plant, particularly if its growth isn't stunted by frequent frost damage. In the colder areas of the desert it can be grown in a pot. Some potted plants develop the character of a bonsai. The small fruits are a favorite food of birds.

---

## Yellow Orchid-vine, Gallineta
### *Callaeum macroptera* (syn., *Mascagnia macroptera*)
MALPIGHIACEAE [MALPIGHIA FAMILY]

**Description** Delicately fringed five-petaled yellow flowers adorn Yellow Orchid-vine in late spring. The vine's young stems are medium green; as the plant ages the stems turn gray. Without support, the plant is a twining shrub to 6 feet high, but it can climb to 30 feet if given support. Smooth green leaves are about 2 inches long and 1 inch wide, tapering to a point. After flowering, the showy, papery winged fruits develop, turning from light green to tan at maturity.

**Native Distribution** Baja California, Sonora, and southward throughout most of Mexico is Yellow Orchid-vine's natural range. It is usually found growing along rocky washes, on hillsides, and on sandy plains.

**Culture** Yellow Orchid-vine is a vigorous, fast-growing plant slowed only by temperatures below the mid-20s F. It recovers rapidly from cold damage, though the flowering period might be delayed. The vine should be planted in full sun and, for best growth, given support. A deep soaking once or twice a month in the summer will encourage lush foliage. When stressed for water, the foliage wilts noticeably. Yellow Orchid-vine grows best in well-drained soil.

**Landscape Use** Trained on a trellis, Yellow Orchid-vine can shade a western or southern exposure. The fast-growing foliage will quickly cover a chain link fence or any other feature that needs screening. Its flowers and fruits merit a featured place in the landscape.

---

Purple Mascagnia (*Mascagnia lilacina*), from Coahuila, Mexico, in the Chihuahuan Desert, is similar to Yellow Orchid-vine; however, the leaves are smaller and more rounded, while the flowers are lavender. Small hairs on the foliage can cause skin irritation for some people. Purple Mascagnia is evergreen or cold-deciduous, depending on the microclimate in which it grows. It is somewhat more cold hardy than Yellow Orchid-vine, though not as fast-growing. Otherwise, cultural requirements and landscape use are the same.

*Bouteloua gracilis* Blue Grama

*Buddleia marrubifolia* Woolly Butterfly Bush; detail above left

*Bursera microphylla* Elephant Tree

*Callaeum macroptera* Yellow Orchid-vine

*Mascagnia lilacina* Purple Mascagnia

## Baja Fairy Duster
### *Calliandra californica*
FABACEAE [PEA FAMILY]

*Description* Brilliant red powder puff–like flowers 1½ inches across are the most conspicuous feature of Baja Fairy Duster. The blooms, from which small seedpods ¼ inch wide and 2 inches long develop, occur throughout much of the year. Deep green foliage divided into many tiny leaflets persists through the year unless damaged by frost. The loosely branched shrubs can reach 4 feet high and equally wide.

*Native Distribution* As the common name suggests, Baja Fairy Duster is native to Baja California, Mexico. It usually is found on gravelly flats, on hillsides, and in desert washes.

*Culture* The most important consideration in growing Baja Fairy Duster is temperature. Below about 25° F the branch tips will be damaged. You should plant it in a protected location such as a courtyard. A fairly wide range of soil types is acceptable, although the soil should be well drained. Full sun promotes the most prolific flowering. Once established, Baja Fairy Duster is drought tolerant, although supplemental water several times a month during the summer will boost flower production. The natural growth form of Baja Fairy Duster is very attractive and needs no shaping.

*Landscape Use* As a specimen plant Baja Fairy Duster is hard to beat, with spectacular flowers occurring over a long period. Use it to accent an entryway or to provide interest around a patio area. The shrub would be an excellent complement to a hummingbird garden. Baja Fairy Duster's relatively dense habit could create an attractive, informal hedge. The plants needn't be planted in a straight line; rather, they could be offset for a more natural effect. Because this moderately cold-tender shrub benefits from a sheltered location, you might use it as a foundation planting near the house to relate the structure to the landscape visually. People in colder desert areas who would like to grow Baja Fairy Duster might consider planting it in a large pot, which could be given shelter on cold nights.

## Fairy Duster, False-mesquite
### *Calliandra eriophylla*
FABACEAE [PEA FAMILY]

*Description* When in full bloom, Fairy Duster appears to be covered with a pink mist. The delicate flowers, which vary from light pink to deep rose, have many threadlike stamens crowded together, making a fluffy ball about 1 inch in diameter. The primary bloom period is from February to May, with occasional spurts in summer or fall. Slender, rigid stems are light gray. They are loosely covered with medium green leaves divided into tiny leaflets. The foliage is evergreen to semi-evergreen, depending on temperature and moisture availability. A small, flat pod splits open at maturity, often into a curled shape. In the wild, Fairy Duster is a low shrub to 2 feet high. However, under favorable landscape conditions, it generally takes on a rounded shape 3 feet high and 4 feet wide.

*Native Distribution* Fairy Duster is usually found in sandy washes and on dry gravelly slopes and mesas, between 1,000 and 5,000 feet in elevation. It has a wide distribution, from southeastern California through southern Arizona and New Mexico to western Texas, and in Mexico from Sonora east to Coahuila, south to Jalisco and Puebla, and west to the Baja California peninsula.

*Culture* As suggested by its broad geographical distribution, Fairy Duster is able to grow under a wide range of conditions.

It is hardy to at least 15° F, losing some of its foliage only in extreme cold. Coarse, well-drained soil is preferred, as is full sun. Plants will grow in partial shade, but with sparser foliage and fewer flowers. Established plants are very drought tolerant, able to survive on natural rainfall. In a landscape situation, you may want to give Fairy Duster a deep watering once or twice a month during hot weather to improve its appearance. Supplemental water will also increase the growth rate. Little or no pruning should be necessary for Fairy Duster; indeed, much of its graceful appearance is due to the upright, arching branches, a feature that heavy pruning would ruin.

**Landscape Use** Fairy Duster lends a light texture to the landscape through both its flowers and its foliage. A nice contrast can be achieved by interplanting it with cacti or other succulents such as Agave. The plant's compact size suits it for use in small spaces. In a naturalistic desert landscape, this shrub combines well with Creosote Bush (*Larrea tridentata*), Bursage (*Ambrosia deltoidea*), and Palo Verde (*Cercidium* species). Artificial washes in the landscape will attain more of a natural character with several Fairy Duster plants scattered along the edges. A dense root system provides a deterrent to soil erosion; mass plantings create functional, attractive groundcover for either level areas or slopes. Since hummingbirds are attracted to the flowers, you may wish to plant Fairy Duster where the tiny birds' aerial antics can be enjoyed. Birds and rodents eat the seeds.

## Crucifixion Thorn
### Canotia holacantha
KOEBERLINIACEAE [JUNCO FAMILY]

**Description** The light green branches of this plant closely resemble those of Palo Verde (*Cercidium* species), but Crucifixion

Thorn has a more upright growth form than the Palo Verdes. A mature specimen can reach 15 feet in height with a 10-foot spread. Tiny leaves, about $\frac{1}{16}$ inch long, drop early in the season. The spine-tipped branches are flexible when young, becoming rigid as they grow larger with age. Crucifixion Thorn blooms from May to August, although the small white flowers are inconspicuous. The fruit is an oblong $\frac{1}{4}$-inch-long capsule that turns brown and woody and eventually splits into two slender parts.

**Native Distribution** Crucifixion Thorn is found on dry slopes and mesas, between 2,000 and 4,500 feet in elevation. It occurs in southern Utah, southeastern California, western Arizona, and Sonora, Mexico.

**Culture** Temperatures to 10° F are tolerated by this shrub, which prefers full sun and well-drained soil. After one to two years of establishment, Crucifixion Thorn can be gradually weaned to irrigation once a month through the summer.

**Landscape Use** Crucifixion Thorn can be used as an accent plant for its interesting form, green branches, and clusters of woody fruits. Locate the spiny plant well away from pedestrian areas. Its rather dense branching structure could serve as a screen. The plant would also blend well into naturalistic desert landscapes.

## Saguaro
### Carnegiea gigantea
CACTACEAE [CACTUS FAMILY]

**Description** The main trunk of a mature Saguaro may be 40 feet high and 2 feet in diameter. A woody inner skeleton provides the strength to support ten arms or more. Although the age of a Saguaro is impossible to pinpoint because it doesn't have growth rings like a tree, one indication of age is the appearance of arms. They start to grow when the cactus is

Above and below: *Calliandra eriophylla* Fairy Duster

*Calliandra californica* Baja Fairy Duster

Below left and right: *Canotia holacantha* Crucifixion Thorn

around sixty or seventy years old. Experts believe Saguaros can live to be about two hundred years old. The medium green skin covers twelve to twenty-four ribs, which expand and contract like an accordion depending on the amount of stored moisture within the plant. Stout gray spines occur in crowded clusters along the ribs. The central spine of each cluster is 2–3 inches long, while the radial spines are generally shorter. In May and June, the tips of the arms and the main stem are crowned with funnel-shaped, 3-inch-wide flowers with waxy white petals. Each flower blooms only once, opening at night and staying open into the next day. This is the state flower of Arizona. Smooth-skinned green fruits the size and shape of a chicken egg split open at maturity. The red inner pulp sometimes causes the fruits to be mistaken for flowers. The pulp, which contains tiny black seeds, is edible and very tasty.

**Native Distribution** Saguaros occur mostly below 3,500 feet in elevation, on gravelly slopes. Their distribution is limited to southern Arizona, the extreme southeastern edge of California, and Sonora, Mexico.

**Culture** Saguaros require well-drained soil and full sunlight for best growth. Young nursery-grown plants will probably need protection from the sun after trans-planting. You can cover the plant with a piece of woven shade cloth through its first summer. If you move a Saguaro, keep the same orientation to the south to avoid sunburn on the tender, less exposed skin. Although mature plants can be moved, transplant success decreases with age. Young plants can be watered once a month during extended drought; older, established plants can survive on rainfall alone. Saguaros, particularly seedlings and very old plants, can be severely damaged or killed below 21° F. Bacterial rot can also affect Saguaros; older plants seem to be more susceptible. The rot causes the

normally light green, firm tissue to become brown and mushy, oozing a black, foul-smelling liquid. By the time the problem is noticed, it usually has spread extensively through the plant, and death is imminent. Unless the dying Saguaro poses a danger to buildings, people, or other plants, you can let it decay naturally until just the woody skeleton remains. Some people like to use the skeleton as a decorative element in the landscape.

Gila woodpeckers and gilded flickers make their nesting holes in the main trunk and arms of Saguaros. Other birds such as elf owls and starlings take over the holes after the original occupants move on. Although the nest building is a natural process, the Saguaros in developed communities are affected more heavily because there are fewer per area than in the natural desert. The flickers' holes are potentially the most harmful, because they disturb water-transport tissues in the upper part of the plant. You may be able to discourage the birds' excavations by making a life-size replica of either a Gila woodpecker or a gilded flicker and putting it on the Saguaro. These birds are territorial and may be driven away by the imposter "bird." If the excavation has already begun, you might be able to discourage further activity by wedging a circle of hardware cloth into the opening. Do not fill the hole with any substance like concrete.

**Landscape Use** Saguaros, more than any other plant, say "Southwest." One outstanding specimen could be the focal point of an entire landscape. Locate the cactus well away from structures and pedestrian areas. You might plant "spears" (young plants without arms) of different sizes in a naturalistic desert landscape to mimic the range of sizes found in nature. Because Saguaros are slow growing, they are also well suited to planting in con-tainers. Birds relish the pulp of Saguaro fruits.

# Desert Hackberry

## *Celtis pallida*

ULMACEAE [ELM FAMILY]

**Description** Desert Hackberry is a very densely branched, spiny shrub, though from a distance the spines are not evident and the overall effect is of a medium green mound, to 8 feet high and 10 feet wide. The foliage is evergreen except in extreme cold or drought. Oval leaves 1 inch long and ½ inch wide are coarsely toothed on the edges and rough on both the upper and lower surfaces. Following the spring bloom, greenish yellow flowers turn to small orange berries that ripen in the fall.

**Native Distribution** The typical habitat of Desert Hackberry is along washes, on gravelly plains, and on hillsides, from 1,500 to 4,000 feet in elevation. Its range covers southern and western Texas, southern New Mexico, south-central Arizona, and Sinaloa, San Luis Potosí, and the Baja California peninsula in Mexico.

**Culture** Full sun and well-drained soil are preferred by Desert Hackberry. The normally slow growth rate can be increased with irrigation once or twice a month through the summer. Below 20° F plants will lose their leaves; recovery is quick in the spring, however.

**Landscape Use** The dense habit of Desert Hackberry suits it for informal hedges or screening. Because neither its form nor its foliage is distinctive, the shrub creates a good background for showier accent plants. Perhaps the most common landscape use is to attract wildlife. The flowers are good for honey, the berries provide food for birds and other animals, and the dense growth furnishes excellent cover for quail and other birds. Another functional use of Desert Hackberry is for erosion control.

# Winterfat

## *Ceratoides lanata* (syn., *Eurotia lanata*)

CHENOPODIACEAE [GOOSEFOOT FAMILY]

**Description** Winterfat has a woody base from which herbaceous branches grow upright to a height of 2 feet, spreading to 1½ feet. Both the branches and linear, 1-inch-by-⅛-inch blue-green leaves are woolly with white to rust-colored hairs. Winterfat is evergreen, though the foliage may thin out a bit during summer in the hottest desert areas. Inconspicuous spikes of flowers bloom from April to July, with male and female types on separate plants. The real show begins as the flowers ripen into fruits in fall and winter. Silvery hairs make the fruiting spike glisten, particularly when backlit by the sun. The female plants are the showy ones, but at least one male plant is necessary for cross-pollination. The common name refers to the plant's value as winter forage for livestock, particularly sheep.

**Native Distribution** The natural range of Winterfat is extensive, from eastern Washington to Saskatchewan, Canada, southward to southeastern California and western Texas, and in Mexico from Baja California to Coahuila. Dry plains and mesas from 2,000 to 8,000 feet in elevation are Winterfat habitats.

**Culture** In the hottest desert areas, plant Winterfat in an eastern exposure, where it will be sheltered from the day's worst heat. It needs cool nights, as in its native habitat, to thrive. Winterfat is cold hardy to 0° F. Once established, it is drought tolerant. However, a deep soaking every few weeks in summer will maintain a moderate to fast growth rate. Winterfat is adaptable to most soils, even alkaline. You can keep the plant bushy by pruning it to the ground before the new growth appears in early spring.

**Landscape Use** Winterfat is at its best in fall and winter, a time when the landscape often needs a boost. The showy seedheads

*Celtis pallida* Desert Hackberry

Opposite: *Carnegiea gigantea* Saguaro

*Ceratoides lanata* Winterfat

CM

should be displayed against a dark background of foliage or perhaps against a wall. Even more effective is back-lighting of the plants if they're located on the eastern or western edge of the landscape. In flower gardens, the silvery foliage provides a foil to more vivid colors. Winterfat's spreading roots can provide good erosion control.

---

## Blue Palo Verde

### *Cercidium floridum*
FABACEAE [PEA FAMILY]

**Description** Few desert plants are as beautiful as Blue Palo Verde in bloom. Small, somewhat fragrant yellow flowers occur in such abundance in March or April that the entire plant seems to glow. Flat pods 3 inches long by ½ inch wide mature from medium green to tan. Blue Palo Verde is also distinctive because of its smooth bluish green bark (*palo verde* means "green stick" in Spanish). When the tiny leaflets drop during drought or in winter, the bark, rich in chlorophyll, continues to carry on photosynthesis. Older bark eventually becomes brown and rough. Blue Palo Verde has a very intricate branching pattern, with small spines at each node. Although people usually refer to Blue Palo Verde as a tree, in its natural form it looks more like a large shrub, with branches extending to the ground. The mature size is typically 20 feet high and 25 feet wide.

**Native Distribution** You will usually find Blue Palo Verde growing along dry washes and on floodplains, from sea level to 4,000 feet in elevation. It occurs in southeastern California and southern Arizona and also in Baja California and Sonora, Mexico.

**Culture** Blue Palo Verde is tolerant of most soils, though it prefers sandy soil; good drainage is a must. Plant in full sun, but don't worry about finding a warm spot in your yard; Blue Palo Verde is cold hardy

to 15° F. Give plants a deep soaking once or twice a month in the summer to prevent leaf drop, the natural means of conserving water during drought. This plant will accept a fair amount of irrigation and can even tolerate a lawn situation. If you want to train it into a tree, you'll need to remove the lower branches. Otherwise, pruning can be limited to removal of dead or damaged branches. When you're choosing a location for Blue Palo Verde, keep in mind its abundant production of flowers and seedpods. The litter can be swept from a patio or sidewalk easily enough, but you will probably want to keep the plant away from the pool. An insect called the palo verde root borer (*Derobrachus germinatus*) can infest the plant's roots. Because the borer lives underground, it is hard to control. The best defense against infestation is a healthy plant, so don't let it become seriously drought stressed. Mistletoe, a parasitic plant that looks like a cluster of green sticks, can grow on Blue Palo Verde, weakening or even killing it. A tiny mite can cause distorted clumps of growth, called witches'-broom, that resemble mistletoe. Either condition can be controlled by cutting out the affected branch.

**Landscape Use** A moderately dense shade is cast by Blue Palo Verde. It can cool a patio yet allow enough light through to grow shade-tolerant plants beneath. Blue Palo Verde can also be used to shade the east, west, or southern sides of buildings. As an accent tree it can stand on its own. In an average-sized front yard there may be room for only one plant. On larger properties, a grove of three to five Blue Palo Verdes would be very attractive. The birds would love it too, as they nest in the trees and feed on the flowers and seeds. Desert tortoises have been observed eating the fallen flowers.

## Littleleaf Palo Verde, Foothills Palo Verde
### *Cercidium microphyllum*
FABACEAE [PEA FAMILY]

**Description** Tiny yellow-green leaves clothe the branches of Littleleaf Palo Verde, giving the foliage a delicate, almost hazy look. In contrast, the trunk is often very gnarled. Overall the large shrub or small tree is 12 feet high and 15 feet wide. During winter or in severe drought, Littleleaf Palo Verde drops its leaves. It still looks green, though, because of the chlorophyll in its branches. It blooms in April or May with a profusion of pale yellow ½-inch flowers. The pods contain several pealike seeds that are quite tasty when young and green. Ornamental at close range, the light brown mature pod is constricted between the seeds and pointed at the tip.

**Native Distribution** Littleleaf Palo Verde grows between 500 and 4,000 feet in elevation, in southeastern California, southern Arizona, Baja California, and Sonora, Mexico. It is found most often on rocky slopes in the foothills of desert mountains; it also occurs on plains and sometimes along washes.

**Culture** This plant is tolerant of the harshest conditions. It will grow in rocky or caliche soil, can survive on rainfall alone once established (although summer irrigation speeds the normally slow growth rate), and is hardy to at least 17° F. Put it in a sunny, well-drained site, water it the first year or so to get it going, and then let it be. You can allow the plant to take on its characteristically rugged form or do some pruning to encourage a more refined, small tree shape. The palo verde root borer, mistletoe, and witches'-broom can affect Littleleaf Palo Verde. See the Blue Palo Verde (*Cercidium floridum*) description for more information.

**Landscape Use** Showcase Littleleaf Palo Verde as a specimen tree, even accenting its interesting form with night lighting. The relatively small size allows you to use it in entry courtyards, patios, or other areas where space is limited. Be sure to keep the tree from walkways or play areas, as the branches end in spines. The flowers and seedpods create a fair amount of litter, so keep Littleleaf Palo Verde away from the pool. For an informal screen, place several plants in an uneven line and leave their lower branches unpruned. Littleleaf Palo Verde is also good to include in naturalistic landscapes, along with Creosote Bush (*Larrea tridentata*), Bursage (*Ambrosia deltoidea*), and cacti such as Prickly-pear (*Opuntia* species) or Barrel Cactus (*Ferocactus* species). The flowers reportedly yield good honey. Birds like to nest in Littleleaf Palo Verde, and a variety of desert animals feed on the flowers and seeds.

## Palo Brea, Sonoran Palo Verde
### *Cercidium praecox*
FABACEAE [PEA FAMILY]

**Description** Palo Brea's umbrella-like canopy extends 20 feet high and 25 feet wide above a smooth, lime-green trunk. The small bluish green compound leaves are normally evergreen, though extreme cold can cause the foliage to thin or to shed completely. At each node, the branches bear one or two spines up to ½ inch long. Bright yellow ¾-inch-diameter flowers produced March through May develop into dark tan papery pods 2 inches long and ½ inch wide.

**Native Distribution** Palo Brea grows on desert plains from Sonora and Baja California, Mexico, to Venezuela and Peru.

**Culture** If you live in a cold desert area, you'll need to provide a warm location for Palo Brea. Temperatures in the low 20s F can cause serious damage or death, particularly to young plants. Well-drained

*Cercidium floridum* Blue Palo Verde

*Cercidium microphyllum* Littleleaf Palo Verde

Above and below: *Cercidium praecox* Palo Brea

soil and full sun are recommended for best growth. Palo Brea is very drought tolerant once established. You can increase the normally moderate growth rate by providing supplemental irrigation in the summer. This tree has a naturally high branching pattern; only limited pruning is needed to keep the foliage above people's head level. See the description of Blue Palo Verde (*Cercidium floridum*) for a discussion of pests.

*Landscape Use* Palo Brea's handsome form, attractive foliage, and flowers make it a good choice for almost any landscape. It can serve as the focal point of a planting or create a shady grove with a clustering of several plants. It can also be utilized to shade exposed building faces. The high branching pattern is a good characteristic for street trees or patio and courtyard trees. Try to keep the trunk from being overgrown with nearby shrubs or vines, as the smooth lime-green bark is a most ornamental feature. The tree can provide shelter and nesting sites for birds.

# Desert-willow
## *Chilopsis linearis*
BIGNONIACEAE [BIGNONIA FAMILY]

*Description* Desert-willow isn't really a willow, but its long, slender leaves make it look like one. The foliage is medium green and drops during the winter. Sometimes the leaves turn yellow before falling. Twenty feet high and 15 feet wide is a typical mature size for this large shrub or small tree. Pink to lavender flowers adorn the plant from April through September. The ruffled, trumpet-shaped blooms look something like an orchid, and they are fragrant, too. Desert-willow's white-fringed seeds are enclosed in a slender 8-inch-long pod that turns tan with age. The pods hang on through the winter, making the plant look somewhat shaggy.

*Native Distribution* Desert-willow is commonly found along dry washes between 1,500 and 5,000 feet in elevation throughout much of the southwestern United States and northern Mexico.

*Culture* This tree prefers full sun, though it will grow in partial shade. Once established, rainfall alone will probably keep the plant alive; for more attractive foliage and flowers, provide supplemental irrigation two or three times a month in summer. Desert-willow will grow in a wide range of soil types if the soil is well drained. It is hardy to at least 10° F and probably lower. New growth can be susceptible to frost, so discontinue irrigation by early fall. Left to its own devices, Desert-willow develops a shrubby form, often with basal suckers. Occasional pruning can give it a neater appearance; heavier pruning will be necessary to achieve a tree form. The persistent seedpods can make the plant look ratty, particularly after the leaves drop in the fall. You might want to clip off the pods, although there's no harm in leaving them on, and the seeds can provide food for birds. Desert-willow is a fast-growing plant, given supplemental irrigation.

*Landscape Use* Plant Desert-willow to shade an eastern, southern, or western exposure in the summer, and you'll still be able to enjoy the sun's warming rays in winter. The graceful foliage and beautiful flowers help make this a nice accent tree. Its winter bareness can be softened by incorporating evergreen plants nearby. A grouping of unpruned Desert-willows can provide an informal hedge for visual screening or for blocking the wind. Desert-willow fits well into arroyo plantings and provides shelter for nesting, as well as nectar for hummingbirds.

## Damianita
### *Chrysactinia mexicana*
ASTERACEAE [SUNFLOWER FAMILY]

**Description** Damianita's dark green, needlelike leaves are mostly less than ⅓ inch long, and aromatic when crushed. The evergreen foliage forms a low, shrubby mound 1–2 feet high and about 2 feet wide. Bright yellow daisylike flowers 1 inch in diameter bloom from April to September.

**Native Distribution** Western Texas, New Mexico, and northeastern Mexico are home to Damianita. The plant typically grows on rocky limestone slopes between 1,800 and 7,000 feet in elevation.

**Culture** Sandy to loamy soil and even caliche are tolerated by Damianita. Established plants are very drought tolerant and quite cold hardy, to near 0° F. Give Damianita a location with full sun.

**Landscape Use** Damianita is striking in mass plantings. Its compact size also makes it useful for limited-space areas such as courtyards or median strips. Its extended blooming period suggests its use in flower gardens. If you have a dry, rocky slope that needs some type of vegetative cover, consider Damianita.

## Rabbitbrush
### *Chrysothamnus nauseosus*
ASTERACEAE [SUNFLOWER FAMILY]

**Description** Rabbitbrush produces many erect stems from a woody base that form a rounded evergreen shrub 4 feet high and about as wide. The individual flowers are only about ¼ inch long, but *en masse* they create a stunning bloom from September to November. The flowers develop into golden, bristly seeds. The stems are grayish or whitened with fine, woolly hair. Linear blue-green leaves reach 1–2 inches long and ¹⁄₁₆ inch wide.

**Native Distribution** This plant occurs in western North America, from Canada southward into Mexico. It tends to grow on dry plains, mesas, and slopes, as well as along washes, from 2,000 to 8,000 feet in elevation.

**Culture** The cooler desert areas suit Rabbitbrush best. It is very cold hardy, to below 0° F. However, hot summers cause it to go semi-dormant, and it may look ratty. In the low desert areas it needs water every two weeks or so in the summer. Afternoon shade in those same areas also would ease the stress of summer's heat. Elsewhere, plant Rabbitbrush in full sun. This fast-growing shrub can get leggy, so you may want to prune it nearly to the ground in late spring. It is adaptable to various soil types.

**Landscape Use** A fall show of color can be provided by Rabbitbrush, either scattered throughout a naturalistic landscape or used as an informal, low hedge. Combine it with Autumn Sage (*Salvia greggii*) for complementary flower colors and contrasting foliage colors.

## Arizona Grape Ivy
### *Cissus trifoliata*
VITACEAE [GRAPE FAMILY]

**Description** The deep green, fleshy leaves of Arizona Grape Ivy are three-lobed or divided into three individual leaflets. Overall, the leaves can reach 3 inches long by 2 inches wide. Arizona Grape Ivy will climb by tendrils if given support or crawl on the ground if lacking it. Reportedly the foliage can cause a skin rash in some people, and the plant's underground tubers are poisonous. Small, black, non-edible berries to ¼ inch in diameter develop from inconspicuous flowers that bloom from May to August. The vine is evergreen in mild winters.

Above left and right: *Chilopsis linearis* Desert-willow

*Chrysothamnus nauseosus* Rabbitbrush

*Chrysactinia mexicana* Damianita  <sup>BS</sup>  *Cissus trifoliata* Arizona Grape Ivy

Below left and right: *Clematis drummondii* Old Man's Beard

**Native Distribution** Arizona Grape Ivy clambers over rocks and bushes along washes and in canyons in southern Arizona, Mexico, and tropical America. The elevational range is 3,000–5,000 feet.

**Culture** This vine can grow in full sun or partial shade in various soil types. It requires only occasional watering through extended dry periods. It is somewhat frost tender and can freeze to the ground in the low 20s F, but regrowth is rapid.

**Landscape Use** Arizona Grape Ivy can lend its greenery to walls or fences. An interesting effect can be achieved by planting the vine at the base of a tree such as Velvet Mesquite (*Prosopis velutina*) and letting it climb. It can also be used as a groundcover.

## Old Man's Beard, Virgin's Bower
### *Clematis drummondii*
RANUNCULACEAE [CROWFOOT FAMILY]

**Description** Old Man's Beard is a vine with slender, woody stems climbing to 20–30 feet by twining petioles (leaf stalks). The gray-green, fuzzy compound leaves drop at the onset of winter. Each leaf is composed of three to five lance-shaped, lobed leaflets about 1½ inches long by ½ inch wide. Inconspicuous flowers borne from March to September are followed by showy fruits with many 3-inch-long fuzzy tails that turn from silvery white to rust-colored.

**Native Distribution** This vine is typically found in dry washes and rocky canyons, often climbing over shrubs and trees. Old Man's Beard is found below 4,000 feet in elevation in southern Arizona, New Mexico, and western, central, and southern Texas, as well as in the Mexican states of Baja California, Sonora, Sinaloa, Chihuahua, Coahuila, Durango, Zacatecas, Nuevo León, Tamaulipas, and San Luis Potosí.

**Culture** Old Man's Beard seems content growing either in full sun or in partial shade. It needs support to climb; otherwise it will trail along the ground. Well-drained soil is preferred but not essential. Old Man's Beard will grow moderately fast with supplemental irrigation several times a month through the summer. The vine is cold hardy to at least the low 20s F.

**Landscape Use** Old Man's Beard looks right at home planted near a wash and allowed to clamber over boulders, shrubs, and trees. It can be trained on a trellis to shade the side of a building or provide overhead shade to a patio. The vine's deciduous nature allows sunlight to penetrate in the winter. The unusual fluffy fruits make Old Man's Beard an interesting accent.

## Bitter Condalia
### *Condalia globosa*
RHAMNACEAE [BUCKTHORN FAMILY]

**Description** Bitter Condalia is an intricately branched, rounded shrub or small tree, to 8 feet high and 10 feet wide. Tiny, ¼-inch-long, ⅛-inch-wide, deciduous yellow-green leaves cluster along the spine-tipped branches. The equally diminutive greenish white flowers would go unnoticed if not for their wonderful fragrance. They bloom in March and again in October and November. Black fruits ⅛ inch in diameter have a thin, fleshy, very bitter outer coat around the seed.

**Native Distribution** This plant is usually found along sandy washes and on slopes and gravelly flats, between 1,000 and 2,500 feet in elevation. It occurs in southeastern California and southwestern Arizona and also in Baja California and Sonora, Mexico.

**Culture** Bitter Condalia should receive full sun. It is quite drought tolerant, although you can provide supplemental irrigation monthly through the summer. The ideal soil is well drained. Temperatures as low as 18° F are tolerated without damage.

**Landscape Use** Place Bitter Condalia where its fragrant flowers can be enjoyed, but keep in mind how spiny the branches are. A grouping of these plants could form an impenetrable security barrier. Birds seek shelter among the branches.

---

A similar species, Warnock Condalia (*Condalia warnockii*), is somewhat smaller than Bitter Condalia, yet its fruits are larger (¼-inch diameter) and not bitter. *Condalia warnockii* variety *kearneyana* occurs in southeastern Arizona and Sonora, Mexico, while the variety *warnockii* is found in western Texas, southern New Mexico, and Chihuahua, Coahuila, and Zacatecas, Mexico. Cultural requirements and landscape use are the same as for Bitter Condalia.

---

## Littleleaf Cordia
### *Cordia parvifolia*
BORAGINACEAE [BORAGE FAMILY]

**Description** Evergreen, gray-green leaves 1 inch long and ½ inch wide serve as backdrop to a dazzling display of white bell-shaped flowers on Littleleaf Cordia. The 1½-inch-wide flowers appear sporadically from February to November in response to rain or irrigation. At maturity the open-branched shrub can reach 6 feet high and 8 feet wide.

**Native Distribution** Littleleaf Cordia occurs in Mexico from Sonora to Coahuila, Durango, Zacatecas, and central Baja California. Its usual habitat includes arroyos, alluvial flats, and rocky plains.

**Culture** Once established, plants are drought tolerant. Supplemental irrigation in the summer will help extend the blooming period. Prolonged drought will cause the leaves to drop. Minimal pruning is needed to keep this shrub looking attractive. Littleleaf Cordia will grow on most soil types, though it prefers well-drained soils. It does best in full sun. Cold hardiness is quite good, to about 18° F.

**Landscape Use** Not many desert plants have white flowers, so Littleleaf Cordia can be an interesting addition to the landscape. White accentuates the colors of other flowers while providing a visual cooling effect. Blues, purples, and pinks are especially nice in combination with the white. Littleleaf Cordia can be planted singly, as an accent, or massed for an informal hedge or screen.

---

## Coursetia, Baby Bonnets
### *Coursetia glandulosa* (syn., *Coursetia microphylla*)
FABACEAE [PEA FAMILY]

**Description** The intriguing common name Baby Bonnets is explained come springtime (March and April), when this open-branched shrub displays numerous tiny pea-shaped white, yellow, and pink flowers. Twisted pods 1 to 2 inches long and ¼ inch wide follow the flowers. Coursetia is winter deciduous, the small, compound leaves reappearing about the same time as the flowers. Overall size of the shrub is 8 feet high by 12 feet wide.

**Native Distribution** Typically found in canyons and on gravelly hillsides from 2,000 to 4,000 feet in elevation, Coursetia occurs in southern Arizona and in Baja California, Sonora, and Sinaloa, Mexico.

**Culture** Drought tolerant and cold hardy to about 20° F, Coursetia prefers full sunlight and well-drained soil. Pruning should be limited to the removal of dead branches; the natural form is very beautiful and graceful. The growth rate is moderate with supplemental watering.

*Condalia warnockii* Warnock Condalia ᴮˢ

*Condalia globosa* Bitter Condalia; detail above left

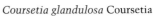

*Cordia parvifolia* Littleleaf Cordia

*Coursetia glandulosa* Coursetia

Irrigation should not be necessary during the dormant (leafless) period, but plants can be deep-watered in the summer for a lusher appearance.

**Landscape Use** Coursetia's informal, open habit looks best in a naturalistic landscape. The fine-textured foliage could provide a contrast to larger-leaved plants. The small flowers are best viewed at close range; however, because of its winter bareness, you may wish to use Coursetia as background to complement an evergreen accent plant. It also makes a nice informal screen.

---

## Silver Dalea
### *Dalea bicolor* var. *argyraea*
FABACEAE [PEA FAMILY]

**Description** Fine hairs cover the evergreen foliage of this rounded shrub, giving it a silvery appearance. A typical mature size is 3 feet by 3 feet. Silver Dalea blooms from July to September, producing short dense purple spikes, about ¾ inch long. Seven to thirteen ¼-inch oval leaflets comprise the 1-inch-long compound leaf.

**Native Distribution** Silver Dalea is found on rocky limestone hills between 1,500 and 5,000 feet in elevation, in western Texas and southern New Mexico and in Chihuahua, Coahuila, and Nuevo León, Mexico.

**Culture** Silver Dalea is hardy to near 10° F. It prefers well-drained soil and full sun. Although it is drought tolerant, periodic irrigation through the warm months will maintain the normally fast growth rate.

**Landscape Use** Silver Dalea makes a good groundcover for hillsides or exposed sites prone to erosion. The fine-textured foliage lends a soft appearance to the landscape; the plant would be appropriate around pools or patios. Silver Dalea's delicate foliage and the strong form of a succulent

such as *Yucca* species or Desert Spoon (*Dasylirion wheeleri*) would be striking together.

---

## Baja Dalea
### *Dalea bicolor* var. *orcuttiana*
FABACEAE [PEA FAMILY]

**Description** The flowering season of Baja Dalea begins in the fall and continues into spring. The rose-purple flower cluster is shaped like an elongated cone, to 2 inches long. Gray-green evergreen foliage covers stiff branches that form a rounded shrub to 3 feet high and equally wide. The compound leaves are 1 inch long, divided into nine to twenty-one leaflets that are ¼ inch long.

**Native Distribution** As the common name indicates, Baja Dalea occurs in Baja California, Mexico, along washes, in canyons, and on rocky hillsides.

**Culture** Full sun promotes the best growth and flowering, although Baja Dalea will tolerate light shade. Well-drained soil is preferred. The biggest challenge in growing Baja Dalea is protecting it from frost. Damage to stem tips can occur at 28° F; however, regrowth is normally rapid. Wait to prune any frost-damaged foliage until all danger of frost is past.

**Landscape Use** You can create an attractive low border with Baja Dalea. It can also be used as a foundation planting to link a structure visually with the surrounding landscape. Baja Dalea can add a bit of color to poolside plantings.

---

## Feather Dalea
### *Dalea formosa*
FABACEAE [PEA FAMILY]

**Description** Feather Dalea is a low, rounded shrub with a mature height and width of 2 feet. It is semi-evergreen, the ¼-inch leaves divided into seven to fifteen tiny light green leaflets. Small violet flowers occur in short clusters about 1 inch long. Each flower is surrounded by feathery plumes, the inspiration for the common name. The seeds also have feathery tails. The blooming season extends from March to September, with the heaviest flowering in spring.

**Native Distribution**  This shrub occurs over a wide portion of the southwestern United States and northern Mexico, including Oklahoma, Colorado, southern Utah, Arizona, New Mexico, western Texas, Sonora, Chihuahua, and Coahuila. It usually grows on gravelly or rocky slopes between 2,000 and 6,500 feet in elevation.

**Culture**  Feather Dalea prefers full sun. It can get leggy with less light or too much water. Once established, the shrub is very drought tolerant. As might be expected from the northerly extent of its range, it is cold hardy, to 0° F. Good drainage is the only important requirement of soil for Feather Dalea; otherwise it is quite adaptable. Feather Dalea's compact form should require little pruning, if any.

**Landscape Use**  This low-growing shrub can form an effective groundcover when used *en masse*. Another use would be as a low border. The pretty, feathery flowers lend interest with both color and texture. Feather Dalea could be used in courtyard gardens or other areas where the flowers could be viewed up close.

---

## Black Dalea
### *Dalea frutescens*
FABACEAE [PEA FAMILY]

**Description**  Black Dalea blooms from August through November. Tiny violet flowers occur in ¾-inch-long clusters above medium green, fine-textured deciduous foliage. The compound leaves

are about ½ inch long, with eight to twenty oval ⅛-inch-long leaflets. This rounded or spreading shrub reaches a height of 3 feet with a 4-foot spread.

**Native Distribution**  This shrub is found on rocky hillsides and along washes in Oklahoma, the western two-thirds of Texas, New Mexico, and the Mexican states of Chihuahua and Coahuila.

**Culture**  Black Dalea grows moderately fast. If it gets leggy, it can be pruned severely to promote a more compact shape. A site with good drainage and full sun is preferred, although light shade is tolerated. Once established, Black Dalea needs minimal water to survive. Supplemental irrigation through the summer will prevent the plant from dropping its leaves to conserve water. Some thinning of the foliage also occurs during cold weather. This plant is cold hardy to about 15° F.

**Landscape Use**  Black Dalea has an attractive, rounded shape that could be used for foundation plantings near buildings. It also looks good in other landscape situations, such as courtyard gardens and patios, or even in naturalistic desert plantings. The fall-flowering Black Dalea could be combined with Autumn Sage (*Salvia greggii*) for a spectacular late-season show.

---

## Trailing Indigo Bush, Gregg Dalea
### *Dalea greggii*
FABACEAE [PEA FAMILY]

**Description**  Delicate gray-green foliage on wiry stems forms a low mound, usually about 1 foot high and up to 4 feet in diameter. Roots grow at any node touching the ground, making Trailing Indigo Bush a good soil stabilizer. The foliage is evergreen. Half-inch purple balls bloom spring through summer. The flowers are pretty at close range, though hardly noticeable from a distance.

*Dalea bicolor* var. *argyraea* Silver Dalea

*Dalea bicolor* var. *orcuttiana* Baja Dalea

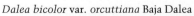

*Dalea formosa* Feather Dalea    CM

*Dalea frutescens* Black Dalea

**Native Distribution** Trailing Indigo
Bush occurs from western Texas south-
ward into Mexico, including the states of
Chihuahua, Coahuila, Tamaulipas, Nuevo
León, Hidalgo, Durango, San Luis Potosí,
Puebla, and Oaxaca. Its typical habitat is
rocky limestone hillsides between 2,000
and 4,500 feet in elevation.

**Culture** Once established, Trailing Indigo
Bush is very drought tolerant, although its
foliage looks sparse with rainfall only.
Some irrigation in the summer will
promote a denser groundcover. Likewise,
full sun encourages the lushest growth,
while partial shade produces sparser
foliage. The plant can tolerate temperatures to 15° F without damage. Hard frost
will cause it to die back to the roots. The
preferred soil type is well drained, but
Trailing Indigo Bush is fairly tolerant of
poor soil. Pruning shouldn't be necessary
unless the size of plants in small areas
must be controlled. If you do prune,
clip the stems back to different lengths
rather than shearing them to a straight,
unnatural edge.

**Landscape Use** Trailing Indigo Bush's
delicate gray foliage softens the landscape.
Allow the plants to clamber over boulders,
mingle with succulents such as Agave, or
cover a slope, preventing soil erosion
from wind or rain. A very restful, monochromatic scene can be created by
combining Trailing Indigo Bush with other
gray-foliaged plants. To avoid monotony,
vary the texture of the plants' foliage; for
example, use fine-textured Trailing Indigo
Bush with medium-textured Brittlebush
(*Encelia farinosa*) and coarse-textured
Desert Agave (*Agave deserti*). Some
white can help brighten the gray foliage;
try Blackfoot Daisy (*Melampodium
leucanthum*) or Desert Zinnia (*Zinnia
acerosa*).

## Bush Dalea, Smoke Bush
### *Dalea pulchra*
FABACEAE [PEA FAMILY]

**Description** Small, gray-green compound
leaves ½ inch long and ½ inch wide give
Bush Dalea a delicate texture. The
evergreen, rounded shrub can reach 4 feet
high by 5 feet wide. March and April bring
a profuse bloom of ¾-inch purple flower
clusters.

**Native Distribution** Bush Dalea occurs in
locations between 2,500 and 5,000 feet in
elevation in southeastern Arizona and
Sonora, Mexico, typically on gravelly
slopes.

**Culture** Full sun encourages the best
growth, as does supplemental irrigation
once or twice a month through the
summer. Bush Dalea is cold hardy to 15° F.
It prefers well-drained soil, though it is
fairly tolerant of other types.

**Landscape Use** Bush Dalea's spectacular
spring bloom merits a prominent spot in
the landscape. Be sure to allow it ample
room to grow without being crowded or
having to be pruned. Try contrasting the
delicately textured foliage with coarser-
textured gray-green plants such as
Brittlebush (*Encelia farinosa*), Desert
Spoon (*Dasylirion wheeleri*), or *Agave*
species. Bush Dalea can make an attractive informal hedge.

---

## Wislizenus Dalea
### *Dalea versicolor* var. *sessilis* (syn., *Dalea wislizeni*)
FABACEAE [PEA FAMILY]

**Description** Wislizenus Dalea is an open-
branched evergreen shrub that reaches
3 feet high and 4 feet wide at maturity.
Compact flower spikes to 1 inch long
create a bloom of violet from fall through
spring. The dark green compound leaves
are about ¾ inch long and ⅜ inch wide,

with eleven to twenty-three leaflets. The fruit is a small, inconspicuous pod.

**Native Distribution**  This plant occurs among hills and canyons of the upper desert, into desert grassland, from 3,000 to 5,000 feet in elevation. The natural distribution includes southeastern Arizona, Sonora, and Chihuahua, Mexico.

**Culture**  Wislizenus Dalea can grow in light shade or full sun. It is cold hardy to 20° F and probably lower. Supplemental irrigation will boost this plant's naturally fast growth rate. Good drainage is necessary for the best growth. To encourage fuller growth, leggy plants can be cut back nearly to the ground. This type of pruning should be done in spring, after the plants have finished blooming.

**Landscape Use**  A number of potential landscape uses suit Wislizenus Dalea. Used near a building as a foundation planting, it can help blend the structure with its surroundings. It can also be utilized in a naturalistic landscape with other desert trees and shrubs. Because of its attractive evergreen foliage and long blooming season, you might include this shrub in a flower garden.

---

## *Dasylirion* species
AGAVACEAE [AGAVE FAMILY]

A mature *Dasylirion* shows graceful symmetry, with its long, slender leaves arching forth from a central trunk into a rounded form. In spring a tall flower stalk emerges from the center of the plant. Few desert plants have as much potential for accents in landscapes. *Dasylirion* is most effective when complemented by fine-textured groundcovers or shrubs. An innovative use of *Dasylirion*—massed in groups of five or more—creates a large-scale focal point. The plant is also striking in large containers. Interesting contrasts in form occur when *Dasylirion* is planted

with cacti such as Saguaro (*Carnegiea gigantea*), Prickly-pear (*Opuntia* species), or Barrel Cactus (*Ferocactus* species). Most *Dasylirion* species have saw-toothed leaves, which might be utilized in security plantings.

*Dasylirion* species are tolerant of cold and drought. You can get them well established with summer irrigation in the first year or two; then they can make it on their own. The normally slow to moderate growth rate can be increased with supplemental watering. Provide *Dasylirion* with well-drained soil. Full sunlight encourages the best growth, although plants will grow in light shade. The flower stalk can be removed after it has finished blooming. It doesn't hurt to leave it on, though. Some people cut off the lower leaves as they dry and turn tan. This "poodle-izing" takes away much of the plant's natural character, and there's no horticultural reason to do it.

---

## Green Desert Spoon
### *Dasylirion acrotriche*

The straplike leaves of Green Desert Spoon are medium green and edged with curved teeth. Individual leaves measure about 2 feet long and ½ inch wide. They create a rounded form 3–4 feet high. Green Desert Spoon is native to San Luis Potosí, Veracruz, Hidalgo, and Querétaro, Mexico.

---

## Sotol
### *Dasylirion leiophyllum*

Glossy green leaves, sometimes with a bluish cast, measure 2½ feet long and nearly 1 inch wide. Rust-colored teeth, ⅛ inch long and hooked, line the leaf margins. In May and June, cream-colored flowers bloom on a 12-foot-high stalk. A mature plant measures about 4 feet high

*Dalea greggii* Trailing Indigo Bush

*Dalea pulchra* Bush Dalea

*Dalea versicolor* var. *sessilis* Wislizenus Dalea SP

*Dasylirion acrotriche* Green Desert Spoon

*Dasylirion leiophyllum* Sotol

and 4 feet wide. Sotol grows on limestone hills and grasslands, at elevations from 2,200 to 6,500 feet, in southwestern Texas, southern New Mexico, and adjacent Chihuahua, Mexico.

### *Dasylirion longissimum*

Stiff green leaves with smooth edges radiate outward to form a more or less rounded shape, 5 feet high and equally wide. Individual leaves can reach 3 feet in length, yet they are only ¼ inch wide. *Dasylirion longissimum* occurs from Tamaulipas to Hidalgo, Mexico.

## Texas Sotol
### *Dasylirion texanum*

Texas Sotol's light green leaves are 3 feet long and about ⅓ inch wide, with tiny hooked teeth along the leaf edges. A spectacular flowering stalk to 15 feet high with cream-colored flowers appears between May and July. Texas Sotol can reach a height and spread of 5 feet. It grows on rocky limestone hills in southwestern Texas and Chihuahua, Mexico.

## Desert Spoon, Sotol
### *Dasylirion wheeleri*

The short, woody trunk with its covering of 3-foot-long, ¾-inch-wide blue-green leaves reaches 4 feet high and a little wider. Sometimes a plant has more than one head. The leaves are toothed along the edges and spoon-shaped where they attach to the trunk. Cream-colored flowers cluster near the top of a 12-foot stalk from May to July. Desert Spoon is native to southern Arizona, New Mexico, and southwestern Texas, as well as to Sonora and Chihuahua, Mexico. Gravelly hillsides

of limestone or granite are common habitat. The elevational range is 3,000–6,000 feet.

## Sacred Datura, Jimson Weed, Angel's Trumpet
### *Datura wrightii* (syn., *Datura meteloides*)
SOLANACEAE [NIGHTSHADE FAMILY]

**Description** The white, trumpet-shaped flowers of Sacred Datura open in early evening, perfuming the air until they close the next day, usually by mid-morning. The sphinx moths that pollinate them are dwarfed by the 6- to 8-inch-long, 5-inch-wide flowers. The blooming period lasts from May to October. Golfball-sized fruits covered with spines hang from the plant like Christmas tree ornaments, maturing from medium green to tan. Sacred Datura's more-or-less heart-shaped leaves are dark gray-green and velvety. They measure about 5 inches long and 4 inches wide. This herbaceous plant dies to the ground each winter but grows back in spring from a thick perennial root. By the end of the growing season, Sacred Datura can reach a height of 3 feet, with a 6-foot spread. All parts of the plant are poisonous. Some people develop a rash just from touching the foliage.

**Native Distribution** Sacred Datura is found along sandy washes and on desert flats. It is also common to see the plant in roadside ditches. It grows at elevations from 1,000 to 6,500 feet in southern California, Arizona, New Mexico, and Texas, and south to South America.

**Culture** Sacred Datura grows best in full sun but will tolerate partial shade. It is moderately drought tolerant; supplemental water in the growing season will promote better flowering. This plant prefers well-drained, deep soil. The foliage dies back in winter, but the perennial root is cold hardy.

**Landscape Use** Sacred Datura is most effective used as a seasonal accent. Choose a location where the night-blooming flowers will be noticeable, perhaps near a patio or entry courtyard. This prolific bloomer would also be good to include in a flower garden. Remember that the entire plant is poisonous, and it might be a hazard to children or pets.

---

## Dicliptera
### *Dicliptera resupinata*
ACANTHACEAE [ACANTHUS FAMILY]

**Description** From May through October, ¾-inch-long rose-purple flowers bloom against lush, medium green foliage. This herbaceous perennial has erect or spreading stems that can reach 2 feet high and 3 feet wide at maturity. The leaves are 2 inches long, narrowing to a point from the ¾-inch-wide base.

**Native Distribution** Washes and rocky slopes in southeastern Arizona, south-western New Mexico, and south to west-central Mexico are home to Dicliptera. The plant's elevation range is from 3,000 to 6,000 feet.

**Culture** Dicliptera can grow in full sun to fairly deep shade. The plant will be more leggy under low light conditions. Any temperature below freezing will knock Dicliptera to the ground; however, its roots are cold hardy to the low 20s F. Water new plants every seven to ten days through their first summer; thereafter only moderate irrigation is required, about every two weeks in summertime.

**Landscape Use** The small but vivid flowers are most effective at close range. Incorporate Dicliptera into courtyard gardens or flower gardens, or use at poolside.

## Texas Persimmon, Mexican Persimmon, Black Persimmon
### *Diospyros texana*
EBENACEAE [EBONY FAMILY]

**Description** Texas Persimmon is a multitrunked shrub to small tree that can reach 15 feet high and a similar width. The bark is the most interesting feature: the thin gray outer layers peel off to reveal the smooth, white and gray mottled trunk beneath. Small dark green leathery leaves are oval in shape, about 2 inches long and 1 inch wide. The foliage is evergreen except in extreme cold. The tiny white bell-shaped flowers are not as noticeable as their sweet fragrance. The fruit is a dark purple to black berry with sweet, edible pulp surrounding the seeds. Birds and other wildlife relish the fruit, and reportedly it makes good jelly.

**Native Distribution** As you might guess from the common names, this plant occurs in central and western Texas and in Coahuila, Nuevo León, and Tamaulipas, Mexico. It can be found along arroyos, rocky slopes, and woodlands, at elevations from 1,100 to 5,700 feet.

**Culture** Full sun is best for Texas Persimmon, though it will tolerate partial shade. Its cold hardiness extends to at least the low 20s F. Fairly adaptable as far as soil is concerned, Texas Persimmon can grow in limestone, caliche, clay, or loamy soil, preferably well drained. The water requirement is quite low once the plant is established. Supplemental water can speed growth and result in a better summertime appearance. Pruning isn't necessary if you want a shrub, but for a small tree, you will need to prune the lower branches to expose the trunk.

**Landscape Use** With its dark green foliage and ornamental trunk, Texas Persimmon makes a beautiful small tree. Its size is appropriate for courtyard, patio, or poolside gardens. Nighttime accent lighting on the trunk can create a dra-

*Dasylirion longissimum*

*Dasylirion texanum* Texas Sotol

*Dasylirion wheeleri* Desert Spoon

*Datura wrightii* Sacred Datura

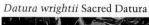

*Dicliptera resupinata* Dicliptera

*Diospyros texana* Texas Persimmon

matic effect. As a shrub, it can provide privacy screening when several plants are massed. The color contrasts nicely with light green or gray-foliaged plants. If you want to attract wildlife to your landscape, Texas Persimmon can furnish both food and cover.

## Green Sprangletop
### *Diplachne dubia* (syn., *Leptochloa dubia*)
POACEAE [GRASS FAMILY]

*Description* The seedhead of Green Sprangletop consists of a central stem with three to fifteen slender, flexible side branches. These are usually about 4 inches long. Green Sprangletop blooms from July to October. The blue-green leaf blades are 6 inches long by ⅛ inch wide and slightly rough to touch. Overall, this perennial bunchgrass reaches 2 feet high and nearly as wide.

*Native Distribution* Green Sprangletop occurs from Oklahoma to Arizona and southward through Mexico. The grass also occurs in disjunct populations in southern Florida and Argentina. It grows mostly on dry, rocky slopes and open areas, from 2,500 to 6,000 feet in elevation.

*Culture* This grass tolerates cold to 0° F. It is not quite as drought tolerant as some of the other desert grasses; provide established plants with irrigation about twice a month through the warm months. Green Sprangletop prefers a loamy soil with good drainage and full sun. You can rejuvenate straggly-looking plants by cutting them back to the ground.

*Landscape Use* The seedheads of Green Sprangletop are quite attractive. Provide a plain background to best display that feature, as well as the foliage. The grass can be used as an accent or massed. Try using Green Sprangletop as a backdrop for a flower garden.

## Hopbush
### *Dodonaea viscosa*
SAPINDACEAE [SOAPBERRY FAMILY]

*Description* Hopbush is an erect evergreen shrub, reaching 10 feet high and 6 feet wide at maturity. The bright green leaves are 2–3 inches long by ½ inch wide, and often shiny with a resinous coating. Small yellowish green flowers are barely noticeable; more ornamental are the ½-inch papery, winged fruits. They are green at first, then turn either tan or a rose color in late summer. The common name refers to the fruits, which have been used as a substitute for hops in making beer.

*Native Distribution* Hopbush grows at elevations from 2,000 to 5,000 feet in canyons, along arroyos, and on dry rocky slopes. It occurs not only in Arizona but also throughout the warmer parts of the world, including the tropics.

*Culture* Hopbush grows fast in full sun to partial shade. Its cold tolerance extends to 15° F. Soils ranging from rocky to clayey are acceptable. Hopbush's natural form is quite attractive, although it does accept pruning and can be trained into a formal hedge. Hopbush can grow under a wide range of irrigation amounts, from nothing (assuming plants are established) to ample. The growth rate and ultimate size of Hopbush will vary accordingly.

*Landscape Use* Hopbush's bright green color can help create an oasis feeling around a patio or pool area. A mass planting can form a backdrop for other plants of contrasting color or form. Either natural or clipped, Hopbush makes a good hedge for privacy screening or wind control. Quail and dove eat the seeds and no doubt seek shelter among the branches.

## Shrubby Dogweed
### *Dyssodia acerosa*
ASTERACEAE [SUNFLOWER FAMILY]

*Description* This perennial branches from a woody base to form an evergreen subshrub 6 inches high and 1 foot wide. Shrubby Dogweed has medium green, ½-inch needlelike leaves that emit a spicy fragrance when touched. Bright yellow, ½-inch daisy-type flowers crown the plant from April through October.

*Native Distribution* Shrubby Dogweed's range includes southern Nevada and Utah, much of Arizona, central and southern New Mexico, western Texas, and Sonora, Chihuahua, Coahuila, Zacatecas, San Luis Potosí, and Hidalgo, Mexico. It normally grows on dry, rocky slopes and mesas, between 1,900 and 6,000 feet in elevation.

*Culture* This plant isn't fussy about growing conditions; most soil types are acceptable. Full sun is preferred, and little supplemental water is required for good growth. Shrubby Dogweed is hardy to at least 10° F.

*Landscape Use* Shrubby Dogweed could be incorporated into a flower garden or simply scattered throughout the landscape. It makes a good edging plant for sidewalks or patios. Used *en masse*, it not only presents a pleasing combination of fine-textured foliage and dainty flowers, but it also provides erosion control. Its low water requirement makes Shrubby Dogweed suitable for cactus gardens.

---

*Dyssodia pentachaeta*, called Dogweed or Golden Dyssodia, is a short-lived herbaceous perennial that otherwise closely resembles *Dyssodia acerosa* and has the same cultural requirements and landscape use. Dogweed grows on dry slopes and mesas between 2,500 and 4,500 feet in elevation in Arizona and New

Mexico, western, central, and southern Texas, and Coahuila, Nuevo León, Tamaulipas, and San Luis Potosí, Mexico.

---

## Hedgehog Cactus
### *Echinocereus engelmannii*
CACTACEAE [CACTUS FAMILY]

*Description* Black, brown, red, yellow, white, and even variegated flexible spines 2–3 inches long nearly hide the green stems of Hedgehog Cactus. Up to thirty 1-foot-high, 3-inch-wide stems can grow from the plant's base into a clump 3 feet across. This is one of the earliest cacti to bloom in the spring, producing 2½-inch-wide magenta flowers over a period of three to four weeks anytime between February and May. The red, spine-covered oval fruits to 1 inch in length are said to taste like strawberries.

*Native Distribution* Hedgehog Cactus is found from sea level to 5,000 feet in elevation on desert plains, gravelly slopes, and mesas, in the southern regions of California and Arizona and in Baja California and Sonora, Mexico.

*Culture* A site with well-drained soil and full sun is ideal for Hedgehog Cactus. Moisture stored in the plant's succulent tissues maintain it through extended dry periods. It is hardy to 15° F or lower.

*Landscape Use* The bright magenta flowers would be noticeable anywhere in the landscape, but if you put Hedgehog Cactus near a patio or walkway, the blooms will be better appreciated. This cactus can be incorporated into a mixed planting of desert trees, shrubs, and succulents, or planted in a cactus garden. It can also be grown in a pot. It grows slowly, but keep in mind its potential mature size when choosing a planting site.

*Diplachne dubia* Green Sprangletop

*Dyssodia acerosa* Shrubby Dogweed

*Dodonaea viscosa* Hopbush

*Dyssodia pentachaeta* Dogweed

*Echinocereus engelmannii* Hedgehog Cactus

## Spiny Strawberry Hedgehog
### *Echinocereus stramineus*
CACTACEAE [CACTUS FAMILY]

**Description** A mature specimen of this cactus can have more than a hundred 3-inch-wide stems, which create a mound to 2 feet high and 3 feet across. Long straw-colored spines nearly obscure the green stems. The magenta flowers, which appear in spring, are 3–4 inches across, followed by red oval to round fruits 1½ inches in diameter.

**Native Distribution** Rocky hills between 2,000 and 5,000 feet in elevation in southeastern New Mexico, western Texas, and Chihuahua, Mexico, are home to Hedgehog Cactus.

**Culture** Full sun and well-drained soil are important elements in growing Spiny Strawberry Hedgehog. It is very drought tolerant, and it is cold hardy to 10° F or lower.

**Landscape Use** Be sure to give Hedgehog Cactus ample room for development, as it will eventually grow quite large. It could be incorporated into a cactus garden, perhaps among dark boulders to contrast with the golden spines. It would also be an interesting feature in a mixed planting of trees, shrubs, and herbaceous plants.

## Brittlebush
### *Encelia farinosa*
ASTERACEAE [SUNFLOWER FAMILY]

**Description** A dense covering of white hairs gives Brittlebush leaves a silvery-green appearance. Well-watered plants will be greener, while the foliage of plants grown under very dry conditions is almost white. Brittlebush leaves are lance-shaped or triangular, about 2 inches long by 1½ inches wide. The plant is evergreen, though some leaves will drop during severe drought and cold. The rounded shrub is typically 3 feet high and 4 feet wide. Daisylike, yellow flowers 1½ inches across rise on slender stems above the foliage from March through May. Brittlebush can bloom at other times during the year following rain or supplemental irrigation.

**Native Distribution** This heat-loving shrub most often grows on south- and west-facing rocky slopes, gravelly plains, or along washes, below 3,000 feet in elevation. It is native to southwestern Utah, southern Nevada, southern and western Arizona, southern California, and Baja California, Sonora, and Sinaloa, Mexico.

**Culture** Too much water and/or not enough sunlight produces gangly, weak growth. Water Brittlebush until it is established, then irrigate only a few times throughout the summer. Temperatures below 28° F damage the foliage, and at 15° F plants may freeze to the ground. Be sure to discontinue irrigation by early fall to discourage new growth and allow plants to harden off. Brittlebush prefers soil with good drainage. Aphids love its new growth and flower stalks. The infestations are usually more unsightly than harmful, but you can control them with a spray of insecticidal soap repeated every few days. It helps to keep plants on the dry side, since aphids prefer the tender, succulent growth encouraged by abundant water. Overgrown or gangly plants can be pruned nearly to the ground to rejuvenate. Clip the dried flower stalks off for a neater appearance. If Brittlebush has been damaged by frost, wait on pruning until new growth appears, so you can determine the extent of damage.

**Landscape Use** The versatile Brittlebush can be used poolside, near patios, in naturalistic desert landscapes, and in parking lot or highway median strips. Dazzling flowers create a stunning accent in spring. It looks great among dark boulders, which set off the silvery foliage. Dramatic contrasts can be achieved by pairing Brittlebush with green-foliaged plants such as Chihuahuan-sage (*Leucophyllum laevigatum*), Autumn Sage (*Salvia greggii*), or Ruellia (*Ruellia peninsularis*). Birds and other desert animals eat the seeds. Brittlebush can provide erosion control on slopes, and it is a common component of many revegetation seed mixes.

## Green Brittlebush
### *Encelia frutescens*
ASTERACEAE [SUNFLOWER FAMILY]

***Description*** The medium green leaves of Green Brittlebush feel like sandpaper. They are ¾ inch long and ½ inch wide at the base, narrowing to a pointed tip. The evergreen shrub acquires a mounded shape with maturity, to 3 feet high and 4 feet wide. Yellow flowers ½ inch wide appear at the ends of branches from March through October. They are like daisies, minus the petals.

***Native Distribution*** The native habitat of Green Brittlebush includes southern Utah and Nevada, southeastern California, most of Arizona, and Sonora and Baja California, Mexico. It grows from sea level to 4,000-foot elevations on rocky slopes and mesas.

***Culture*** Green Brittlebush prefers a site with full sun and well-drained soil. It requires very little water once established; however, in a landscape situation, supplemental irrigation once or twice a month in the summer promotes a better appearance. The cold hardiness extends to about 5° F. The dried flower stalks can be clipped for a neater look.

***Landscape Use*** An interesting effect could be achieved by combining the similar forms but contrasting foliage colors of Green Brittlebush and Brittlebush (*Encelia farinosa*). Individual Green Brittlebush

plants also display a mix of colors due to the green leaves and white stems. The shrub would make a good addition to a naturalistic desert landscape. Birds eat the seeds.

## Joint-fir, Mormon-tea
### *Ephedra* species
EPHEDRACEAE [JOINT-FIR FAMILY]

Several species of Joint-fir occur in the Southwest. All of them look pretty much alike, with some differences in overall size and stem color. The plants are medium-sized shrubs with very slender green stems, usually about ⅛ inch thick. The leaves are minute and have no function in photosynthesis. Joint-fir is a gymno-sperm, like pine trees and junipers, so its "flowers" occur as tiny, ¼-inch cones from March to April. The male and female cones are on separate plants.

Joint-fir makes an interesting accent in the landscape, since it looks so different from other plants. The slender green stems combine well with "leafy" plants such as Brittlebush (*Encelia farinosa*) or Creosote Bush (*Larrea tridentata*). Joint-fir also looks good in naturalistic desert landscapes scattered among other plants.

Good drainage is essential for Joint-fir. It is generally quite cold hardy and drought tolerant. Be careful not to overwater. Full sunlight is best. Prune only to remove dead wood.

### *Ephedra antisyphilitica*

This species of *Ephedra* occurs in southwestern Oklahoma, most of the western two-thirds of Texas, and north-eastern Mexico, on gravelly plains and hills, in arroyos, and in canyons. It grows to 4 feet high and 4 feet wide. Young stems are green, turning to yellowish green and eventually gray-green.

Above and left:
*Echinocereus stramineus*
Spiny Strawberry Hedgehog

Opposite:
*Ephedra*
species
Joint-fir
(detail)

*Encelia farinosa*
Brittlebush

Above and left:
*Encelia frutescens*
Green Brittlebush

## Ephedra aspera

The stems of *Ephedra aspera* are greenish yellow and rough to touch. It reaches a mature height and width of 3 feet. Gravelly plains and slopes, mesas, and canyons, from 1,000 to 4,000 feet in elevation, are typical habitats. The plant is found in southern Nevada, southwestern Utah, southeastern California, and much of Arizona, and in southern New Mexico and western and southern Texas. In Mexico it occurs from Baja California to Coahuila and south to Zacatecas and Tamaulipas.

## Ephedra californica

As its name suggests, this species is found in southern California and northern Baja California, Mexico. Three thousand feet in elevation is generally its upper limit of occurrence. *Ephedra californica* grows on desert plains, gravelly slopes, and mesas, and in arroyos. The stems of the 3-foot-by-3-foot shrub are pale green.

## Ephedra nevadensis

Three feet in height and width is a typical mature size of *Ephedra nevadensis*. Its stems are pale green to gray. The shrub occurs at elevations from 2,000 to 6,000 feet on dry plains and slopes in Nevada, southern Utah, eastern California, and western Arizona, and in the Mexican states of Baja California and Sonora.

## Ephedra trifurca

This is the largest of the Southwestern *Ephedra* species, reaching 6 feet in height and 8–10 feet in width. The yellow-green branches are spine-tipped. Southern

Nevada, southwestern Utah, southern California, Arizona, southern New Mexico, western Texas, and Baja California, Sonora, and Chihuahua, Mexico are home to *Ephedra trifurca*. The shrub is found on sand dunes, gravelly plains and hills, mesas, and along arroyos, to 5,000 feet in elevation.

## Ephedra viridis

Bright green stems are characteristic of *Ephedra viridis*. A typical size is 3 feet in height and width. It occurs on the upper edges of the desert and into grassland and the pinyon-juniper woodland plant community, from 3,000 to 7,000 feet in elevation. Its distribution includes Nevada, Utah, southwestern Wyoming, western Colorado, and northern Arizona.

## Plains Lovegrass
### Eragrostis intermedia
POACEAE (GRASS FAMILY)

**Description** Plains Lovegrass grows to 2 feet high in the form of a bunchgrass. The leaves are about 6 inches long, ⅛ inch wide, and rough-textured on the upper side. The broadly pyramidal seedheads are open and delicate-looking, growing to 10 inches long and 8 inches wide. The spikelets are grayish green to purple-tinged. Plains Lovegrass blooms from June to October.

**Native Distribution** This grass is found between 3,500 and 6,000 feet in elevation in canyons and on sandy plains or rocky slopes. Its range extends from Georgia to Oklahoma and Arizona and south through Mexico and Central America.

**Culture** You can make summertime easier on Plains Lovegrass by giving it a deep soaking every two to three weeks. It prefers well-drained soil. This grass can grow in full sun or light shade. Plains Lovegrass is cold hardy to at least 0° F.

**Landscape Use** The airy appearance of Plains Lovegrass can lend a lighter appearance to the landscape. It looks good combined with other grasses and wildflowers for a meadow effect. Planted *en masse*, it could provide excellent erosion control.

## Turpentine Bush, Larchleaf Goldenweed

### *Ericameria laricifolia*
ASTERACEAE [SUNFLOWER FAMILY]

**Description** The bright green needlelike leaves of Turpentine Bush are ½ inch long and covered with a sticky resin. If you rub the evergreen foliage, it gives off an aroma like turpentine. The shrub's many branches form a compact mound 2 feet high and 3 feet wide. Clusters of yellow flowers bloom at the ends of the branches from September to November. Plants from the Chihuahuan Desert have ray flowers (petals) on the ¼-inch flowering heads, while the Sonoran Desert types do not. Light brown, bristly seeds develop from the flowers.

**Native Distribution** Turpentine Bush is found in southeastern California, southern Arizona, southern New Mexico, western Texas, and Sonora and Chihuahua, Mexico. It frequents rocky slopes, canyons, and mesas, between 3,000 and 6,000 feet in elevation.

**Culture** Once Turpentine Bush is established, keep it on a very lean water ration to control its size. Once a month during the summer should be adequate. If the plant becomes lanky, cut it back to the ground and it will regrow with dense foliage. Turpentine Bush is hardy to 5° F. It grows best in full sun in any well-drained soil.

**Landscape Use** The bright green, fine-textured foliage contrasts nicely with gray-foliaged plants such as Texas Ranger (*Leucophyllum frutescens*) and Guayule (*Parthenium argentatum*). Turpentine Bush's gorgeous fall display of color is most effective when three or more plants are massed together. It makes a good informal hedge or foundation planting near buildings. Another use for this hardy shrub is roadside or median strip plantings.

## Flattop Buckwheat

### *Eriogonum fasciculatum* var. *poliofolium*
POLYGONACEAE [BUCKWHEAT FAMILY]

**Description** Flattop Buckwheat is a low, rounded evergreen shrub to 1½ feet high and 2 feet wide. The leaves are ¾ inch long and ⅛ inch wide, dark gray-green above and often white and woolly beneath. Dense, flattened clusters of tiny white or pale pink flowers to 2 inches across bloom from March to November, most abundantly in spring.

**Native Distribution** Dry, rocky slopes from 1,000 to 4,500 feet in elevation comprise the typical habitat of Flattop Buckwheat. The plant occurs in southwestern Utah, southern Nevada, southeastern California, Arizona, and northern Baja California, Mexico.

**Culture** Flattop Buckwheat grows best in coarse, well-drained soil, with full sunlight. It is very drought tolerant once established; however, it will benefit from supplemental irrigation every two to three weeks in summer. Flattop Buckwheat is hardy to at least 15° F. This shrub's naturally rounded form often looks as if it has been sheared; pruning generally isn't necessary.

*Ephedra viridis* Joint-fir

*Eragrostis intermedia* Plains Lovegrass

*Ericameria laricifolia* Turpentine Bush

*Eriogonum fasciculatum* var. *poliofolium* Flattop Buckwheat

*Landscape Use* Flattop Buckwheat can be incorporated into naturalistic desert landscapes, where it is particularly useful on slopes for controlling soil erosion. A mass planting of Flattop Buckwheat would be striking whether in bloom or just displaying the attractive fine-textured foliage. The plant's compact size suits it to highway medians, parking lot planting strips, and other limited-size spaces. The seeds provide food for birds and other desert animals such as ground squirrels.

## Wright Buckwheat
### *Eriogonum wrightii*
POLYGONACEAE [BUCKWHEAT FAMILY]

*Description* Wright Buckwheat is a perennial subshrub, with many slender stems rising from a woody base to a mound 1½ feet high by 2 feet wide. The leaves occur on the lower half of the plant, with wiry flower stalks filling out the upper half. Small leaves, ½ inch long by ¼ inch wide and narrowed to a point, are silver-green from a covering of white hairs. From July through October, tiny white or pinkish flowers appear in clusters along the stalks.

*Native Distribution* Typical habitat for Wright Buckwheat includes gravelly slopes and rocky hillsides from 3,000 to 7,000 feet in elevation. The plant grows in Arizona, southern New Mexico, and western Texas, as well as in northern Mexico.

*Culture* Wright Buckwheat develops a compact form and blooms best in full sun. It is cold hardy to near 0° F and is drought tolerant once established. Supplemental irrigation once or twice a month through the summer is advisable. This plant needs well-drained soil.

*Landscape Use* Wright Buckwheat blooms after many other desert plants have finished, so it can be used in flower gardens to extend the flowering season. A mass planting could be used for ground-cover on either flat areas or slopes. Wright Buckwheat can be planted throughout naturalistic landscapes.

## Southwest Coral Bean
### *Erythrina flabelliformis*
FABACEAE [PEA FAMILY]

*Description* In springtime, before bright green foliage clothes Southwest Coral Bean's spiny branches, it bears 6-inch clusters of bright red, tubular flowers. After blooming for several weeks during the period from March through May, Southwest Coral Bean often has a second flowering period in September in response to summer rains. Eight-inch-long, 1-inch-wide pods contain the bright red ½-inch seeds for which the plant is named. The seeds are reportedly poisonous. In frost-free areas, Southwest Coral Bean develops into a tree to 20 feet high, but repeated freezing will keep the plant shrubby, about 6 feet high and equally wide. The compound leaves have three parts, with each leaflet 2 inches long and 3 inches wide and shaped like a triangle with rounded edges. The broad-based spines are only ¼ inch long.

*Native Distribution* Southwest Coral Bean occurs in southeastern Arizona, south-western New Mexico, and northern Mexico, including Baja California, Chihuahua, Durango, Zacatecas, and San Luis Potosí. It is normally found in rocky canyons, on hillsides, and along washes, between 3,000 and 5,500 feet in elevation.

*Culture* A warm location is important for successfully growing Southwest Coral Bean, which can freeze at 28° F. Wait until new foliage appears before pruning any frost-damaged wood, to be sure that no more than necessary is removed. In well-drained soil, the plant will have a moderate growth rate with supplemental irrigation. It will also tolerate drought. Full sun is recommended for best growth and flowering.

**Landscape Use** Situate Southwest Coral Bean so that its attractive flowers and the hummingbirds that visit them can be appreciated at close range. The extra warmth provided by a south- or west-facing wall or an enclosed courtyard will help protect the tender plant from frost. The bold foliage could lend a tropical feeling to poolside landscapes. Interplanting evergreen plants with Southwest Coral Bean will help camouflage its winter bareness.

## Candelilla
### *Euphorbia antisyphilitica*
EUPHORBIACEAE [SPURGE FAMILY]

**Description** The common name, Spanish for "little candle," refers to the slender, pale green stems. Each stem is about ¼ inch in diameter and 1 foot tall. The plant spreads by rhizomes (creeping underground stems) and at maturity may form a clump to 3 feet across. The tiny leaves are drought deciduous, present only on new growth. Pink and white flowers cluster along the stem tips anytime during the warm season but particularly following rains.

**Native Distribution** Candelilla grows at elevations between 100 and 3,800 feet on rocky slopes, ridges, and hills, usually on limestone. Southwestern Texas to Hidalgo and Querétaro, Mexico, is its geographic range.

**Culture** Candelilla is very drought hardy, though not cold hardy below 15° F. If frozen to the ground, it may grow back from the roots. It prefers full sun, and soil that is well drained. The slow growth rate keeps plants a reasonable size; pruning shouldn't be needed.

**Landscape Use** Use Candelilla as a distinctive vertical accent in the landscape. It looks good planted with cacti and other succulents, or on its own with just a boulder for company. A background of darker-colored plants could be used to highlight its pale foliage. Gardeners in cold winter areas can utilize Candelilla as a potted plant on a patio.

## Apache Plume
### *Fallugia paradoxa*
ROSACEAE [ROSE FAMILY]

**Description** Clusters of pink or purple 1-inch-long feathery seed tails form a fuzzy ball 2½ inches in diameter. The showy fruit's resemblance to an Apache headdress inspired the common name. Five-petaled white flowers 1½ inches across bloom from May to September, with the heaviest bloom early on. The upright, multibranched shrub spreads slowly by woody rhizomes (creeping underground stems) to a mature size of 6 feet high and 4 feet wide. Apache Plume's flaky bark is grayish white. The evergreen to semi-deciduous leaves are dark green above, white or reddish below. They measure ½ inch long by ¼ inch wide and are divided into three to seven fingerlike lobes.

**Native Distribution** This shrub is often found along arroyos or on gravelly slopes in the upper desert and into chaparral vegetation, from 3,500 to 8,000 feet in elevation. Its range is considerable, including southern Nevada, southern Utah, southern Colorado, southeastern California, much of Arizona, southern New Mexico, and western Texas. In Mexico, Apache Plume occurs in Coahuila, Chihuahua, and Durango.

**Culture** Apache Plume prefers full sun, although in the hottest desert areas afternoon shade is beneficial. Provide well-drained soil. In the summer, par-

*Eriogonum wrightii* Wright Buckwheat

*Euphorbia antisyphilitica* Candelilla

*Erythrina flabelliformis* Southwest Coral Bean

Above, left and right, and below:
*Fallugia paradoxa* Apache Plume

ticularly in the low desert, give Apache Plume extra water once or twice a month. That will encourage flowering and faster growth. It is very cold hardy, to at least 0° F. Pruning is generally not necessary, although Apache Plume can be made into a hedge.

**Landscape Use** The dense, dark green foliage of Apache Plume makes a good background for other plants, particularly those with light-colored foliage. It can also be used for hedges or screening. The ornamental flowers and fuzzy fruits enable the shrub to stand on its own as well. Apache Plume is a good plant for soil erosion control, and it affords cover for wildlife.

## Compass Barrel
### *Ferocactus cylindraceus* (syn., *Ferocactus acanthodes*)
CACTACEAE [CACTUS FAMILY]

**Description** When young, Compass Barrel has a globular form, but with maturity it becomes cylindrical. Very old plants can be 8 or 9 feet tall, although 3–5 feet is a more typical height, with a diameter of 1½ feet. The plant is usually single, though sometimes it branches near the ground to form multiple heads. Compass Barrel's thick green skin covers ribs ¾ inch high. The stout central spines can be yellow, red, or brown; they are at least 2 inches long and often curved at the tip. Compass Barrel's yellow to orange, funnel-shaped, 2-inch-wide flowers occur in a ring at the top of the plant. Following the March to June blooming period, oval fruits 1 inch long and ¾ inch wide ripen to a yellow color.

**Native Distribution** Compass Barrel grows on rocky slopes and bajadas (outwash fans), up to 3,000 feet in elevation. It occurs in southern California and Nevada, southwestern Arizona, and northwestern Sonora and Baja California, Mexico.

**Culture** Compass Barrel's common name refers to its supposed tendency to lean toward the south. Two explanations are that the plant exposes its growing tip to the brightest light, or that the side of the plant in the shade (north) grows faster, so the plant leans in the opposite direction. In a landscape setting the cactus may or may not show any directional preference. However, plants in the shade may extend toward brighter light. Always give mature Compass Barrel plants full sunlight. Young plants grown in a greenhouse or shadehouse should be gradually accustomed to direct sunlight. A piece of woven shade cloth can be used to shield plants from the intense summer sun for the first season or two in the open. You can put the cloth directly on the plant, using a few spines as anchors. Compass Barrel needs loose, well-drained soil. The inner succulent tissues can store water to sustain the plant through dry periods, so you shouldn't need to water established plants. Supplemental irrigation once or twice a month to young plants during their first summer can speed establishment. It is cold hardy to 15° F or lower.

**Landscape Use** The solid form of Compass Barrel creates a strong focal point, accentuated when the flowers or fruits are present. A background of fine-textured shrubs or trees contrasts well with Compass Barrel. It can add variety of form to a cactus and succulent garden. Birds and squirrels like the fruits. Be sure to keep the cactus a conservative distance from walkways or patios.

## Coville Barrel, Sonoran Barrel
### *Ferocactus emoryi* (syn., *Ferocactus covillei*)
CACTACEAE [CACTUS FAMILY]

**Description** Coville Barrel's rounded form can reach 6 feet tall with a diameter of 2 feet. The thick green skin covers twenty to thirty ribs, which support clusters of 2-inch-long, hooked central spines with several smaller radial, or secondary, spines. The spines are reddish, turning gray with maturity. Yellow, orange, or maroon flowers to 2 inches wide bloom atop the plant from June to August. The flowers develop into yellow oval fruits to 2 inches long and ½ inch in diameter.

**Native Distribution** Sonora, Mexico, is the primary geographic location of Coville Barrel, although it also occurs in southern Arizona and is common in Organ Pipe Cactus National Monument. The plant's habitat is rocky hills and gravelly flats between 1,500 and 3,500 feet in elevation.

**Culture** Coville Barrel is very drought tolerant thanks to its succulent tissue. Supplemental watering would be advisable only during extended drought. The cactus is hardy to about 15° F. Provide full sun and well-drained soil.

**Landscape Use** The reddish spines of Coville Barrel could provide extra color to a cactus and succulent garden. The rounded form would stand out most when contrasted with spiky plants such as *Yucca* species or the fine-textured foliage of Creosote Bush (*Larrea tridentata*) and Whitethorn Acacia (*Acacia constricta*). Coville Barrel planted in a pot would make a fine accent for the patio.

---

## Fishhook Barrel
### *Ferocactus wislizenii*
CACTACEAE [CACTUS FAMILY]

**Description** Maturing from a globular to a cylindrical form, Fishhook Barrel can reach 6 feet high and 2 feet wide. Occasionally multiple heads will occur near the base of the main plant. Fishhook Barrel's central spines are gray to red and 2–3 inches long, with a definite hook at the end. The spines have cross-ridging on their flattened surface. Twenty to thirty 1-inch-high vertical ribs appear like accordion pleats on the body of the plant. With abundant moisture the pleats are less pronounced, but they become deeper as the cactus uses its reserves of water during drought. From July through September, 2-inch-wide funnel-shaped flowers, red to yellow but primarily orange, form a crown atop Fishhook Barrel. The fruits, to 2 inches long and 1 inch wide, resemble miniature yellow pineapples.

**Native Distribution** Fishhook Barrel's range includes southern Arizona, southern New Mexico, southwestern Texas, and Sonora, Sinaloa, and Chihuahua, Mexico, below 4,500 feet in elevation. The cactus typically grows on rocky hillsides, desert flats, or grasslands.

**Culture** Provide Fishhook Barrel with full sun and well-drained soil. Very drought-tolerant, it can survive on rainfall alone. There's much more danger of it dying from overwatering than from drought. Slow-growing Fishhook Barrel is hardy to near 0° F.

**Landscape Use** Use Fishhook Barrel to lend a desert feeling to the landscape. It combines well with other cacti such as Prickly-pear or Cholla (*Opuntia* species). Just don't overdo the cactus, or you'll end up with a hostile landscape, visually and literally. Shrubs, trees, and herbaceous perennials all help to soften the appearance of this cactus. For a strong contrast in form, pair the rotund Fishhook Barrel with a vertical form such as Desert Milkweed (*Asclepias subulata*) or Slipper Plant (*Pedilanthus macrocarpus*). The ripe fruits of Fishhook Barrel are relished by desert animals.

Opposite page and above:
*Ferocactus cylindraceus*
Compass Barrel

*Ferocactus emoryi* Coville Barrel

Below left and right: *Ferocactus wislizenii* Fishhook Barrel

## Tarbush
### *Flourensia cernua*
ASTERACEAE [SUNFLOWER FAMILY]

**Description** Tarbush is a densely branched evergreen shrub, typically 3 feet high and about as wide. The 1-inch-long, ½-inch-wide pointed leaves are medium green and resinous, with a slight odor of tar. Yellow flowers ½ inch long and ¼ inch wide appear among the foliage from September to December.

**Native Distribution** Southeastern Arizona, southern New Mexico, western Texas, and Sonora, Chihuahua, Coahuila, Nuevo León, Durango, and Zacatecas, Mexico, are home to Tarbush. It occurs on desert plains, slopes, and mesas, from 2,300 to 6,500 feet in elevation.

**Culture** Full sun is necessary for proper development of Tarbush. It can grow in relatively heavy soils or well-drained ones. Once established, the shrub requires supplemental irrigation only during prolonged drought. Temperatures below 10° F can damage the foliage.

**Landscape Use** Tarbush could be incorporated into naturalistic desert landscapes among other shrubs and trees. Another possible use is as a low, informal hedge.

## Desert-olive, New Mexico–privet
### *Forestiera neomexicana*
OLEACEAE [OLIVE FAMILY]

**Description** Desert Olive's light gray bark provides a pleasing contrast to its bright green foliage. Oblong, finely toothed leaves are 1 inch long by ½ inch wide and either blunt or pointed at the tip. The foliage is deciduous in winter and under severe moisture stress. This upright, stiffly branching shrub or small tree typically reaches a height of 12 feet and a spread of 8 feet. Inconspicuous greenish white flowers occur in clusters before the leaves, in March and April. Oval, fleshy fruits ¼ inch long turn from blue to black between June and September.

**Native Distribution** Desert-olive is found in valleys and canyons and on desert flats and rocky slopes, from 3,000 to 7,000 feet in elevation. The plant's distribution includes southern California, Nevada, and Utah; southwestern Colorado; Arizona and New Mexico; western Texas; and northern Mexico.

**Culture** Established plants tolerate drought but grow faster and are more attractive if given supplemental water during the summer. Desert-olive can grow in all types of soil. It prefers full sun. The plant's cold tolerance extends to at least 10° F. Desert-olive can be left in its natural form or pruned into a hedge. A tree form can be achieved by removing the lower branches.

**Landscape Use** Desert-olive makes an interesting small tree for patio gardens if pruned to reveal the lower branches, or let it develop as a shrub, to provide background foliage for other plants. Wildlife will eat the fruits and utilize the foliage for cover and nesting.

## Mexican Tree Ocotillo
### *Fouquieria macdougalii*
FOUQUIERIACEAE [OCOTILLO FAMILY]

**Description** As its common name indicates, this relative of Ocotillo (*Fouquieria splendens*) is treelike, with a short, stocky, yellowish green trunk to 1 foot thick. In frost-free climates, Mexican Tree Ocotillo can reach a height of 20 feet, but elsewhere a typical mature size is 6 feet high and 4 feet wide. The brown or reddish branches bear ½-inch gray spines. Mexican Tree Ocotillo blooms from February to September, following rains, with loose clusters of 1-inch-long tube-shaped bright red flowers.

*Native Distribution* Mexican Tree Ocotillo grows mostly on desert flats and gentle slopes in Sonora and Sinaloa, Mexico.

*Culture* Protect this tender plant from temperatures below 28° F. It prefers well-drained soil and full sun. Once it is established, supplemental irrigation every two to three weeks in summer will promote flowering and maintain a moderate to fast growth rate.

*Landscape Use* Courtyard or patio gardens are logical places to use Mexican Tree Ocotillo, because it requires protection from cold. Where temperatures consistently drop below freezing, you can put the plant in a pot and move it to shelter when frost threatens. The flowers make Mexican Tree Ocotillo a fine accent plant.

---

## Ocotillo, Coachwhip
### *Fouquieria splendens*
FOUQUIERIACEAE [OCOTILLO FAMILY]

*Description* Ocotillo is one of the most distinctive shrubs of the desert. Its gray, thorny branches rise from a central base to 15 feet high, fanning outward to a diameter of 10 feet. Green leaves 1 inch long and ½ inch wide hug the branches during times of adequate moisture but drop under drought stress. Amazingly, the leaves can regrow within a few days following summer rains. The cycle of leaf drop and regrowth may occur several times a season. In the spring, bright red tubular flowers clustered at the branch tips are like beacons, attracting nearby hummingbirds.

*Native Distribution* All three of the warm Southwestern deserts (Chihuahuan, Sonoran, and Mojave) have this plant. Its range extends from Texas to California in the United States and from Baja California to Coahuila and Zacatecas in Mexico. Ocotillo typically grows on desert flats, rocky slopes, and mesas, from sea level to 5,000 feet in elevation.

*Culture* Ocotillo needs full sun and well-drained soil. It can tolerate long periods of drought; however, if you want the plant to retain its leaves, water twice a month during the summer. The rest of the year, rainfall alone should provide adequate moisture. Don't overwater or you may kill the plant, especially an older one. Ocotillo plants are usually sold bare-root. Newly set-out plants should be watered about once a week until established. The plants can be frustratingly slow to leaf out after transplant, but some people report success by misting the stems with water for several minutes daily. It is cold hardy to about 10° F. Never prune Ocotillo branches part-way. If it is necessary to remove a branch, cut it all the way back to the base.

*Landscape Use* Few plants are as striking in the landscape as Ocotillo. Its distinctive form is especially effective when silhouetted against a plain wall or the skyline. The thorny stems need to be kept away from sidewalks and patios. An impenetrable living fence can be created by planting individual branches close together in a line. The branches should develop roots and eventually leaves—sometimes even flowers.

---

## Gregg Ash, Littleleaf Ash
### *Fraxinus greggii*
OLEACEAE [OLIVE FAMILY]

*Description* Gregg Ash develops into a shrub or small tree, averaging 15 feet high and 10 feet wide. The semi-evergreen foliage drops for a short time in the spring. The dark green, leathery leaves are 1½ inches long and divided into three oval to oblong leaflets, each 1 inch long and ¼ inch wide. As the branches age, the bark turns from dark green to gray. Although

*Flourensia cernua* Tarbush

*Forestiera neomexicana* Desert-olive

Above and right:
*Fouquieria macdougalii*
Mexican Tree Ocotillo

*Fouquieria splendens* Ocotillo

*Fraxinus greggii* Gregg Ash

the small flowers that bloom from March through May aren't conspicuous, the ¾-inch-long slender winged seeds are interesting.

**Native Distribution** The range of Gregg Ash includes western Texas, New Mexico, and southern Arizona, as well as Coahuila, Nuevo León, Zacatecas, and Tamaulipas, Mexico. It occurs at elevations between 1,200 and 6,000 feet along arroyos, in canyons, and on rocky hillsides.

**Culture** Provide Gregg Ash with full sun in the cooler desert areas and partial shade in the low-elevation, hottest deserts. Once established, it requires little water, although supplemental irrigation in prolonged drought is beneficial. Gregg Ash prefers well-drained soil. The ultimate form of this plant depends on whether or not it receives pruning. Left to develop naturally, Gregg Ash will have a shrubby form, with branches to the ground. You can remove the lower branches to develop a small tree.

**Landscape Use** As an accent tree, Gregg Ash adds interesting form and fresh green foliage to the landscape. It works well in patio and courtyard gardens. Another use would be as an informal hedge or screen.

## Wright Silktassel
### *Garrya wrightii*
CORNACEAE [DOGWOOD FAMILY]

**Description** The leathery gray-green leaves of Wright Silktassel are generally oval in shape yet pointed at the tip. They are 2 inches long and 1 inch wide. Inconspicuous greenish white flowers occur in silky clusters from May through August, followed by dark blue fruits ¼ inch in diameter. This evergreen, erect shrub reaches 8 feet high and 6 feet wide.

**Native Distribution** Wright Silktassel occurs in western Texas, southern New

Mexico, and Arizona, and Chihuahua and Sonora, Mexico. Its usual habitat is dry, rocky slopes between 3,000 and 8,000 feet in elevation.

**Culture** Full sun is best for Wright Silktassel, except in the hottest desert areas, where afternoon shade is recommended. Once established, Wright Silktassel does well with only supplemental water during the summer. It tolerates cold to 10° F. The preferred soil is well drained.

**Landscape Use** An excellent informal hedge could be created with Wright Silktassel. The gray-green, coarse-textured foliage would be an interesting foil to dark green, fine-textured plants such as Creosote Bush (*Larrea tridentata*). The fruits provide food for wildlife.

## Goodding-verbena
### *Glandularia gooddingii* (syn., *Verbena gooddingii*)
VERBENACEAE [VERVAIN FAMILY]

**Description** Flat-topped spikes of fragrant lavender flowers cover Goodding-verbena's 1-foot-high, 1½-foot-wide mounded form from March through June. The herbaceous stems and leaves are covered with short white hairs. Gray-green leaves measure between 1 and 2 inches long and 1 inch wide; they are usually three-cleft, with the divisions coarsely toothed.

**Native Distribution** Goodding-verbena grows in the southern parts of Utah, Nevada, California, Arizona, and New Mexico, and in southwestern Texas, northern Baja California, and Sonora, Mexico, mostly below 5,000 feet in elevation. It prefers canyons, washes, dry rocky slopes, and grassy hillsides.

**Culture** Full sun promotes the best flowering, as does periodic irrigation. Weekly soakings during the blooming season should elicit a glorious display, after which you can cut back to watering about twice a month through the summer. Goodding-verbena is adaptable to most soils. Clip the dried flower stalks for a neater appearance. Pruning the foliage severely in mid-summer can help rejuvenate this plant and prevent woodiness, although its life span is typically short— usually about three years. The plants may reseed; otherwise you should plan on planting replacements. Goodding-verbena is cold hardy to at least the mid-20s F.

*Landscape Use* Incorporate Goodding-verbena with other perennial wildflowers such as Blackfoot Daisy (*Melampodium leucanthum*), *Penstemon* species, and Desert-marigold (*Baileya multiradiata*) to make a colorful flower garden. Annual wildflower seed can be sown to enhance the display. Walkways, courtyards, and pool areas will all benefit from plantings of this colorful, long-blooming perennial. Large masses of Goodding-verbena are stunning in bloom but can look ragged in the off-season unless interplanted with some evergreen shrubs. Creosote Bush (*Larrea tridentata*) and Bur-sage (*Ambrosia deltoidea*) are two possible choices. In naturalistic desert landscapes, Goodding-verbena can be scattered along a wash or clustered near boulders. Its size lets you tuck it into small areas. Butterflies are attracted to the flowers.

---

Wright-verbena (*Glandularia wrightii*, syn., *Verbena wrightii*) has a form and size much like Goodding-verbena. The foliage of Wright-verbena, however, is greener and more finely divided. Wright-verbena produces pink or rose to magenta flowers from February to October. It grows on gravelly flats and slopes in Kansas, Oklahoma, Colorado, Texas, New Mexico, Arizona, and northern Mexico. Guidelines for culture and landscape use are the same as for Goodding-verbena.

## San Marcos–hibiscus
### *Gossypium harknessii* (syn., *Hibiscus harknessii*)
MALVACEAE [MALLOW FAMILY]

*Description* This rounded shrub blooms from October to May in mild-winter areas, but where it freezes back, flowering can be expected from June to October. Each 2-inch-wide flower has five yellow petals with a maroon spot at the base. The fruit is a rounded capsule, about ½ inch long. The heart-shaped leaves are entire (smooth-margined) to shallowly three-lobed, 1½ inches wide and 2 inches long. San Marcos–hibiscus reaches a height of 3 feet and a width of 4 feet at maturity.

*Native Distribution* Baja California, Mexico, is the only place where San Marcos–hibiscus occurs naturally. It grows mostly near the sea, in sandy or rocky arroyos and on slopes.

*Culture* San Marcos–hibiscus is cold tender, but even though it freezes to the ground at 28° F, it will grow back from the roots. The frost-damaged stems can be removed in early spring, when all danger of frost is past. Provide a planting site with well-drained soil and full sun. A deep soaking about twice a month during the summer will promote faster growth and more profuse flowering.

*Landscape Use* Use San Marcos–hibiscus for a foundation planting; the moderate-sized shrub can help provide a visual link between the building and landscape while deriving some protection from cold temperatures. In mild-winter areas, it could be incorporated into mixed desert plantings. The shrub's bloom could lend color to patio areas or courtyard gardens. San Marcos–hibiscus's deep green foliage would create a striking contrast to gray-leaved plants.

*Garrya wrightii* Wright Silktassel

*Glandularia gooddingii* Goodding-verbena

*Gossypium harknessii* San Marcos–
hibiscus; detail below

*Glandularia wrightii* Wright-verbena

## Guayacan, Soapbush
### *Guaiacum angustifolium*
ZYGOPHYLLACEAE [CALTROP FAMILY]

**Description** Guayacan is in the same family as Creosote Bush (*Larrea tridentata*); you can see the similarity in the flowers. Like those of Creosote Bush, Guayacan flowers are about ¾ inch across and have five petals, although they are deep bluish purple (rather than yellow) and fragrant. The blooming season is from March through September. Guayacan's gnarled branches grow mostly upright into a large shrub, 10 feet high and the same width. The foliage is evergreen, crowded close to the gray branches. The tiny dark green leaflets fold up at night and often in the heat of the day to conserve water. Shiny red fruits ½ inch in diameter adorn the plants in fall. The common name Soapbush refers to the use of its root bark as a source of soap in Mexico.

**Native Distribution** This Guayacan species is frequently found in arroyos and canyons among brushy vegetation, at 1,600 to 4,000 feet in elevation. The plant's distribution includes central, southern, and western Texas and the Mexican states of Chihuahua, Coahuila, Nuevo León, and Tamaulipas.

**Culture** Cold hardiness and drought tolerance are two attributes of Guayacan. Occasional summer watering can boost the normally slow growth rate. Full sun to partial shade is acceptable, as are most well-drained soils. Much of the plant's character is in its gnarled branches, so keep pruning to a minimum.

**Landscape Use** The size and dense foliage suggest a use in screening. Rather than attempting to manipulate Guayacan into a traditional straight hedge, you can stagger the plants and let them assume their natural form. You can use this attractive shrub as an accent plant or focal point in the landscape. Its fragrant flowers will be best appreciated near a walkway or patio, and it can provide good cover and food for wildlife.

---

## Guayacan
### *Guaiacum coulteri*
ZYGOPHYLLACEAE [CALTROP FAMILY]

**Description** Deep blue-violet, ¾-inch flowers appear sporadically from April to September, clinging tightly to Guayacan's twisted branches. Deep green leaves are divided into six to ten ½-inch-long oval leaflets that similarly cluster along the branches. The fruit is ½ inch long and has light green, fleshy wings that turn golden upon ripening. The size of Guayacan is often determined by temperature. In areas that experience light frost, the shrub will reach a height and width of about 5 feet. In frost-free areas, it becomes a large shrub or small tree, to 20 feet high. The foliage is evergreen unless damaged by frost.

**Native Distribution** This Guayacan species grows on gravelly plains and slopes in the western part of Mexico, from Sonora to Oaxaca.

**Culture** A location that is sheltered from cold yet receives full sun is most appropriate for Guayacan. The branch tips can suffer damage below 30° F, and the foliage will be severely harmed by temperatures in the low 20s F. Well-drained soil is preferred by this plant, which does well on minimal water. Supplemental irrigation in the summer will encourage heavier flowering. If the foliage sustains frost damage, wait to prune until new growth appears in spring.

**Landscape Use** It is worth the effort to find a warm microclimate for this plant or to cover it on cold nights. The deep blue-violet flowers are stunning and should be featured near a pool or patio. Try planting Guayacan with Creosote Bush (*Larrea tridentata*) to bring out the similarities in the related shrubs.

## Snakeweed, Broomweed
### *Gutierrezia sarothrae*
ASTERACEAE [SUNFLOWER FAMILY]

**Description** Snakeweed is smothered with tiny yellow flowers from June to November. Bright green, resinous leaves 1½ inches long and ⅛ inch wide provide color the rest of the year. The semi-evergreen foliage forms a rounded shrub, woody at the base but herbaceous above. A typical mature height is 1½ feet, with a spread of 2 feet.

**Native Distribution** Snakeweed occurs on dry plains and slopes between 1,500 and 7,000 feet in elevation. It is especially abundant on overgrazed rangeland. The plant's range extends from southern Canada to northern Mexico; in the United States it occurs as far east as Kansas.

**Culture** A wide range of soils is acceptable to Snakeweed. It prefers full sun, and once established, it is drought tolerant. The plant is aggressive, so supplemental irrigation should be kept to a minimum. Snakeweed tolerates temperatures to 0° F or lower.

**Landscape Use** This low-growing shrub would make an excellent groundcover if massed. Its colorful flowers and foliage could brighten a naturalistic desert planting or a flower garden—just be sure to keep the seedlings from taking over. Its hardiness is an attribute for roadside and median plantings and other harsh landscape situations.

## Texas False-agave
### *Hechtia texensis* (syn., *Hechtia scariosa*)
BROMELIACEAE [PINEAPPLE FAMILY]

**Description** The succulent rosette of Texas False-agave is typically 6 inches high and 8 inches wide, but as the plant matures it develops offsets that eventually form a clump to 1½ feet in diameter. The medium green leaves usually turn reddish in the fall. A loose cluster of small, inconspicuous flowers occurs on a 2-foot stalk between February and May. Texas False-agave's flowers develop into ½-inch dark brown capsules.

**Native Distribution** This plant's distribution is limited to southwestern Texas and northeastern Mexico, between 1,800 and 3,700 feet in elevation. It grows on rocky limestone slopes and ridges.

**Culture** Texas False-agave does best in well-drained soil. Once established, plants are very drought tolerant. They can be treated much like *Agave* or *Yucca* species, with supplemental irrigation during drought. Cold to 15° F is tolerated. Full sun is preferred, although light shade is acceptable.

**Landscape Use** This attractive plant would lend interest to a cactus and succulent garden. In a naturalistic desert landscape, it could be planted in the company of a shrub such as Creosote Bush (*Larrea tridentata*). It could also be grown in a pot.

## Coahuilan Hesperaloe
### *Hesperaloe funifera*
AGAVACEAE [AGAVE FAMILY]

**Description** The light green leaves of Coahuilan Hesperaloe rise stiffly to 4 feet. A mature plant can spread to 4 feet wide. Coarse hairs appear along the edges of 1½-inch-wide, sharp-tipped leaves. In spring, Coahuilan Hesperaloe sends up a 10-foot candelabra-type flower spike with 1-inch-long, bell-shaped white flowers. The woody fruiting capsules are generally oval and 1–2 inches long.

**Native Distribution** Coahuilan Hesperaloe occurs in Coahuila, Nuevo León, and San Luis Potosí, Mexico.

Above left and right: *Guaiacum angustifolium* Guayacan

*Guaiacum coulteri* Guayacan

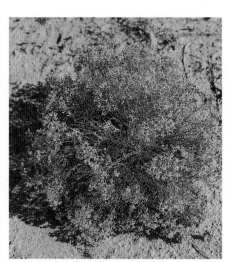

*Gutierrezia sarothrae* Snakeweed

*Hechtia texensis* Texas False-agave

*Hesperaloe funifera* Coahuilan Hesperaloe

*Culture* Well-drained soil is ideal, although Coahuilan Hesperaloe will grow in other soil types. Full sun is required for proper development. Once a plant is established, it needs supplemental irrigation only during prolonged dry periods. It is cold hardy to about 15° F.

*Landscape Use* Coahuilan Hesperaloe's stiff, vertical rosette contrasts with other desert plant forms, so it would stand out in any landscape. The plant could be used singly or, for added impact, in groupings of three to seven. Highway median or roadside plantings could be spiced up by incorporating Coahuilan Hesperaloe. A plain wall or a background of fine-textured foliage such as Velvet Mesquite (*Prosopis velutina*) would show off Coahuilan Hesperaloe's angular form. Be sure to keep the pointed leaves a safe distance from walkways or patios.

# Red Hesperaloe, Red-yucca
## *Hesperaloe parviflora*
AGAVACEAE [AGAVE FAMILY]

*Description* Dark green, semi-succulent leaves 3 inches long and ½ inch wide, with fibrous threads along the edges, form a grasslike clump 3–4 feet across. From late spring through fall, deep pink bell-shaped flowers bloom atop 5-foot stalks that emerge from the center of the plant. The flowers develop into rounded capsules about 1 inch long, at first light green, then brown and woody.

*Native Distribution* Red Hesperaloe grows in central and southwestern Texas and the northern part of Coahuila, Mexico.

*Culture* Red Hesperaloe adapts to most soil types; good drainage is desirable. A deep soaking once a month in the summer will keep the plant looking good. A location with full sun is best, although it can grow in partial shade. It is cold hardy to about 12° F, with a slow to moderate growth rate. The flower stalks can be pruned back to the foliage when the bloom is finished.

*Landscape Use* Hummingbirds are attracted to the long-blooming flowers of Red Hesperaloe. It is a fine accent around patios and swimming pools and in flower gardens. The plant's form and texture are compatible with other succulents and cacti, while an interesting contrast can be achieved by combining Red Hesperaloe with "leafy" plants. It also makes a good container plant.

# Desert Rose-mallow
## *Hibiscus coulteri*
MALVACEAE [MALLOW FAMILY]

*Description* Desert Rose-mallow is a shrubby perennial to 3 feet high and nearly as wide. The lower leaves are coarsely toothed, with a round or oval shape, while the upper leaves are divided into three narrow, toothed lobes. Despite the difference in shape, both the lower and upper leaves are about 1 inch long and ¾ inch wide. The deciduous foliage is dark green, with sparse, stiff hairs. The 2-inch-wide, cup-shaped flowers vary in color from white to bright yellow, typically with a red spot at the base of each petal. Desert Rose-mallow blooms predominantly from April through September, in response to moisture. The fruit is a ½-inch capsule containing hairy seeds.

*Native Distribution* Rocky slopes and the sides of canyons, between 1,500 and 4,500 feet in elevation, are the preferred habitat of Desert Rose-mallow. Its distribution includes western Texas, southern New Mexico, and southwestern Arizona. In Mexico, it occurs from Sonora and Chihuahua to Hidalgo.

*Culture* Desert Rose-mallow likes well-drained soil. The nicest foliage and flowers will be produced in full sun. Selective pruning can encourage denser growth. Temperatures to 20° F are tolerated without damage.

**Landscape Use** Incorporate Desert Rose-mallow into a flower garden with other drought-tolerant perennials. Because of its potential height, place it near the back. The plant would also be a nice addition to a naturalistic desert landscape. In a more formal setting, Desert Rose-mallow could be massed for a low hedge. In nature Desert Rose-mallow often grows under other shrubs, which provide some shelter from the cold. If you live in a colder desert area, you may wish to replicate that situation in your landscape.

## Paleface Rose-mallow
### Hibiscus denudatus
MALVACEAE [MALLOW FAMILY]

**Description** Greenish yellow fuzzy leaves are borne on Paleface Rose-mallow's herbaceous stems, which grow to 2 feet high and 1 foot wide from a woody base. The drought-deciduous leaves are oval, ending in a point, and are edged with coarse teeth. They measure 1 inch long and ¾ inch wide at the base. Dark lavender to nearly white flowers appear from March to October. The five petals that form the 1½-inch-wide flower are often reddish at the base.

**Native Distribution** Paleface Rose-mallow has a broad distribution, including southeastern California, southern Nevada, southern Arizona, southern New Mexico, and western Texas, plus Baja California, Sonora, Chihuahua, Coahuila, and Durango, Mexico. It is normally found between 200 and 4,600 feet in elevation, in washes and canyons and on rocky slopes.

**Culture** A planting site with well-drained soil is preferred. Paleface Rose-mallow is hardy to 5° F and drought tolerant once established. In a landscape situation,

supplemental irrigation every other week will promote faster growth with denser foliage. Some extra water, combined with full sun, encourages prolific flowering.

**Landscape Use** The delicate lavender flowers of Paleface Rose-mallow are best appreciated at close range, in a patio or courtyard planting, or flower garden.

## Big Galleta
### Hilaria rigida
POACEAE [GRASS FAMILY]

**Description** At maturity this coarse, almost woody perennial bunchgrass can reach 3 feet high with a similar spread. The stiff leaf blades are 3 inches long by ⅛ inch wide, and sometimes covered with a light, woolly fuzz. The foliage is dull bluish green, drying to gray. Dense flowering spikes up to 4 inches long are produced from February to September.

**Native Distribution** Big Galleta is found in southern California, Utah, Nevada, and Arizona, as well as in Baja California and Sonora, Mexico. The grass grows to 4,000 feet above sea level, usually on desert flats, rocky hillsides, and sand dunes.

**Culture** The soil in a landscape situation should be like that of Big Galleta's natural habitat: well drained and either sandy or gravelly. It is very drought tolerant once established, able to survive on rainfall alone. Big Galleta grows best in full sun. Temperatures to at least 10° F are tolerated without damage. You can rejuvenate this bunchgrass by cutting it to the ground every few years.

**Landscape Use** Big Galleta is a coarse-looking grass best suited for use in a naturalistic landscape. You could inter-mingle it with desert shrubs such as Creosote Bush (Larrea tridentata) or use it in a mass planting. It can provide excellent erosion control.

*Hibiscus coulteri* Desert Rose-mallow

*Hilaria rigida* Big Galleta

*Hibiscus denudatus* Paleface Rose-mallow

Opposite:
*Hesperaloe parviflora*
Red Hesperaloe

## Burrobrush, Cheese Bush
### Hymenoclea monogyra
ASTERACEAE [SUNFLOWER FAMILY]

**Description** Threadlike, yellowish green leaves to 2 inches long give Burro-brush a delicate appearance. The densely branched, rounded shrub grows to 5 feet high and 5 feet wide. It is drought deciduous. In September and October, Burrobrush produces small, inconspicuous greenish white flowers. The ¼-inch fruits, with a single whorl of papery wings, are more noticeable.

**Native Distribution** Burrobrush grows naturally in southern California, Arizona, New Mexico, western Texas, and the Mexican states of Baja California, Sonora, and Chihuahua. It is most commonly found along sandy washes from 1,000 to 5,000 feet in elevation.

**Culture** Soil conditions like those in its habitat, loose and well drained, suit Burrobrush best. It is hardy to 15° F or lower. Provide full sun and just enough water to keep the shrub green.

**Landscape Use** Burrobrush could be incorporated into naturalistic desert landscapes, particularly those with a wash. The plant is useful for erosion control. Allergy sufferers may want to pass on Burrobrush, as its pollen is said to cause irritation.

---

*Hymenoclea salsola*, also called Burrobrush or Cheese Bush, differs from *Hymenoclea monogyra* by flowering from March to May. Also, the fruits have several whorls of papery wings instead of just one. The plant overall is less erect (to about 3 feet high and 3 feet wide) and less leafy than *Hymenoclea monogyra*. *Hymenoclea salsola* grows along sandy washes and on desert flats and slopes, usually below 4,000 feet in elevation. Its range includes southern California, southern Nevada, southwestern Utah, western Arizona, and Baja California and Sonora, Mexico. Culture and landscape use are the same as for *Hymenoclea monogyra*.

---

## Desert-lavender
### Hyptis emoryi
LAMIACEAE [MINT FAMILY]

**Description** The gray leaves of Desert-lavender are covered with fine hairs and are soft to the touch. A pleasant lavender scent is released following rains or if you brush against the foliage. Individual leaves are 1 inch long by ¾ inch wide, broader at the base than at the tip. The edges have rounded teeth. The branches grow upright to form an evergreen shrub to 10 feet high and 8 feet wide. Spikes of silvery-blue flowers develop at the ends of branches anytime throughout the year, but they appear most heavily in spring.

**Native Distribution** Desert-lavender occurs to 3,000 feet elevation, in southern California, Nevada, Arizona, New Mexico, and Baja California and Sonora, Mexico. It grows on dry, rocky slopes, along washes, and in canyons.

**Culture** Full sun encourages dense growth; in partial shade the foliage will be sparser. Well-drained soil is recommended. Desert-lavender is drought tolerant once established, though extended drought will cause some leaf drop. It will benefit from infrequent deep soakings during the warm season, until late summer, when water should be withheld to harden the plant for winter. Temperatures in the low 20s F will cause foliage damage. Even though the plant may freeze to the ground in severe winters, it should resprout and will probably grow back bushier than before. The natural growth form of Desert-lavender is fairly compact, so pruning is optional. Fall pruning, which would stimulate frost-sensitive new growth, should be avoided.

**Landscape Use** Desert-lavender's silvery foliage would look attractive in most desert landscapes, either combined with similarly colored plants for a restful, monochromatic effect, or contrasted with green-foliaged plants. You could take advantage of the upright form by making an informal hedge or privacy screen of several plants. The fragrant foliage can best be appreciated near a patio or in an entryway. Bees frequent the flowers, and birds often nest among the branches.

---

## Bladderpod
### *Isomeris arborea* (syn., *Cleome isomeris*)
CAPPARIDACEAE [CAPER FAMILY]

**Description** Clusters of ¾-inch, four-petaled yellow flowers adorn the rounded form of Bladderpod most abundantly from February through May, and to some extent almost throughout the year. From the flowers develop 2-inch-long oval inflated fruits, which are the inspiration for the common name. The fruits, at first light green, turn tan and persist on the plant through the summer. The strongly scented evergreen leaves are divided into three oblong leaflets, 1 inch long and ½ inch wide. The foliage is yellow-green to gray-green. At maturity, Bladderpod averages 4 feet high and 6 feet wide.

**Native Distribution** Bladderpod often grows in disturbed areas, and also on dry slopes and along washes. The shrub's home is southern California and Baja California, Mexico, from 200 to 3,000 feet in elevation.

**Culture** Areas with alkaline soil can support Bladderpod. Good drainage is preferable. Bladderpod can grow in partial shade, although the best growth is attained in full sun. Likewise, the plant

can survive extreme drought once established, but it looks better with a deep soaking every few weeks in summertime. Temperatures to 15° F are tolerated by this fast-growing shrub.

**Landscape Use** Bladderpod can be used for a moderate-sized, informal hedge, and for soil stability on slopes. The flowers are a nice bonus in naturalistic desert landscapes.

---

## Slender Janusia
### *Janusia gracilis*
MALPIGHIACEAE [MALPIGHIA FAMILY]

**Description** Slender Janusia is a deciduous, shrubby vine that often climbs within other shrubs. Linear to lance-shaped deep green leaves, ¾ inch long and ⅛ inch wide, occur sparsely along the slender, twining branches. Without support, the plant will only reach a height and width of about 2 feet. The ½-inch delicate yellow flowers have five fringed petals. Flowering occurs sporadically from April to October in response to moisture. Slender Janusia's ⅓-inch-long winged fruits turn red upon ripening.

**Native Distribution** The natural range of Slender Janusia includes Arizona, southern New Mexico, and western Texas, as well as Chihuahua, Sonora, and Baja California, Mexico. It grows on rocky hillsides and in arroyos, between 1,000 and 5,000 feet in elevation.

**Culture** Slender Janusia can grow in full sun or light shade. It needs well-drained soil. Once established, plants need no supplemental watering, although some irrigation during the warm season will increase flowering. In order to climb, it needs the support of another plant or a trellis. It is hardy to at least 18° F.

**Landscape Use** Slender Janusia's subtle beauty is best appreciated at close range. It

*Hymenoclea monogyra* Burrobrush

*Hymenoclea salsola* Burrobrush

*Hyptis emoryi* Desert-lavender

*Isomeris arborea* Bladderpod

*Janusia gracilis* Slender Janusia

could be used in an entry courtyard or near a patio. Train the vine on a fence or trellis, or simply allow it to climb on a shrub such as Creosote Bush (*Larrea tridentata*). The plant lends interest to naturalistic desert landscapes.

---

# Limber Bush
## *Jatropha cardiophylla*
EUPHORBIACEAE [SPURGE FAMILY]

**Description**  The flexible stems of Limber Bush are covered with reddish bark, a nice contrast to the deep green, glossy foliage. The heart-shaped leaves are 1 inch long and equally wide, with shallow, rounded teeth on the margins. This drought-deciduous shrub grows to 3 feet high and 3 feet wide. Small, inconspicuous pink flowers bloom in July and August, followed by rounded greenish brown seed capsules about ½ inch long.

**Native Distribution**  Limber Bush frequents desert plains, rocky slopes, and mesas, from 2,000 to 3,000 feet in elevation. It occurs in southern Arizona and Sonora, Mexico.

**Culture**  A sheltered location is necessary for this plant; it shows foliage damage at temperatures near 20° F. Limber Bush survives periods of drought by shedding its leaves; however, it will remain evergreen with supplemental water through the summer. It prefers well-drained soil and full sun.

**Landscape Use**  Limber Bush can be incorporated into naturalistic desert landscapes. The cold protection the shrub requires can be provided by using it near a building, either as a foundation planting or in a courtyard garden. Its semi-succulent appearance would be appropriate for a cactus and succulent garden.

# Leatherplant, Limber Bush
## *Jatropha cuneata*
EUPHORBIACEAE [SPURGE FAMILY]

**Description**  Many thick, leathery stems rise from a central base to form a 3-foot-high, 4-foot-wide semi-succulent shrub. Leatherplant's medium green fleshy leaves are ½ inch long and ¼ inch wide, ending in a broadened tip. They appear when the humidity rises during the summer rains. Inconspicuous, pinkish white ¼-inch tube-shaped flowers bloom in July and August. The fruit is a capsule about ½ inch long and 1 inch broad.

**Native Distribution**  Leatherplant is typically found in washes and on dry plains, slopes, and mesas, between 1,000 and 2,000 feet in elevation. Its native range includes southwestern Arizona and Baja California and Sonora, Mexico.

**Culture**  Leatherplant will grow well in a sunny location sheltered from cold. Temperatures below 32° F can damage the foliage. The plant is extremely drought tolerant once established, so supplemental irrigation really isn't necessary. The semi-succulent leaves will react to drought stress by wrinkling. Leatherplant needs well-drained soil. If the plant suffers frost damage, wait until new growth appears, then prune away the dead portions. Otherwise, let it grow to its natural form without being pruned.

**Landscape Use**  This plant could be incorporated into a cactus and succulent garden to provide some variety in form. Leatherplant can also be mixed with other desert shrubs in a naturalistic landscape or planted as a low, informal hedge. The protection afforded by a patio, courtyard, or swimming pool will increase its chances of escaping cold damage.

## Leatherstem, Sangre de Drago
### Jatropha dioica
EUPHORBIACEAE [SPURGE FAMILY]

**Description** Common names are often quite descriptive of a plant. The first one refers to the upright to arching leathery stems, which can reach 1½ feet high. The stems rise from an underground rootstock rather than an above-ground base, so the plant's mature spread is variable, to as much as 6 feet. If a stem is broken, the meaning of the other common name becomes obvious. The clear to yellow sap turns blood red upon exposure to air. *Sangre de Drago* means "blood of the dragon" in Spanish. Leaf shape distinguishes the two varieties of *Jatropha dioica*. *Jatropha dioica* variety *dioica* has leaves about 1 inch long and ¼ inch wide at the broad, blunt tip. Longer, narrower leaves, sometimes three-lobed, occur on *Jatropha dioica* variety *graminea*. The foliage of both varieties is deciduous. Leatherstem's tiny white or pink flowers bloom in clusters in spring and early summer. The fruit is a small, leathery capsule.

**Native Distribution** Leatherstem occurs in southwestern Texas and northern Mexico, often on limestone.

**Culture** Temperatures below 15° F can damage Leatherstem. It needs full sun and well-drained soil. Give young plants supplemental irrigation once or twice a month through the summer, then gradually wean them to rainfall only.

**Landscape Use** Leatherstem is an odd-looking plant, especially in winter, when the bare, upright stems look like dead sticks. The rest of the year, the plant can contribute rich green color to the landscape. The best use of Leatherstem might be in a cactus and succulent garden among other uniquely-shaped plants. Another possibility would be to put it in a pot and move it to the background during the off-season.

## Chuparosa
### Justicia californica
ACANTHACEAE [ACANTHUS FAMILY]

**Description** Chuparosa's gray-green branches and leaves form an open, twiggy shrub 3 feet high and 4 feet wide. The heart-shaped leaves, about 1 inch long and ¾ inch wide, drop in cold weather or extreme drought. Deep red, tubular 1-inch-long flowers occur in clusters and appear throughout much of the year, most abundantly in spring.

**Native Distribution** This shrub grows from sea level to 2,500 feet in elevation in southeastern California and southern Arizona as well as in Sonora, Sinaloa, and the Baja California peninsula in Mexico. Look for Chuparosa along washes and on rocky slopes.

**Culture** Chuparosa needs a location protected from hard frost. The foliage will be damaged at about 28° F and frozen to the ground in the low 20s F. Regrowth is usually rapid, especially with supplemental water. Wait until all danger of frost has passed before you do any pruning of damaged foliage. Don't encourage frost-sensitive new growth by pruning in the fall. Although very drought tolerant, Chuparosa will look better if given a deep soaking once or twice a month in the summer. The growth rate is moderate to fast, depending upon availability of water. Sometimes in the desert you'll see Chuparosa intertwined with another shrub or tree, but an open location receiving full sun is better. Soil should be well drained.

**Landscape Use** If you want to attract hummingbirds to your garden, be sure to plant Chuparosa. The common name is derived from *chupar*, Spanish for "to suck," referring to the plant's popularity with hummingbirds. Chuparosa's moderate size suits it for use in courtyard gardens, near the house for foundation

172

*Jatropha cardiophylla* Limber Bush

*Jatropha cuneata* Leatherplant

*Jatropha dioica* var. *dioica* Leatherstem

*Justicia californica* Chuparosa

plantings, and even along streets and in parking lot planters. One or more plants can lend authenticity to a simulated wash in the landscape. The shrub's abundant red flowers not only please the hummers but also create a colorful accent in the landscape.

would look most natural planted along a wash, though it could also be used more formally as a low hedge or foundation planting near the house. Planting Red Justicia near a swimming pool or in a courtyard garden would give it the best protection against cold damage.

## Red Justicia, Hummingbird Bush
### *Justicia candicans* (syn., *Justicia ovata*)
ACANTHACEAE [ACANTHUS FAMILY]

*Description* Red Justicia's leaves and young branches are soft to touch, as they are covered with fine hair. The bright green evergreen leaves are heart-shaped, to 1 inch or more long and ¾ inch wide. At maturity the shrub is 3 feet high and equally wide, with numerous upright to somewhat spreading branches. Bright red tube-shaped flowers 1 inch long appear sparsely over a long period from fall to spring, particularly if the winter is mild.

*Native Distribution* Desert washes and rocky canyons are typical habitat. Red Justicia grows at elevations between 1,500 and 3,500 feet in southern Arizona and in Sonora, Sinaloa, and Chihuahua, Mexico.

*Culture* This plant will grow in full sun or partial shade, blooming well in either situation. The planting location should be sheltered from frost, since Red Justicia can be damaged around 25° F. The fast-growing plants recover quickly, though. Well-drained soil is the best type, and supplemental water every two to three weeks will give Red Justicia a boost during the warm season. Selective pruning can create denser growth, but the natural form is more graceful.

*Landscape Use* This plant would be a good addition to a hummingbird garden. The bright green foliage sprinkled with red flowers would also make a nice backdrop to a perennial flower garden. Red Justicia

## Allthorn, Crucifixion Thorn
### *Koeberlinia spinosa*
KOEBERLINIACEAE [JUNCO FAMILY]

*Description* The common name Allthorn is appropriate, as this shrub looks like a tangle of thorns. Its form is typically rounded, but at times it becomes treelike. A typical mature size is 8 feet high and 6 feet wide. The branches are pale green, stiff, and spine-tipped. Tiny leaves drop early in the season. The March-through-October display of tiny greenish white flowers is not nearly as showy as the clusters of shiny, ¼-inch red and black berries that follow.

*Native Distribution* Allthorn's range extends from southeastern California through southern Arizona and southern New Mexico to western Texas, and from Baja California to Tamaulipas and Hidalgo, Mexico. Its habitat includes arroyos, desert plains, and rocky slopes, from 2,500 to 5,000 feet in elevation.

*Culture* Allthorn is very cold hardy, to at least 0° F, and drought tolerant, although supplemental irrigation once or twice a month during hot weather would be appreciated. It is tolerant of various soil types. Choose a planting site that receives full sun.

*Landscape Use* A formidable security barrier could be made by planting a group of Allthorn. Birds find cover among the branches and eat the berries.

## Creosote Bush

### *Larrea tridentata* (syn., *Larrea divaricata*)

ZYGOPHYLLACEAE [CALTROP FAMILY]

**Description** Whenever it rains in the desert, Creosote Bush lends a distinctive fragrance to the air. Tiny resinous olive green leaves are the source of the fragrance, though not the source of real creosote, as the common name would suggest. Twisted gray stems rising from a central base are sparsely foliated, giving the plant an open, airy appearance. Under favorable soil and moisture conditions, Creosote Bush can reach 10 feet in height and width. A more typical size is 6 feet high and 8 feet wide. Throughout the year, but heaviest in spring, ½-inch yellow flowers sprinkle the foliage. Pea-sized fruits with a dense covering of silver hairs follow the flowers.

**Native Distribution** One of the most common shrubs of the Southwestern deserts, Creosote Bush occurs from western Texas to southeastern California, north to southern Utah and Nevada, and south to Baja California, Querétaro, and Hidalgo, Mexico. It usually grows in loose, well-drained soil on dry plains, mesas, and slopes, between sea level and elevations of 5,000 feet.

**Culture** Creosote Bush is extremely drought tolerant once established. It is also very cold hardy, to 5° F. Full sun is preferred; plants in shade become leggy and sparse. Typically, Creosote Bush grows at a slow to moderate rate. Additional water and fertilizer can speed things along, though the resulting growth lacks the distinctive gnarled, irregular appearance. Pruning is recommended only to remove dead wood. A tiny fly called a midge (*Asphondylia* species) causes galls, 1-inch balls of distorted foliar growth, to form on Creosote Bush's branches. The galls usually occur on water-stressed plants, but they don't seem to cause serious harm.

**Landscape Use** Creosote Bush works well in revegetated or naturalistic desert landscapes. Plants can be massed for screening or used singly to showcase their distinctive form. A plain background is particularly effective for accenting the irregular, twisted branches. The delicate foliage of Creosote Bush is a good contrast to the bold forms of cacti and other succulents such as *Agave* species.

## Golden Ball Lead Tree

### *Leucaena retusa*

FABACEAE [PEA FAMILY]

**Description** One-inch golden puffball flowers dot the branches of Golden Ball Lead Tree in spring, like miniature Christmas tree ornaments. A narrow woody pod about 6 inches long contains several shiny brown seeds. Golden Ball Lead Tree is a large rounded shrub, often multiple-trunked. It can be pruned to a small tree 15 feet high and nearly as wide. The wood is weak and brittle. The shrub sheds its bright green, feathery foliage in the fall.

**Native Distribution** Golden Ball Lead Tree typically grows on rocky limestone slopes or in canyons, between 1,200 and 5,500 feet in elevation, in western Texas, southern New Mexico, and Coahuila, Mexico.

**Culture** This plant can adapt to a wide range of soils. Good drainage is preferred. Irrigation is necessary only for new plants and during extended drought. Provide full sun for Golden Ball Lead Tree, which usually has a fast rate of growth. It needs no special protection from cold, being hardy to 5° F, although a location sheltered from the wind is advised, since the brittle wood breaks easily.

**Landscape Use** Golden Ball Lead Tree is a good medium-sized tree for courtyards or

Above left and right: *Justicia candicans* Red Justicia

*Koeberlinia spinosa* Allthorn

*Leucaena retusa* Golden Ball Lead Tree

*Larrea tridentata* Creosote Bush; flower above left

patios. The flowers are very ornamental, suiting the plant for use as an accent in the landscape. The feathery foliage casts moderate shade in summer yet allows the sun's warming rays to penetrate in winter. Perennials that bloom in the spring and prefer some protection from the summertime sun would do well under Golden Ball Lead Tree. Left unpruned, the plant can provide visual screening.

## Violet Silverleaf
### *Leucophyllum candidum*
SCROPHULARIACEAE [FIGWORT FAMILY]

**Description** Short whitish hairs cover the foliage and young stems of this densely branched evergreen shrub. It will reach a height of 2–3 feet and a width of 3 feet. The silvery leaves are about ½ inch long and ¼ inch wide at the broadened tip. Violet, bell-shaped ½-inch flowers cover Violet Silverleaf in September and October and occasionally after spring and summer rain showers.

**Native Distribution** Violet Silverleaf grows naturally in western Texas and in Chihuahua, Coahuila, Durango, and Zacatecas, Mexico. It frequents limestone hillsides and plains between 2,200 and 4,900 feet in elevation.

**Culture** This shrub prefers full sun. Light shade is okay, but the shaded plant will develop a looser form. Well-drained soil is best. Violet Silverleaf tolerates drought once established; an extra watering once a month in summer would be appreciated. It is cold hardy to about 10° F.

**Landscape Use** Violet Silverleaf can serve as a focal point in the landscape, or it can just as easily blend into a grouping of other shrubs. Its silver foliage makes a good contrast with green plants such as Desert-fern (*Lysiloma microphylla* variety *thornberi*) or Desert Broom (*Baccharis*

*sarothroides*). The soft foliage is good around patios and pool areas.

A cultivar (cultivated variety) of *Leucophyllum candidum* developed by Texas A&M University, called 'Silver Cloud,' has very silver, almost white, foliage and deep purple flowers.

## Texas Ranger, Texas-sage, Cenizo
### *Leucophyllum frutescens* (syn., *Leucophyllum texanum*)
SCROPHULARIACEAE [FIGWORT FAMILY]

**Description** Texas Ranger is the largest species of *Leucophyllum*. It can reach 6 feet in height, with an 8-foot spread. The evergreen foliage is silver-gray, soft to the touch, and densely clustered along spreading branches. One-inch-long leaves broaden at the tip to ½ inch across. Warm temperatures and high humidity trigger blooming in summertime. Texas Ranger's 1-inch bell-shaped flowers range in color from white to pinkish lavender to purple.

**Native Distribution** Southwestern Texas and northeastern Mexico are home to Texas Ranger, which grows on rocky hillsides, along arroyos, and in brushlands, between 1,000 and 4,500 feet in elevation.

**Culture** Texas Ranger is hardy to about 10° F and will grow in a wide range of soils, preferably those that are well drained. Full sun encourages full, dense growth. Texas Ranger is drought tolerant once established. In extreme dryness, the plant will shed some leaves. Supplemental irrigation every few weeks in the summer will keep the foliage looking better. Be careful not to overwater. Texas Ranger is a popular choice for hedges, so it is unusual to see an unpruned specimen, although the natural form is quite attractive. If you must prune Texas Ranger, do it in the spring before the flower buds form or in the fall after blooming has finished.

*Landscape Use*  This dense shrub could be used for visual screening and wind control. A dramatic contrast of foliage color could be achieved using Texas Ranger and green-leaved plants. The silvery foliage harmonizes with other gray- or blue-toned plants—for example, Bush Dalea (*Dalea pulchra*) or Golden-flowered Agave (*Agave chrysantha*). With its showy summer flowering, Texas Ranger could certainly be used as an accent plant.

Several attractive cultivars (cultivated varieties) of *Leucophyllum frutescens* are available. 'Green Cloud' has green foliage, while the name 'White Cloud' refers not to foliage color but to the large, white flowers. The smaller, denser *Leucophyllum frutescens* variety *compactum* matures to 4 feet high and about as wide. 'Green Cloud' and 'White Cloud' are similar in size to the species.

---

## Chihuahuan-sage
### *Leucophyllum laevigatum*
SCROPHULARIACEAE [FIGWORT FAMILY]

*Description*  Medium green leaves are somewhat sparsely arranged, yet they cling tightly along the erect to spreading branches of Chihuahuan-sage. Individual leaves measure ½ inch long and ¼ inch wide at the bluntly rounded tip. This evergreen shrub normally reaches a height of 4 feet and a width of 5 feet. The ½-inch-long flowers, like the leaves, are closely attached to the stems. During the summer blooming season, the shrub looks like a big bouquet of pale bluish lavender spikes. The flowers have a pleasant fragrance. Chihuahuan-sage doesn't seem to be as dependent on humidity and warmth to bloom as the other *Leucophyllum* species. A thorough watering can prompt blooming.

*Native Distribution*  Chihuahuan-sage occurs on rocky limestone hillsides from 4,000 to 7,800 feet in elevation in Chihuahua, Coahuila, Durango, Zacatecas, and San Luis Potosí, Mexico.

*Culture*  Full sun or light shade is acceptable to Chihuahuan-sage. It is drought tolerant once established; supplemental irrigation once or twice a month through the hottest months will maintain a moderate growth rate and attractive appearance. The ideal soil type is limestone based and well drained, although Chihuahuan-sage can adapt to other soils. It has endured temperatures to 18° F with no cold damage. Pruning is unnecessary, as Chihuahuan-sage naturally takes on a uniform, rounded shape.

*Landscape Use*  The fragrance of Chihuahuan-sage's summer-blooming flowers would be nice around a patio or pool or in an entry courtyard. Chihuahuan-sage could be used near the house as a foundation planting, visually blending the structure with the landscape. It also could be used in a naturalistic desert landscape or, more formally, as a medium-height hedge. Chihuahuan-sage and Texas Ranger (*Leucophyllum frutescens*) make an interesting combination in hedges or mass plantings because of their similar forms yet different foliage and flower color.

---

## Big Bend Silverleaf
### *Leucophyllum minus*
SCROPHULARIACEAE [FIGWORT FAMILY]

*Description*  Big Bend Silverleaf is a small, many-branched shrub with a height and width of about 3 feet. From June to November, usually after periods of high humidity or rain, ¾-inch violet flowers stand out against the silvery evergreen foliage. The leaves are ⅜ inch long by ¼ inch wide, and oval to broad-tipped.

*Leucophyllum candidum* Violet Silverleaf; 'Silver Cloud' cultivar ^SP

*Leucophyllum frutescens* Texas Ranger

*Leucophyllum laevigatum* Chihuahuan-sage

*Leucophyllum frutescens* 'White Cloud'  *Leucophyllum minus* Big Bend Silverleaf

**Native Distribution** Gravelly plains, rocky foothills, and mountains, typically of limestone, are habitat for Big Bend Silverleaf. It is found at elevations between 2,300 and 6,600 feet in south-western Texas, southeastern New Mexico, and Chihuahua and Coahuila, Mexico.

**Culture** Provide well-drained soil and full sun for Big Bend Silverleaf. After a young plant becomes established it can be weaned from irrigation, with supple-mental watering only during prolonged dry spells. This shrub is hardy to about 25° F. Although it grows fairly rapidly under favorable conditions, pruning to control size usually isn't necessary.

**Landscape Use** A background such as a dark stucco wall would most effectively showcase Big Bend Silverleaf's striking coloration. Contrasting this plant with deep green plants is another way to accentuate the silvery foliage. The shrub can be planted near patios, walkways, or swimming pools. Median strips and parking lot planting islands are also likely destinations for this compact plant.

Blue Ranger
*Leucophyllum zygophyllum*
SCROPHULARIACEAE [FIGWORT FAMILY]

**Description** The leaves of Blue Ranger are silver-gray, thick, ½ inch long by ¼ inch wide, and oval to broadened at the tip. The young branches are silvery, becoming gray to tan with age. Overall, the evergreen shrub has a rounded form, to 3 feet high and 3 feet wide. Bell-shaped purple to light violet flowers nearly ½ inch long bloom in the summer. The flowers have a slight lavender fragrance.

**Native Distribution** Blue Ranger grows in rocky limestone and caliche habitats between 4,000 and 6,900 feet in elevation in Nuevo León, Tamaulipas, and San Luis Potosí, Mexico.

**Culture** Once established, this drought-tolerant shrub requires supplemental irrigation only to improve its summer appearance. It is cold hardy to 20° F. Well-drained soil and full sun are preferred.

**Landscape Use** Blue Ranger is useful in relatively small spaces, where some of the other *Leucophyllum* species would be too large. The silvery foliage and purple flowers combined make an attractive accent in the landscape. Several plants can be massed as a background for smaller plants of contrasting color. Blue Ranger can also be used as an informal, low hedge.

Senita
*Lophocereus schottii*
CACTACEAE [CACTUS FAMILY]

**Description** Gray hairlike spines 2 inches long crowd the tips of mature Senita stems. Lower on the plant, short, stouter spines occur along the five to seven broad ribs. Senita's numerous gray-green 4-inch-thick stems rise from a central base to 10 feet high. An individual plant can be 12 feet wide. Night-blooming pink flowers 1 inch across appear from April through August. The red, spineless fruit is 1 inch in diameter.

**Native Distribution** Senita grows on desert plains and rocky hillsides, from 1,000 to 2,000 feet in elevation. Its distribution is limited to extreme southern Arizona, Baja California, and Sonora, Mexico.

**Culture** Well-drained soil is a must for Senita. The cactus is very drought tolerant, though it is somewhat cold tender. Temperatures in the low 20s F can cause damage. Senita needs full sun for proper development.

**Landscape Use** An entire landscape could be developed around one outstanding specimen of Senita. Plants such as Palo

Verde (*Cercidium* species), Creosote Bush (*Larrea tridentata*), and Bur-sage (*Ambrosia deltoidea*) would complement Senita yet not compete for attention. Senita grows slowly, but in time it can become quite large and difficult to relocate, so be sure to keep it away from buildings, driveways, and sidewalks. Young plants can be potted for use on the patio.

---

Totem Pole Cactus (*Lophocereus schottii* forma *monstrosus*), the monstrous form of Senita, rarely has spines except at the tips of the older branches. Light green skin covers irregularly placed bumps, which some people have compared to blobs of wax on a candle. Its growth form, cultural requirements, and landscape use are similar to those for Senita. Totem Pole Cactus is found only in Baja California, Mexico.

---

## Deer-vetch
### *Lotus rigidus*
FABACEAE [PEA FAMILY]

**Description** Yellow and orange pea-shaped, ½-inch-long flowers are scattered over Deer-vetch's rounded form from February to May. Narrow pods about 1 inch long develop from the flowers. Numerous stems branch from a woody base to 1½ feet high and 2 feet wide. The medium green compound leaves are ½ inch long and divided into three to seven leaflets, which are ⅓ inch long. They drop during times of drought.

**Native Distribution** Deer-vetch is found on dry, rocky slopes and along washes, below 5,500 feet in elevation. Its range includes southern Utah, southern Nevada, Arizona, and southeastern California, as well as Baja California, Mexico.

**Culture** This plant is tough—cold hardy to near 0° F, and very drought tolerant. Provide supplemental water only during extended dry periods, or Deer-vetch will become leggy. It can be pruned severely once a year or so to promote more compact growth. Grow Deer-vetch in well-drained soil and in full sun.

**Landscape Use** Deer-vetch's small but numerous blooms can brighten a flower garden. The plant looks best nestled against a boulder or planted along a wash in a naturalistic desert landscape.

---

## *Lycium* species
SOLANACEAE [NIGHTSHADE FAMILY]

The dense, spiny branches of *Lycium* species provide excellent cover and nesting sites for desert birds. The bright orange to red berries that cover the scraggly shrubs in late summer and fall are relished by dove, quail, and other animals. Besides attracting wildlife, *Lycium* species can also be used for barrier plantings.

The ornamental value of *Lycium* species is limited by their unattractive appearance when leafless due to drought or cold. *Lycium* species prefer full sun or light shade and well-drained soil. Cold hardiness varies among species. Choose a species native to your area, or at least one that grows at your elevation. Once established, *Lycium* species tolerate long periods of drought. The irregular form and branching pattern defy shaping. Let the shrubs grow their own way and only prune dead material.

---

## Anderson Thornbush, Desert Wolfberry
### *Lycium andersonii*

The fleshy leaves of Anderson Thornbush are about ½ inch long and only

*Leucophyllum zygophyllum* Blue Ranger

*Lophocereus schottii* Senita, left; *L. schottii,* forma *monstrosus* Totem Pole Cactus, right

*Lotus rigidus* Deer-vetch

*Lycium* species Wolfberry

⅛ inch wide, sometimes broader at the tip than the base. Red, oval ¼-inch-long berries develop from pale lavender, ½-inch tubular flowers that bloom from February through May. Anderson Thornbush matures to a height and width of 6 feet. It is found in desert washes and on rocky slopes to 6,000 feet in elevation, in southern Utah, southern Nevada, much of Arizona, and southwestern New Mexico, as well as in Baja California, Sonora, and Sinaloa, Mexico.

## Berlandier Wolfberry
### Lycium berlandieri

This species is nearly unarmed, with just a few, if any, needlelike spines at the ends of young branches. The leaves are dark green, linear to somewhat broadened at the tip, and ¾ inch long by ⅛ inch wide. Berlandier Wolfberry is typically 6 feet high and 5 feet wide. Pale lavender bell-shaped flowers bloom from March through September. The round berries are less than ¼ inch in diameter. Berlandier Wolfberry's native distribution includes south-central and western Texas, southern New Mexico, Arizona, and northern Mexico, from 2,000 to 4,600 feet in elevation. The shrub grows in washes and on desert plains and rocky hillsides.

## Thornbush
### Lycium exsertum

The leaves, twigs, and flowers of Thornbush are covered with fine hair. The oval leaves are ½ to ¾ inch long, while the bell-shaped, white to purplish flowers average ½ inch in length. The flowering season lasts from January through April. The oval red berries are ¼ inch long. Overall the shrub measures 8 feet high and 8 feet wide. Thornbush can be found in southwestern Arizona and northern Baja California, to Sonora and northern Sinaloa, Mexico. Typical habitat includes washes, desert plains, and rocky hillsides, between 2,000 and 4,000 feet in elevation.

## Fremont Thornbush
### Lycium fremontii

White to lavender ½-inch tubular flowers appear during two seasons: from February to May and from August to December. Fremont Thornbush's leaves are fleshy, ¾ inch long by ¼ inch wide, and broader at the tip than at the base. The oval fruit is ¼ inch long. Fremont Thornbush occurs from near sea level to 3,000-foot elevations, in washes and on desert plains and rocky hillsides, from western and southern Arizona and southeastern California to Baja California and Sonora, Mexico.

## Pale Wolfberry, Tomatillo, Squawberry
### Lycium pallidum

The leaves of this species are relatively large, 1 inch long and ⅓ inch wide. They are pale green and oval in shape. The ½-inch, funnel-shaped greenish white flowers bloom from April to June, followed by ¼-inch round berries. Mature size is 4 feet high by 6 feet wide. Pale Wolfberry is the most widespread species of Lycium, occurring in southern Colorado and Utah, much of Arizona, southwestern New Mexico and Texas, and in Mexico south to Zacatecas and San Luis Potosí. Pale Wolfberry grows in canyons and on desert plains and rocky slopes from 3,000 to 7,000 feet.

## Torrey Thornbush
### *Lycium torreyi*

Torrey Thornbush's oval, ¼-inch-long berries are the sweetest of those of the *Lycium* species. The grayish green leaves are 1 inch or more long, ¼ to ½ inch wide, broadened at the tip, and somewhat fleshy. Greenish white to lavender funnel-shaped flowers bloom from March to May. Torrey Thornbush occurs on desert flatlands, often in silty, alkaline soil, between 1,000 and 4,500 feet in elevation. Its range includes southwestern Utah, southern Nevada, southeastern California, southern Arizona, southern New Mexico, and western Texas. In Mexico it occurs from Sonora and Chihuahua south to Hidalgo.

## Palo Blanco
### *Lysiloma candida*
FABACEAE [PEA FAMILY]

**Description** Palo Blanco's straight trunk supports a rounded crown of foliage that spreads to 15 feet. The tree's mature height is typically 25 feet. The bark on the trunk and older branches is smooth and chalky white. From March through May, cream-colored, lightly fragrant puffball flowers appear among the gray-green fernlike foliage. The pods turn a coppery red at maturity, when they reach 5 inches long by 1 inch wide. The 7-inch-long leaves are twice-compound, with the individual oval leaflets measuring ½ inch long and ¼ inch wide. In very mild winters the foliage is evergreen.

**Native Distribution** Palo Blanco occurs only on the Baja California peninsula and near Guaymas, on the coast of Sonora, Mexico. Typical habitat is rocky hillsides and arroyos.

**Culture** Temperatures below 25° F can damage this tree. It prefers a location with full sun and well-drained soil. After its establishment, provide supplemental irrigation once a month through the summer. You may want to prune the lower branches to show off the attractive pale trunk.

**Landscape Use** Palo Blanco needs a warm, sheltered location. You can fulfill this requirement and make the most of the tree's ornamental qualities by planting it in an entry courtyard or near a patio. A dark background would make the light-colored trunk most obvious.

## Desert-fern, Feather Bush
### *Lysiloma microphylla* var. *thornberi*
FABACEAE [PEA FAMILY]

**Description** Desert-fern is aptly named. The bright green fernlike leaves are twice-divided into primary leaflets 6 inches long and 4 inches wide, with tiny oval ¼-inch-long secondary leaflets. The foliage is evergreen in mild winters, but Desert-fern will drop its leaves or even freeze to the ground in severe cold. The plant also drops its leaves in spring, just before releafing. Where the winters are harsh, Desert-fern remains a shrub, usually 5 feet high and about as wide. If the plant is not regularly frozen back, it can eventually attain a size of 15 feet high and 18 feet wide. Creamy white puffball-shaped flowers ½ inch in diameter are produced in May and June. The dark brown papery pods that follow are 6 inches long and 1 inch wide.

**Native Distribution** Desert-fern is found only in the Rincon Mountains of southern Arizona, where it grows on rocky hillsides between 2,800 and 4,000 feet in elevation.

**Culture** Desert-fern prefers full sun, though it will grow in light shade, producing sparser foliage. Place it in a warm spot, since the plant sustains damage at about 25° F. Even if severely frozen, Desert-fern recovers quickly in the

*Lycium fremontii* Fremont Thornbush;
detail below left

*Lysiloma candida* Palo Blanco

Above and below: *Lysiloma microphylla*
var. *thornberi* Desert-fern

spring. It prefers well-drained soil but tolerates other types. Desert-fern is tolerant of drought, although it looks best with a deep soaking twice a month in hot weather. Overwatering can cause Desert-fern to become chlorotic, or lacking in iron, which is indicated by yellowed foliage. Supplemental irrigation, combined with selective pruning, can coax Desert-fern into a small tree. When the plant is young, select several major stems, and prune away the other lower branches. Continue to remove side branches or basal sprouts as the main stems mature into trunks. The papery seed pods can be a nuisance when they drop, particularly into a pool or onto paved areas. Some people remove the pods before they fall.

*Landscape Use* When trained as a small tree, Desert-fern can provide shade to patio areas or serve as an accent plant in the landscape. Its lush foliage creates an excellent backdrop to other plants. Desert-fern could be used as a large informal hedge, its screening ability greatest when not pruned. The shrub lends an exotic feeling to patio or swimming-pool plantings.

## Wild-cucumber
### *Marah gilensis*
CUCURBITACEAE [GOURD FAMILY]

*Description* This perennial vine arises from a large tuberous root. Although it is in the same family as cucumber, its fruit is very different. After small greenish white flowers bloom from February to April, prickly fruits 1 inch in diameter develop. The fruits are somewhat succulent when green, but dry upon ripening to a dark tan color. Wild-cucumber has thin, medium green leaves that are slightly rough on the upper surface. They are 2½ inches long and about as wide, and three- to seven-lobed. The vine climbs by slender tendrils.

*Native Distribution* Wild-cucumber occurs in thickets along streams, often using other plants for support and shade. It is found to 5,000 feet in elevation in the southern part of Arizona and New Mexico.

*Culture* When Wild-cucumber's foliage emerges from the underground tuber in spring, supplemental water will promote faster growth. A deep soaking two or three times a month through the warm season should be sufficient. This vine needs shelter from direct afternoon sun. It can grow in an eastern exposure or partial shade. Wild-cucumber does best in loamy soil. Temperatures below 25° F will damage the foliage; however, the tuber is more cold hardy.

*Landscape Use* This vine can be trained on a trellis or allowed to twine among the branches of a shrub, as it does in nature. The foliage and fruits are both attractive features. Wild-cucumber is useful in areas that receive too much shade for other desert vines.

## Snapdragon-vine
### *Maurandya antirrhiniflora*
SCROPHULARIACEAE [FIGWORT FAMILY]

*Description* This vine has a delicate appearance, with slender, twining stems and thin, triangular medium green leaves. In winter the plant dies to the ground. The common name refers to the small pink or purple snapdragon-like flowers. The blooming season extends from spring to fall, encouraged by rainfall or irrigation. Snapdragon-vine can reach 8 to 10 feet high given something to climb upon.

*Native Distribution* Snapdragon-vine ranges from Texas, through Arizona and New Mexico, to California, and south to central Mexico. Plants typically grow in sandy or lime soil, sprawling in dunes, on hills, or on bluffs, and often climbing among shrubs, between the elevations of 1,500 and 6,000 feet.

*Culture* In a garden Snapdragon-vine can grow in full sun or partial shade, with a broad range of soil types as long as they are well drained. Summer irrigation several times a month promotes blooming and faster growth. Although it dies back in winter, the plant is quite cold tolerant, to about 20° F. Snapdragon-vine often reseeds itself.

*Landscape Use* Snapdragon-vine's fragile beauty would be overlooked in a large-scale landscape. Use it near an entryway or patio so that it will be noticed. Another way of focusing attention on the vine is to plant it in a pot or hanging basket. The vine can be planted at the base of a tree or shrub to twine among the branches; otherwise, provide a trellis for support.

## Blackfoot Daisy
### *Melampodium leucanthum*
ASTERACEAE [SUNFLOWER FAMILY]

*Description* When Blackfoot Daisy is at the peak of its bloom, in springtime, the plant is smothered with 1-inch white daisies. Scattered blooms can occur throughout warm weather. The leaves of this herbaceous perennial are long and slender, about 2 inches long by ¼ inch wide. A mature plant can reach 8 inches high, with a spread of 18 inches. Although the fruit is rather small and inconspicuous, it inspired the common name. A papery black foot-shaped husk encloses the seed.

*Native Distribution* The range of Blackfoot Daisy extends from Kansas, Oklahoma, and Colorado, through western Texas, New Mexico, and Arizona, to Chihuahua and Sonora, Mexico. It occurs at elevations between 2,000 and 5,000 feet on plains, dry rocky slopes, and mesas, often on limestone.

*Culture* Blackfoot Daisy requires well-drained soil. Full sun to filtered shade is okay. As you might guess from its northerly distribution, the plant is not affected by cold weather. Overwatering tends to be more of a problem than underwatering, particularly in heavy soils. A few times a month in the summer should be sufficient to keep a plant healthy and blooming. Don't expect a long life for Blackfoot Daisy. You can rejuvenate the foliage by pruning back in the fall, but after four or five years the plant will look pretty scraggly. Oftentimes volunteer seedlings will sprout, and these can be nurtured as replacements for the older plants.

*Landscape Use* The compact size of Blackfoot Daisy makes it very useful for planting in medians, along walkways, or any other place where space is limited. It would be a nice addition to a flower garden, the white color balancing and brightening darker-colored flowers. Mass the plants for a showy groundcover. Blackfoot Daisy can also be grown in pots or raised planters with good drainage.

## Rough Menodora
### *Menodora scabra*
OLEACEAE [OLIVE FAMILY]

*Description* The blooming period of Rough Menodora extends from March to September. Five-petaled yellow flowers measure about ¾ inch across. The fruit is a capsule with two green, shiny ⅛-inch spheres side by side. Rough Menodora is mostly herbaceous but has a woody base. It reaches 1 foot high, with an equal spread. The medium green foliage is sparse; rough-textured, slender leaves are up to 1 inch long.

*Native Distribution* Rough Menodora grows on gravelly slopes and mesas between 1,500 and 7,500 feet in elevation.

*Marah gilensis* Wild-cucumber

*Menodora scabra* Rough Menodora (detail)

*Maurandya antirrhiniflora* Snapdragon-vine

*Menodora scabra* Rough Menodora

*Melampodium leucanthum* Blackfoot Daisy

The native distribution extends from southern Colorado, Utah, and Nevada, to southeastern California, Arizona, New Mexico, and western Texas. In Mexico, Rough Menodora occurs in Baja California, Sonora, Chihuahua, Durango, Zacatecas, and San Luis Potosí.

**Culture** The ideal situation for Rough Menodora would include well-drained soil, full sun, and supplemental irrigation twice a month in the summer. Of course, this tough plant will make do with less water, but it probably won't bloom as much. It is cold hardy to 15° F or lower.

**Landscape Use** In the desert, Rough Menodora typically grows between, or even in, low shrubs such as Bur-sage (*Ambrosia deltoidea*) and Flattop Buckwheat (*Eriogonum fasciculatum* variety *poliofolium*). You can recreate that effect by interplanting Rough Menodora closely with shrubs. A long blooming season makes this subshrub a nice addition to the flower garden. Rough Menodora can be massed to increase the impact of its small but abundant flowers, or you can line a walkway with it. Plants such as Barrel Cactus (*Ferocactus* species) and Banana Yucca (*Yucca baccata*), which have strong forms, can be softened with a scattering of Rough Menodora.

## Yellow Morning Glory–vine, Yuca
**Merremia aurea**
CONVOLVULACEAE [MORNING GLORY FAMILY]

**Description** Yellow Morning Glory–vine's flowers each last only a day, but what a show! The bright yellow, 3-inch-wide trumpet-shaped flowers look like beacons against the vine's dark green foliage. Yellow Morning Glory–vine blooms throughout the warm season. The fruit, a papery capsule, contains four dark brown, velvety seeds about the size of peas.

Twining, woody stems arise from an underground tuber and can climb to 20 feet high with support. The leaves are often divided into five leaflets spreading 2 inches in diameter. In frost-free areas the vine is evergreen.

**Native Distribution** Yellow Morning Glory–vine is native only to the southern half of Baja California, Mexico, where it clambers over rocks, trees, and shrubs along arroyos and on hillsides.

**Culture** Most critical to success in growing Yellow Morning Glory–vine is a protected location. The foliage will be damaged at temperatures below freezing, although the underground tuber is hardy to 15° F. Provide well-drained soil and full sun. It will thrive under conditions that would fry a less heat-loving plant. The growth rate will be moderate to fast with some supplemental water in summer, but you don't have to pamper it. Yellow Morning Glory–vine climbs via twining stems, which need support if they are to attain any size.

**Landscape Use** This vine is fabulous for a color accent. Use it to hide an exposed wall, or train it on an overhead trellis to shade a patio.

## Catclaw Mimosa
**Mimosa biuncifera**
FABACEAE [PEA FAMILY]

**Description** This open-branched shrub grows to 6 feet high and 6 feet wide. The flexible gray stems bear short, curved spines in pairs among the deciduous, twice-compound leaves. Each of the twelve to twenty-four tiny leaflets is ⅛ inch long and 1/16 inch wide. Half-inch fuzzy ball-shaped white to pink flowers bloom from April to September. Curved prickles may occur along the edges of the reddish brown flattened pods, which reach 1½ inches in length and ½ inch in width.

*Native Distribution* Catclaw Mimosa is found from southeastern Arizona, through southern New Mexico and western Texas, to Chihuahua and Sonora, Mexico. Common habitat is rocky canyons and hillsides, from 2,000 to 6,000 feet in elevation.

*Culture* Choose a site for Catclaw Mimosa that receives full sun. The soil type isn't especially critical. Catclaw Mimosa is hardy to at least the low 20s F. Once established, plants can survive on rainfall alone, or you can provide supplemental irrigation once a month for denser growth. Catclaw Mimosa's straggly form doesn't lend itself to shaping. You're probably better off letting the plant develop its own character.

*Landscape Use* Catclaw Mimosa's nearly impenetrable foliage provides shelter for desert wildlife. The flowers furnish nectar for honey, and various animals eat the seeds. The prickly branches would be a nuisance near pedestrian areas, but they might prove useful for security plantings.

---

A more compact form (3 feet high by 4 feet wide) and showy pink fuzzball flowers from April through July make Fragrant Mimosa (*Mimosa borealis*) suitable for ornamental use. Like Catclaw Mimosa, it has compound deciduous leaves and curved spines. Fragrant Mimosa occurs in central and western Texas, Oklahoma, New Mexico, and northern Mexico, often on limestone, between 1,200 and 4,600 feet in elevation.

---

The purplish pink flowers of Velvetpod Mimosa (*Mimosa dysocarpa*) are spike-shaped, about 2 inches long and ½ inch in diameter. They bloom from May to September. A soft, velvety fuzz covers the 1- to 2-inch-long, ¼-inch-wide pods. Lacy looking deciduous leaves occur among numerous spines along the branches. Velvetpod Mimosa reaches 5 feet high and about the same width. Canyons and brushy hillsides between 3,500 and 6,500 feet in elevation are home to this shrub, which occurs in southeastern Arizona, southern New Mexico, and western Texas, and south to Durango, Mexico.

Fragrant Mimosa and Velvetpod Mimosa have cultural requirements similar to Catclaw Mimosa.

---

## Rough Mortonia
### *Mortonia scabrella*
CELASTRACEAE [BITTERSWEET FAMILY]

*Description* The gray branches of Rough Mortonia are crowded with yellowish green oval leaves ¼ inch long and ⅛ inch wide. The evergreen foliage is thick and leathery, with a texture like fine sandpaper. Small five-petaled white flowers bloom from March through September in 1-inch-long clusters. This erect shrub can reach 6 feet high and 5 feet wide.

*Native Distribution* Rough Mortonia is found in southeastern Arizona, southern New Mexico, western Texas, and Chihuahua and Sonora, Mexico. Typical habitat includes dry plains, gravelly slopes, and mesas, from 2,500 to 6,500 feet in elevation.

*Culture* Full sun and well-drained soil are ideal for Rough Mortonia. Only during prolonged drought will established plants require supplemental irrigation. The shrub can tolerate temperatures to at least the low 20s F.

*Landscape Use* A medium-sized hedge would be a good landscape application of Rough Mortonia's dense foliage. The tiny leaves could be contrasted with coarse-textured plants such as *Yucca* species. Rough Mortonia can be planted on slopes to control soil erosion.

*Mimosa borealis* Fragrant Mimosa

*Mimosa dysocarpa* Velvetpod Mimosa

*Mimosa biuncifera* Catclaw Mimosa

Above and below: *Mortonia scabrella*
Rough Mortonia

*Merremia aurea*
Yellow Morning Glory-vine

## Deer Grass
### Muhlenbergia rigens
POACEAE [GRASS FAMILY]

**Description** Deer Grass produces 1-foot-long flowering spikes from July to October above a 3-foot-high, 4-foot-wide mound of foliage. The 1½-foot-long, ⅛-inch-wide leaves are rough-textured. Deer Grass is perennial, and it may stay green through the winter in warm desert areas.

**Native Distribution** This grass grows on gravelly slopes, in grasslands, and in forests, between 2,500 and 7,000 feet in elevation. Its geographic range extends from southern California to western Texas and into northern Mexico.

**Culture** Deer Grass will thrive given well-drained soil, full sun, and a little extra water through the summer. It is cold hardy to around 10° F. Shearing to ground level will rejuvenate old clumps of Deer Grass.

**Landscape Use** Mass plantings of Deer Grass create a striking effect, with the added benefit of erosion control. Several plants could be intermingled with perennials in a flower garden. Deer Grass would soften any part of the landscape.

## Bamboo-muhly
### Muhlenbergia dumosa
POACEAE [GRASS FAMILY]

**Description** As grasses go, this one has rather thick stems, though nothing like real bamboo. The stem bases can be almost woody, but the leaf blades are very delicate, 3 or 4 inches long and less than ⅛ inch wide. The wispy seedheads, about 1 foot long, add to Bamboo-muhly's graceful appearance. They are produced from February to May. Overall, the perennial bunchgrass grows 4 feet high and equally wide.

**Native Distribution** Bamboo-muhly is found in rocky canyons and valleys, mostly below 4,000 feet in elevation, in southern Arizona and northern Mexico.

**Culture** Although Bamboo-muhly tolerates drought once established, it looks better with extra water several times a month through the warm season. If the stems become straw-colored in response to drought or age, they can be cut to the ground for a better appearance and to stimulate new growth. Full sun or partial shade is okay. Bamboo-muhly prefers well-drained soil but is adaptable to other types. It is cold hardy to 10° F.

**Landscape Use** Bamboo-muhly's fine texture can create a soft feeling around patios or swimming pools. The grass will grow in a large pot. An interesting effect could be achieved by combining Bamboo-muhly with coarse-textured plants such as Giant Bur-sage (*Ambrosia ambrosioides*) or even cacti. The dense network of roots provides good erosion control. Massing the plants multiplies the beneficial effect and provides a nice landscape accent too.

## Bigelow Nolina
### Nolina bigelovii
AGAVACEAE [AGAVE FAMILY]

**Description** Bigelow Nolina resembles a yucca, with its woody trunk to 1 foot thick and a cluster of 3-foot-long, 1-inch-wide gray-green leaves at the top. The leaf margins are slightly toothed when young, later separating into brown fibers. Overall the plant reaches 8 feet high and 6 feet wide. A 5-foot-tall flower stalk bears white flowers that occur in an elongated cluster 2–3 feet long and 1 foot wide in May and June.

**Native Distribution** Bigelow Nolina is generally found in canyons and on dry rocky slopes below 3,500 feet in elevation.

It occurs in southeastern California, western Arizona, and Baja California and Sonora, Mexico.

**Culture** Full sun and good drainage are two keys to success in growing Bigelow Nolina. After two or three years of establishment, it can survive on rainfall. During prolonged drought, provide supplemental irrigation. Bigelow Nolina is hardy to the low 20s F and perhaps lower.

**Landscape Use** Put Bigelow Nolina in a prominent place in the landscape, where its distinctive form and showy flowers will be best appreciated. Fine-textured foliage from plants such as Littleleaf Palo Verde (*Cercidium microphyllum*) makes a good contrast to the coarse texture of Bigelow Nolina.

---

## Beargrass
### *Nolina erumpens*
AGAVACEAE [AGAVE FAMILY]

**Description** Beargrass looks like a clump of coarse grass, at maturity 4 feet high and 6 feet wide. The leaves are 3–4 feet long and about ½ inch wide at the base, narrowing to a frayed tip. The leaf margins are finely toothed. Beargrass blooms from May to July. Many small white or greenish flowers crowd into a 2-foot-long, 1-foot-wide cluster borne on a flowering stem not much taller than the plant.

**Native Distribution** Rocky slopes or grassy hills from 2,100 to 7,500 feet in elevation are home to Beargrass. The plant occurs in southwestern Texas and northern Mexico.

**Culture** In the hottest desert areas, give Beargrass a break with partial shade. Where summer temperatures are less extreme, full sun promotes the best growth. Beargrass is cold hardy to 15° F or lower. Well-drained soil is preferable. Once established, Beargrass is drought tolerant. In the hottest areas lessen the stress of summer with a deep soaking every few weeks. The flowering stalk can be cut off anytime, but it's best to wait until the seeds ripen and fall or are eaten by animals.

**Landscape Use** Beargrass's graceful, mounding form, slender leaves, and large flower cluster attract attention whether featured near a patio or a swimming pool or as a focal point in the landscape. A mass planting on a slope would not only be striking but would also control soil erosion. The plant's arching habit is accentuated when used in a pot or raised planter. Beargrass combines well with broad-leaved succulents such as *Agave* and *Yucca* species.

---

A related Beargrass, *Nolina microcarpa*, is called Sacahuista, and it closely resembles *Nolina erumpens*. Sacahuista's coarse, grasslike leaves, which are about 3 feet long and ¼ inch wide, grow from a woody stem that usually is partly underground. The leaves are edged with tiny sawteeth and end in a frayed tip. Sacahuista can reach 5 feet in height with an 8-foot spread. A loose cluster of greenish white flowers appears on a 3-foot stalk that rises above the plant in May and June. Sacahuista is found throughout much of Arizona, in central and southern New Mexico, and in western Texas, as well as in Chihuahua and Sonora, Mexico. It favors rocky or grassy hillsides from 3,000 to 6,500 feet in elevation.

---

Texas Sacahuista (*Nolina texana*) differs by having white to pinkish flowers that bloom from March to July. The leaves are yellow-green, to 3 feet long and ⅛ inch wide, forming a grasslike mound 3 feet high and 3 feet wide. As the common name suggests, Texas Sacahuista grows in Texas, in the central, southern, and

*Muhlenbergia dumosa* Bamboo-muhly

*Nolina bigelovii* Bigelow Nolina

*Muhlenbergia rigens* Deer Grass

*Nolina erumpens*
Beargrass

*Nolina microcarpa*
Sacahuista

*Nolina texana*
Texas Sacahuista

western parts. Its range extends to northern Mexico. Typical habitats include rocky plains and slopes, grasslands, and brushlands, between 3,500 and 5,000 feet in elevation.

Sacahuista and Texas Sacahuista have the same cultural requirements and landscape use as Beargrass.

## Tufted Evening-primrose
### *Oenothera caespitosa*
ONAGRACEAE [EVENING PRIMROSE FAMILY]

*Description*  White, 3-inch-wide flowers open in the evening atop a dark green mound of leaves 1 foot high and 1½ feet wide. The flowers only bloom once; by mid-morning the following day, the petals begin to turn pink and wither. With extra water, Tufted Evening-primrose will flower spring through fall; normally the heaviest bloom is in spring. The leaves of Tufted Evening-primrose are soft to touch, somewhat toothed, and 4 inches long by ¾ inch wide. In cold desert areas the foliage may die back in fall and reappear the next spring.

*Native Distribution*  Tufted Evening-primrose prefers rocky slopes between 4,000 and 7,500 feet in elevation. Its range includes much of the western United States and northern Mexico.

*Culture*  Healthy foliage and abundant flowers are encouraged by supplemental irrigation several times a month during hot weather. Tufted Evening-primrose grows best in full sun with well-drained soil. Plants are cold hardy to at least 12° F. Foliage that dies back due to cold weather can be trimmed to the ground.

*Landscape Use*  Plant Tufted Evening-primrose near areas that are frequented in the evening or early morning, when the flowers are in bloom. It would also be a

good addition to a flower garden, where the white flowers can balance the intensity of brighter colors.

## Ironwood
### *Olneya tesota*
FABACEAE [PEA FAMILY]

*Description*  As the common name suggests, Ironwood has hard, heavy wood. One cubic foot of the wood, valued for carving and firewood, weighs 66 pounds. Ironwood's bark is light gray when young, turning darker with maturity. The gray-green foliage is evergreen except in extreme cold. The 2-inch-long, 1-inch-wide leaves are divided into oval leaflets to ½ inch long. Pairs of ½-inch, straight spines occur at each leaf base. The pinkish-lavender flowers are ⅓ inch long and arranged in loose clusters. Ironwood blooms in May and June, though the intensity of flowering can vary from year to year. Two-inch-long brown pods develop from the flowers, containing edible seeds that taste somewhat like peanuts. Ironwood develops a thick, sometimes multiple-branched trunk. The branches grow upright at first then spread with age, even brushing the ground. The broad-crowned tree can reach 25 feet high with a similar spread.

*Native Distribution*  Ironwood is common along washes and on rocky slopes in southern Arizona and southeastern California, and also in Baja California and Sonora, Mexico. It occurs at elevations below 2,500 feet.

*Culture*  This tough desert tree can tolerate long periods of drought, although extra water a few times a month in the summer can increase the normally slow growth rate. Good drainage is preferred, as is full sun. The most important cultural requirement is protection from cold. Temperatures around 20° F will damage foliage, and prolonged freezing can kill the tree. Ironwood's natural character is very attractive; pruning should be limited to removal of dead branches. If the tree is used to shade a patio, low-hanging branches will need to be pruned for safety. Do heavy pruning only in the cooler months to avoid sunburn on newly exposed branches.

*Landscape Use* Whether planted along a wash in a naturalistic desert landscape or shading a formal patio, Ironwood is appropriate. It is usually the center of attention, yet it complements other desert plants well. Ironwood may seem an unlikely candidate for planting near a swimming pool, but its litter production is relatively light. In its natural, unpruned form, it could create a formidable security barrier or dense screen for visual control.

*Oenothera caespitosa* Tufted Evening-primrose

*Olneya tesota* Ironwood

## Prickly-pear, Cholla
### *Opuntia* species
CACTACEAE [CACTUS FAMILY]

*Opuntia* is the second largest genus of cactus next to *Mammillaria*, and it is well represented throughout the Southwestern deserts, with a variety of forms. Prickly-pears have flattened stems, called pads, that grow one on top of another to form a succulent shrub. Cholla's stems, or "joints," are cylindrical. Some species of Cholla develop a woody trunk with age and resemble a small, thorny tree. In sharp contrast to the plant's forbidding appearance, the flowers of *Opuntia* species are fragile-looking, with petals in a rainbow of colors. Several Prickly-pears and Chollas have showy fruits, too, either yellow or red.

*Opuntia* species are among the least demanding of landscape plants. They can go long periods without water because of their succulent tissues, and they tolerate the hottest, brightest locations. Well-drained soil is preferred. Prickly-pears and Chollas are generally very cold hardy, with a slow to moderate growth rate. It is easy to propagate *Opuntia* species. Cut off a section of the plant at a joint, let the cut dry and callus over for about a week, then plant the section in the ground. Extra water every other week or so will encourage faster rooting.

Some types of Prickly-pear can become infested with cochineal (*Dactylopius coccus*), a small, scale-type insect with a cottony coating. Usually infestations are most severe during the warm months. Cochineal was actually cultivated by Native Americans, who utilized it as a dye. Puncture one of the insects and you'll see a vivid magenta liquid. The white, cottony coating makes it difficult for pesticide sprays to penetrate to the insect, so often the best control is a forceful stream of water from a nozzle, to knock the insects off. You may need to repeat the process a few times to rid the plants of cochineal. Left untreated, a serious infestation of cochineal will weaken the plant and cause yellowing.

Chollas and Prickly-pears add interest to the landscape with their unusual shapes and beautiful flowers. An attractive cactus garden could be achieved by combining various shapes and sizes of *Opuntia* with other succulent plants. Feature one or several *Opuntia* species as the focal point of a mixed desert planting. Functional uses of Prickly-pears and Chollas include security plantings near the house and barrier hedges along property lines or in the yard to keep people from cutting across. A number of desert animals, including tortoises and ground squirrels, relish Prickly-pear fruits. The spiny branches of Cholla provide well-protected nesting sites for desert birds. The cactus wren is so named because of its preference for nesting in Chollas. The spines of *Opuntia* are an obvious reason to keep the plants away from patios, sidewalks, pools, and play areas. Although some Prickly-pears look deceptively harmless, their glochids (tiny spines) can be very irritating and, because they're hard to see, most difficult to remove.

Should you ever have to prune Chollas or Prickly-pears, use tongs or rolled newspapers to grasp the stems while cutting with a saw or hand pruners. Don't bother to wear gloves, because large spines can go right through even thick leather, and if you get glochids in the gloves they are useless for future wear.

## Buckhorn Cholla
### *Opuntia acanthocarpa*
The open-branched, slender green stems of Buckhorn Cholla look somewhat like deer antlers, hence the common name. Individual joints are 6–12 inches long, 1 inch thick, and covered with yellow to brown 1-inch-long spines. Overall, the plant can measure 4 feet high by 5 feet wide. Buckhorn Cholla's flowers range

*Opuntia basilaris* Beavertail Prickly-pear

*Opuntia acanthocarpa* Buckhorn Cholla; flower above left

from red to brownish yellow; they bloom in April and May. The fruit is roughly oval, about 1 inch long, spine-covered, and dry at maturity. Southern Utah, Nevada, California, and Arizona, as well as Baja California and Sonora, Mexico, are included in the range of this Cholla. It grows on desert mesas and slopes, between 500 and 3,500 feet in elevation.

## Beavertail Prickly-pear
### *Opuntia basilaris*

Beavertail Prickly-pear's common name refers to the shape of its pads, which are 6 inches long, 4 inches wide at the broadest portion, and blue-gray in color. Beavertail Prickly-pear has no large spines; rather, the pad surface is dotted with dense clusters of brown glochids (tiny, hairlike spines). Plants typically branch from the base and remain low, less than

Opposite:
*Opuntia bigelovii* Teddy Bear Cholla

1 foot high, but may spread to 2–3 feet across. Magenta flowers cluster along the tops of the pads for three to four weeks anytime from March through June. The spineless fruits are dry at maturity, oval, and about 1 inch long. Beavertail Prickly-pear is found in southern Utah, Nevada, California, and Arizona, as well as in Sonora and Baja California, Mexico, from sea level to 6,000 feet in elevation. It occurs on desert plains, dry mountain slopes, and in washes.

## Teddy Bear Cholla
### *Opuntia bigelovii*

A dense covering of ¾-inch, straw-colored spines gives Teddy Bear Cholla a soft, fuzzy look, but don't even think about touching it. The 4-inch-long, 2-inch-thick joints detach easily, aided by tiny barbs along the spines. Mature plants can

*Opuntia chlorotica*
Pancake Prickly-pear

*Opuntia echinocarpa* Silver Cholla

*Opuntia engelmannii* Engelmann's Prickly-pear

reach 5 feet in height, with a single main trunk and shorter lateral branches above, spreading to 2 feet. With age, the main trunk becomes black. Flowers occur in clusters at the ends of joints from February to May. They are greenish yellow or sometimes white with lavender streaks, and a little over 1 inch in diameter. The green, fleshy fruits are oval-shaped, with a depression on top. They measure 1 inch long and are spiny or nearly spineless. Teddy Bear Cholla often occurs in dense stands on mesas and dry, rocky slopes. Its range extends from southwestern Utah and southern Nevada, through southern California and Arizona, to Baja California and Sonora, Mexico. It occurs to 3,000 feet in elevation.

## Pancake Prickly-pear
### *Opuntia chlorotica*
The light green, round pads of Pancake Prickly-pear have tufts of yellow glochids and curved spines. The flowers, which bloom from April through June, are also yellow. The reddish purple, fleshy fruits are about 1½ inches long. Pancake Prickly-pear has a stout trunk that supports multiple spreading branches above. A mature plant can reach 6 feet high and nearly as wide. Pancake Prickly-pear tends to grow on rocky slopes and in canyons, between 2,000 and 6,000 feet in elevation. Its range includes southern Nevada and Utah, southeastern California, Arizona, New Mexico, and Sonora and northern Baja California, Mexico.

## Silver Cholla
### *Opuntia echinocarpa*
When the sunlight hits Silver Cholla just right, thousands of silvery 1-inch-long spines form a glistening halo around the entire plant. This plant is bushy, with a woody trunk and a densely branched crown to 3 feet high and a little wider. Yellow flowers tinged with red occur at the ends of branches on joints about 4 inches long and 1 inch in diameter. The blooming period spans March and April. Very spiny fruits 1 inch long become dry with maturity. Silver Cholla is found on dry plains and rocky foothills, from sea level to an altitude of 6,000 feet. Southwestern Utah, southern Arizona, southeastern California, western Arizona, and Sonora and Baja California, Mexico, are home to Silver Cholla.

## Engelmann's Prickly-pear
### *Opuntia engelmannii*
The deep rose to purple egg-shaped fruits of Engelmann's Prickly-pear equal the flowers for display and are longer-lasting. Yellow flowers 3 inches across bloom over a four-week period between April and June. The pads are the largest of any native Prickly-pear in the United States, growing to 12 inches long and nearly as wide. Clusters of white or pale gray spines are widely spaced on the pads. Engelmann's Prickly-pear spreads to form a mound 4 feet high and 10 feet or more wide. It is found in southern California, Arizona, New Mexico, and western Texas, as well as in northern Mexico, on desert plains, hillsides, and desert grasslands.

## Chainfruit Cholla, Jumping Cholla
### *Opuntia fulgida*
Young Chainfruit Cholla plants are shrublike; with age they develop an irregular crown atop a woody, blackened trunk. The mature size can be 10 feet high and 8 feet wide. The pale green joints are about 5 inches long and 2 inches thick, with a dense covering of 1-inch straw-colored spines. The joints detach so easily onto clothing or flesh that it seems as if they jump. The other common name

*Opuntia fulgida* Chainfruit Cholla and fruit (inset)

Below left and right: *Opuntia imbricata* Tree Cholla

refers to the chainlike clusters of light green fruit that develop over the years. Individual fruits are more or less oval, 1½ inches long and 1 inch thick. The 1-inch pink flowers bloom from June to August. This Cholla prefers desert plains and gentle slopes between 1,000 and 4,000 feet in elevation. It occurs in southern Arizona and in Sonora and Sinaloa, Mexico.

## Tree Cholla
### *Opuntia imbricata*
May- or June-blooming deep pink flowers are followed by green fruits, which mature to a bright yellow color and persist into winter. Tree Cholla is shrubby when young, eventually becoming treelike with a woody trunk. The mature size is typically 6–8 feet high and 10 feet wide. Medium green joints 6 inches long and 1 inch thick have few spines and are covered with prominent, elongated bumps (tubercles). In extreme cold the joints can become purplish. Tree Cholla is common between 4,000 and 6,000 feet in elevation on desert plains and grasslands, and it is particularly abundant on overgrazed rangeland. It grows as far north as Kansas, Colorado, and Oklahoma, and south through western Texas, New Mexico, and southern Arizona, into central Mexico.

## Desert Christmas Cholla
### *Opuntia leptocaulis*
Red oval fruits ¾ inch long and ½ inch wide call attention in fall and winter to this otherwise inconspicuous cactus. Desert Christmas Cholla is shrubby, to 2 feet high and 3 feet wide, with slender light green joints 4–6 inches long but only ¼ inch thick. In May and June, yellow to bronze flowers appear along the stems. Desert Christmas Cholla usually grows on desert flats, where the soil is heavier.

*Opuntia leptocaulis* Desert Christmas Cholla

Occasionally it grows in the shelter of other shrubs. Oklahoma, western and southern Texas, New Mexico, Arizona, and northern Mexico, between 1,000 and 5,000 feet in elevation, is the plant's natural range.

## Purple Prickly-pear

### Opuntia macrocentra

Blue-green pads 5 inches long and about as wide have conspicuous 3-inch dark brown or black spines on the upper parts of the pads. In cold weather or drought the pads turn reddish purple. The plant's overall size is 1½ feet high by 2–3 feet wide. Yellow flowers with red centers bloom in April and May, followed by fleshy red to purplish fruits 1 inch long and ¾ inch wide. Purple Prickly-pear grows between 2,000 and 5,000 feet in elevation, on desert slopes in southeastern Arizona, southern New Mexico, western Texas, and southward into Chihuahua, Mexico.

## Diamond Cholla

### Opuntia ramosissima

Diamond Cholla is a low, many-branched shrub reaching 2 feet high, with a spread to 3 feet. The common name refers to the diamond-shaped bumps, called tubercles, that cover this Cholla's gray-green stems. The joints average 3 inches long and ⅓ inch thick, and are armed with 1½-inch-long spines that have a yellow papery sheath. May through September is the blooming season, when greenish yellow flowers tinged with red appear. The fruits are up to 1 inch long and so spiny that they look like burrs. You'll find Diamond Cholla growing on low hills and flats in southwestern Utah, southern Nevada, southern California, and western Arizona, as well as in Baja California and Sonora, Mexico. The elevational range is 500–3,000 feet.

## Blind Prickly-pear

### Opuntia rufida

Blind Prickly-pear's symmetrical, 6-inch blue-green pads are polka-dotted with clusters of rust-colored glochids. The glochids can be dislodged by wind or by the plant's being shaken. Reportedly, these hairlike windborne spines can cause blindness in cattle and other animals. A mature plant can reach 4 feet high and 6 feet wide. Yellow flowers bloom in May and June, followed by bright red fleshy fruits 1 inch long. Blind Prickly-pear occurs on rocky hillsides at 2,000–3,400 feet in elevation in the Big Bend region of southwestern Texas, and in adjacent Coahuila and Chihuahua, Mexico.

## Santa Rita Prickly-pear, Purple Prickly-pear

### Opuntia santa-rita

The purple coloration of this Prickly-pear becomes more pronounced with drought or cold weather. Young pads are a maroon color. The pads are more or less round, 5 inches across, and dotted with clusters of yellow to rust-colored glochids. Long spines sometimes occur along the top edges of the pads. Four feet high and 6 feet across is about as big as this bushy cactus gets. The yellow flowers bloom in April and May, then develop into oval, fleshy purple fruits 1 inch long by ¾ inch wide. Santa Rita Prickly-pear's distribution includes southeastern Arizona, southern New Mexico, and southwestern Texas, as well as Sonora, Mexico. It is typically found on desert slopes between 2,000 and 4,000 feet in elevation.

## Cane Cholla

### Opuntia spinosior

Many spreading branches develop from Cane Cholla's woody trunk, eventually becoming a small tree to 8 feet high and at least as wide. Cylindrical 6-inch-long joints have a dense covering of stiff gray spines. The joints are gray-green with purple tinges, the purple coloration becoming stronger in winter. Cane Cholla's flowers can be yellow, red, maroon, or shades in between. Inch-long fruits clustered at the ends of branches ripen to a yellow color and often persist through the winter. Souvenirs such as canes and lamp bases have been made from the plant's woody inner skeleton. Southern Arizona, southwestern New Mexico, and Sonora, Mexico, constitute Cane Cholla's range. Preferred habitat includes desert flats, grasslands, and lower mountain slopes, from 1,000 to 5,000 feet in elevation and occasionally higher.

## Indian Ricegrass

### Oryzopsis hymenoides
POACEAE [GRASS FAMILY]

**Description** The open, diffuse seedheads of Indian Ricegrass are about 6 inches long and nearly as wide, with the seeds borne on slender, wiry stems. This perennial bunchgrass grows 1–2 feet high with a 1-foot spread. The light green leaf blades are long (to 10 inches), slender, and rolled inward. Indian Ricegrass mellows to a straw color at the end of the season.

**Native Distribution** Dry, sandy desert plains are the most common habitat of Indian Ricegrass, though it also grows on hills and into woodlands. Its elevational range is 3,500–6,500 feet, and it occurs throughout the western United States, north to British Columbia and Manitoba, Canada, and as far south as northern Mexico.

**Culture** Indian Ricegrass tolerates poor soils and requires minimal water once established. It can grow in full sun or light shade. In early spring, cut the grass nearly to ground level to rejuvenate. Allow Indian Ricegrass to reseed itself so that young, vigorous plants can replace the older, declining ones. It is cold hardy to at least 10° F.

**Landscape Use** The delicate, airy texture of Indian Ricegrass can lighten a perennial flower garden. The grass can also be used in a meadow planting with other grass species and wildflowers. A mass planting would be stunning and would have the added benefit of erosion control, particularly when used on slopes. The seeds provide food for a variety of desert animals. As the common name suggests, Indian Ricegrass was also an important food source for Native Americans.

## Guayule

### Parthenium argentatum
ASTERACEAE [SUNFLOWER FAMILY]

**Description** This rounded evergreen shrub to 3 feet high and 4 feet wide has silvery leaves that can vary in shape from broad in the middle and ending in a point to bluntly round at the tip and narrow at the base. Leaf edges can be entire (smooth-margined) or toothed. The normal length is 2 inches. White flowers are borne in flat-topped clusters above the foliage in spring, summer, and—with sufficient moisture—in fall.

**Native Distribution** Guayule occurs in rocky limestone habitats between 2,600 and 4,500 feet in elevation in southwestern Texas and northern Mexico. The Mexican distribution is extensive, including Chihuahua, Coahuila, Nuevo León, Durango, Zacatecas, San Luis Potosí, and Hidalgo.

*Opuntia macrocentra* Purple Prickly-pear

*Opuntia ramosissima* Diamond Cholla

*Opuntia rufida* Blind Prickly-pear

*Opuntia santa-rita* Santa Rita Prickly-pear

*Opuntia spinosior* Cane Cholla

*Oryzopsis hymenoides* Indian Ricegrass  CM

*Parthenium argentatum* Guayule

*Culture* The ideal site for growing Guayule has full sun and well-drained limestone soil, though other soil types are acceptable. The plant is very drought tolerant once established. It responds to severe water stress by dropping some of the lower, older leaves. Periodic irrigation will keep the foliage more attractive and prolong the flowering. Guayule tolerates cold to 15° F or lower. You may want to cut off the old flower stems for a neater appearance. Every few years prune the plant severely to keep it dense and encourage more flowers. The plant's naturally rounded form needs no shaping otherwise.

*Landscape Use* Guayule can be massed for a groundcover, planted on slopes for erosion control, or used in mixed desert plantings. Make the most of the silvery foliage by contrasting it with dark-leaved plants. Gardeners and designers in colder desert areas could utilize it in place of the similar-looking but more tender Brittlebush (*Encelia farinosa*).

## Mariola
### *Parthenium incanum*
ASTERACEAE [SUNFLOWER FAMILY]

*Description* A dense covering of fine white hairs gives Mariola's foliage and stems a silver coloring. The aromatic leaves are more or less oval in outline, but deeply lobed or toothed for a delicate appearance. They average 1 inch long by ½ inch wide. White flowers in flat-topped clusters 2–3 inches across appear from June to October. Overall, the intricately-branched evergreen shrub measures 2 feet high and 3 feet wide.

*Native Distribution* Mariola's broad distribution includes northwestern and southeastern Arizona, southern New Mexico, and southwestern Texas, and in Mexico, Sonora and Coahuila south to Michoacán. It grows in caliche and other soil types on desert plains, gravelly slopes, mesas, and desert grasslands, between 2,200 and 6,500 feet in elevation.

*Culture* Mariola needs full sun for best development. It is very drought tolerant once established, and cold tolerant to at least 12° F. If your site has caliche, Mariola won't mind. The growth rate is moderate.

*Landscape Use* Mariola's delicate appearance belies its hardiness. You can plant it in the hottest sites on poor soil. It would be useful for erosion control on slopes, or for highway plantings. The plant's compact form can fit into many small spaces in the landscape. A strong contrast could be made by planting Mariola against dark, coarse-foliaged plants. On the other hand, it can get lost against a light background such as concrete paving.

## Slipper Plant
### *Pedilanthus macrocarpus*
EUPHORBIACEAE [SPURGE FAMILY]

*Description* Slipper Plant's succulent light green stems grow upright from a woody root crown. The jointed stems are mostly unbranched, ¾ inch thick and up to 3 feet tall. The plant can eventually spread to 2 feet wide. Small leaves along the stems drop soon after they appear. Red, 1-inch-long slipper-shaped flowers appear during two seasons: February to May, and August to October.

*Native Distribution* Slipper Plant is found on the Baja California peninsula and on the mainland from Sonora to Colima, Mexico. It grows mainly on desert plains and hillsides.

*Culture* The young growth of this plant can be damaged by temperatures below 32° F, although mature growth is hardy to the mid-20s F. Place Slipper Plant in an area with well-drained soil and full sun. Once the plant is established, provide extra water twice a month during the summer.

**Landscape Use** This plant can provide a strong vertical accent, grounded by low-growing plants such as Trailing Indigo Bush (*Dalea greggii*) or Blackfoot Daisy (*Melampodium leucanthum*). Slipper Plant's unusual form would stand out among most plants, but a background of deep green foliage would create the strongest contrast. It can be planted in a large pot.

## *Penstemon* species
SCROPHULARIACEAE [FIGWORT FAMILY]

Penstemons bring a splash of color to the landscape. Shades ranging from pale pink to red to purple are displayed by various species. Like their relative, snapdragon, they produce flowers along a spike, which blooms from the bottom upward. On most Penstemons the foliage is clustered in a rosette near the ground, with some leaves along the flower stalk.

Penstemons can be used in flower gardens, entry courtyards, patio plantings, or near swimming pools. Wherever they appear, hummingbirds are sure to follow, attracted to the brightly colored tubular flowers. You might combine different species of *Penstemon* for a tapestry of colors with an extended blooming period, or you can create a stunning accent by massing plants of the same species. An individual plant is best displayed against a plain background such as a wall or a dense, fine-textured shrub. The vertical form of Penstemon looks good paired with a groundcover such as Trailing Indigo Bush (*Dalea greggii*) or Blackfoot Daisy (*Melampodium leucanthum*).

Penstemons generally prefer well-drained soil and bright light. Some of the species that occur at higher elevations benefit from partial shade in summer, especially in low desert areas. Winter deciduous trees or those with sparse foliage, such as Littleleaf Palo Verde (*Cercidium microphyllum*), can provide the needed protection without casting too much shade. Supplemental water during the warm season promotes the best flowers and foliage. A deep soaking every ten to fourteen days should suffice. Excessive irrigation, compounded by poorly drained soil, can cause lanky growth. Floppy flower stalks are a sign of either overwatering or too much shade. Aphids can be a problem on the flower stalks. A spray of insecticidal soap should take care of the pests. After the plants have finished blooming, allow the flower stalks to remain until the seed has ripened. (It will look like coarsely ground pepper.) Then you can clip the stalks back to the basal foliage and collect the seed or just shake it onto the ground. Under good conditions the seed will produce volunteer plants. You may need to do some thinning if you get a bumper crop, or you can try transplanting the young plants. Because they are typically short-lived perennials, Penstemons start to look ratty after a few years. The volunteer plants can be allowed to mature and replace the older plants.

## Bush Penstemon, Pink Plains Penstemon
**Penstemon ambiguus**

This Penstemon's growth form is shrublike, to about 3 feet in height and width. Older plants can become woody at the base; in cold-winter areas plants will probably remain herbaceous because of seasonal dieback. Slender branches carry bright green linear leaves ¾ inch long. The foliage is semi-evergreen to 15° F. White to pink flowers cover the plant from May to August. Bush Penstemon commonly grows in sandy areas at elevations of 4,500–6,500 feet. The plant's broad range

*Parthenium incanum* Mariola

*Pedilanthus macrocarpus* Slipper Plant

*Penstemon eatonii* Firecracker Penstemon

*Penstemon ambiguus* Bush Penstemon

*Penstemon baccharifolius* Baccharisleaf Penstemon

extends from Colorado and Kansas to western Texas and California, and southward to Chihuahua and Coahuila, Mexico.

Fendler Penstemon grows on sandy or gravelly plains from eastern Arizona, through central and southern New Mexico, to western Texas.

## Baccharisleaf Penstemon, Rock Penstemon

### *Penstemon baccharifolius*

Bacharisleaf Penstemon's scarlet flowers bloom on short spikes from June to September. Thick green leaves about ½ inch long and ¼ inch wide have small teeth along the edges. The mature size of this multiple-branched, shrublike Penstemon is 1 foot high and equally wide. Bacharisleaf Penstemon occurs in western Texas and northeastern Mexico, growing in limestone crevices at 1,100–4,400 feet in elevation. It is hardy to at least 20° F.

## Firecracker Penstemon

### *Penstemon eatonii*

Dark green pointed leaves 3–4 inches long and 1 inch wide form a basal cluster of foliage, from which 2-foot-tall flower stalks arise. Inch-long tube-shaped red flowers open along the stalk from March through June. Firecracker Penstemon typically grows on rocky slopes at 2,000–7,000 feet in elevation in eastern California, southern Nevada, southern Utah, southwestern Colorado, northeastern New Mexico, and Arizona.

## Fendler Penstemon

### *Penstemon fendleri*

From April to August the violet-blue, 1-inch-long flowers of Fendler Penstemon appear in distinct whorls along 1- to 2-foot-tall flower stalks. Thick gray-green leaves with a pointed tip measure 3 inches long and 1½ inches at the widest part.

## Havard Penstemon, Big Bend Penstemon

### *Penstemon havardii*

Thick leaves of pale blue-green measure about 4 inches long by 2 inches wide, with a rounded tip. The bright red tubular flowers are borne on a stalk 4–5 feet high in spring and summer. Havard Penstemon occurs only in western Texas, on desert plains and hillsides.

## Palmer Penstemon, Scented Penstemon

### *Penstemon palmeri*

Palmer Penstemon's waxy gray-green leaves are densely toothed along the edges and measure 3–4 inches long by 1½ inches wide. From a dense basal rosette of leaves, 3-foot-tall flower stalks arise, carrying puffy pale pink flowers with purple lines inside. The sweetly fragrant flowers bloom from spring into early summer. Gravelly washes and open rocky areas between 4,000 and 6,000 feet in elevation are the preferred habitats of Palmer Penstemon, which occurs in eastern California, southern Utah, Arizona, and central and western New Mexico.

## Parry Penstemon

### *Penstemon parryi*

The deep pink flowers of Parry Penstemon cluster along 3-foot-high stalks that rise from a basal rosette of foliage. Parry Penstemon blooms from late February through April. The smooth, dark green leaves are broader at the tip than at the base, measuring 4 inches long and 1 inch wide. You'll find it growing along washes, on desert slopes, and in canyons in southern Arizona and Sonora, Mexico. It occurs between 1,500 and 5,000 feet in elevation.

April through June and sometimes also in the fall. Southern California, Arizona, New Mexico, and Baja California, Mexico, are home to this Penstemon, which prefers sandy or rocky flats, and slopes at 2,000–5,000 feet in elevation.

## Canyon Penstemon
### *Penstemon pseudospectabilis*
Canyon Penstemon's medium green, arrow-shaped, toothed leaves clasp tightly around the 3-foot-high stems. Rose-purple flowers about 1 inch long bloom from March to May. The range of Canyon Penstemon extends from eastern California, across southern Arizona, to southeastern New Mexico. It grows in desert washes and canyons and on dry slopes, at 2,000–6,000 feet in elevation.

## Superb Penstemon
### *Penstemon superbus*
Vivid coral flowers bloom along Superb Penstemon's 3-foot-long flower stalks in April and May. The leaves are blue-green, about 4 inches long and 1½ inches wide, with pointed or oval tips. The foliage and flower stalk are often purplish-colored. Superb Penstemon is found in washes and rocky canyon areas in southeastern Arizona, southwestern New Mexico, and Chihuahua, Mexico, from 3,500 to 5,500 feet in elevation.

## Thurber Penstemon
### *Penstemon thurberi*
Thurber Penstemon is a shrubby perennial with a woody base. It typically reaches 1½ feet high and 1 foot wide. The leaves are bright green and linear, 1 inch long and less than ⅛ inch wide. Lavender-rose or bluish flowers about ½ inch long bloom at the ends of the branches from

## Desert-fir, Pigmy-cedar
### *Peucephyllum schottii*
ASTERACEAE [SUNFLOWER FAMILY]

**Description** The evergreen foliage of Desert-fir resembles a conifer, but the plant actually belongs to the sunflower family. The shrub is many-branched and rather dense, reaching 4 feet high and 5 feet wide. Needlelike leaves are aromatic, about ½ inch long, and crowded along the gray stems. Yellow flowers adorn the ends of the branches from March to June. They are ½ inch in diameter and lack ray flowers (petals). Tan bristly seeds develop from the flowers.

**Native Distribution** Rocky slopes and arroyos at elevations below 3,000 feet are home to Desert-fir. The species occurs in southern California and Nevada, western Arizona, southwestern Utah, Baja California, and Sonora, Mexico.

**Culture** Desert-fir is cold hardy to about 20° F and is drought tolerant once established. It prefers well-drained soil and develops the most attractive foliage in full sun. You shouldn't need to prune the plant other than removing dead or damaged branches.

**Landscape Use** Desert-fir's fine-textured green foliage contrasts well with broad-leaved silvery plants such as Brittlebush (*Encelia farinosa*) or Desert-lavender (*Hyptis emoryi*). The medium-sized shrub could be used for foundation plantings near buildings to link the structures with the landscape visually. An uneven row of plants creates a fine informal hedge. Desert-fir could also be utilized in

*Penstemon fendleri* Fendler Penstemon

*Penstemon havardii* Havard Penstemon

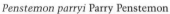

*Penstemon palmeri* Palmer Penstemon

*Penstemon parryi* Parry Penstemon

*Penstemon pseudospectabilis* Canyon Penstemon

*Penstemon superbus* Superb Penstemon

*Penstemon thurberi* Thurber Penstemon

naturalistic desert landscapes. Try planting it near a walkway, where people brushing against the foliage will release its fragrance. Small animals eat the seeds.

## Desert Phlox
### *Phlox tenuifolia*
POLEMONIACEAE [PHLOX FAMILY]

**Description** Slender herbaceous stems rise in a tuft from Desert Phlox's woody base to a height of 1–2 feet and a width of 2 feet. The light green, sparsely distributed leaves are linear, 1½ inches long and ⅛ inch wide. From March through May, white funnel-shaped 1-inch-long flowers crown the plant, releasing a sweet or sometimes musky scent.

**Native Distribution** Desert Phlox occurs only in central Arizona, on rocky slopes and in canyons, from 1,500 to 5,000 feet in elevation.

**Culture** Desert Phlox can grow in full sun or partial shade, though brighter light will encourage better flowering. Provide well-drained soil for this plant, which is cold hardy to at least 15° F. A deep soaking every two weeks through the summer will benefit Desert Phlox.

**Landscape Use** A garden of herbaceous flowering plants would be a likely destination for Desert Phlox. The mounded form and white flowers combine nicely with the tall, slender form of pink-blooming Parry Penstemon (*Penstemon parryi*) or other *Penstemon* species. Desert Phlox could also be used to edge a walkway, patio, or even a swimming pool. The delicate, airy foliage could be contrasted with coarse-textured plants.

## Mexican-ebony, Palo Chino
### *Pithecellobium mexicanum*
FABACEAE [PEA FAMILY]

**Description** Mexican-ebony's gray-green deciduous foliage is divided into tiny, rounded leaflets ¼ inch long. The slender branches bear pairs of ⅛-inch curved thorns. In March and April, fluffy cream-colored flowers almost 1 inch in diameter appear. Brown leathery pods 1 inch wide and 3 inches long follow the flowers. The plant's natural form is a rounded shrub or small tree to 20 feet high and about 15 feet wide.

**Native Distribution** The Mexican states of Baja California, Sonora, and Sinaloa are home to Mexican-ebony. It grows along arroyos, on desert slopes, and on valley floors.

**Culture** In spite of its origin in warm climates, Mexican-ebony is relatively frost tolerant, enduring temperatures to at least 18° F. The plant prefers loose, well-drained soil. Supplemental irrigation in the summer, combined with good soil, can encourage fast growth. Mexican-ebony needs full sun for proper development.

**Landscape Use** Mexican-ebony can be used in courtyards or other limited-space areas. Complement its delicate foliage with medium- or coarse-textured plants. Its winter bareness can be played down by incorporating evergreen plants nearby. Small hooked thorns make the plant effective for security or barrier plantings.

## Plumbago
### *Plumbago scandens*
PLUMBAGINACEAE [PLUMBAGO FAMILY]

**Description** Plumbago's dark green 3-inch-long leaves are 1¼ inch wide, narrowing to a point at the tip. The stems are woody at the base but herbaceous above, sprawl-

*Peucephyllum schottii* Desert-fir

*Phlox tenuifolia* Desert Phlox

*Pithecellobium mexicanum* Mexican-ebony

ing and often vinelike. At maturity the plant is 2 feet high and 3 feet wide. White five-petaled flowers ¾ inch across occur in clusters from May through September. The leaves and roots are reported to be poisonous if taken internally.

**Native Distribution** This plant's distribution is mostly in the tropics, though it occurs on the Baja California peninsula in Mexico, and in southern Arizona, western and southern Texas, and southern Florida. It usually grows along washes, in canyons, and on shaded brushy hillsides between 2,500 and 4,000 feet in elevation.

**Culture** Plumbago grows best in a semi-shaded location, protected from extreme cold. It can suffer damage at temperatures in the low 20s F. A variety of soil types are acceptable. Plumbago requires irrigation every seven to ten days during summer to keep it looking good. If the plant gets scraggly, prune it back in spring or early summer.

**Landscape Use** This plant can fill those semi-shady spots in your landscape where sun-loving plants don't do well. The white flowers stand out against the dark foliage, even in lower light. Because of its sprawly habit, Plumbago could be used in a hanging pot or allowed to trail over the edge of a planter. With support, it could climb as a vine.

## Hoary Rosemarymint
*Poliomintha incana*
LAMIACEAE [MINT FAMILY]

**Description** The leaves of Hoary Rosemarymint are needlelike, to ½ inch long, and silvery from fine white hairs. The evergreen foliage is fragrant. At maturity the shrub reaches a height of 4 feet, with a 4–6 foot spread. Half-inch pale blue flowers or lavender-speckled white flowers cluster among the leaves near the branch tips from May to September.

**Native Distribution** Hoary Rosemarymint is typically found on desert flats and slopes with sandy or gypsum soils. It ranges between elevations of 3,600 and 6,000 feet in western Texas, New Mexico, northern Arizona, southern Utah, and southeastern California. The plant also occurs in Sonora and Chihuahua, Mexico.

**Culture** This shrub tolerates cold to at least 10° F. A planting site with very well-drained soil, preferably sandy, is best for Hoary Rosemarymint. It prefers full sun. You can give established plants a deep soaking once or twice a month through the warm season.

**Landscape Use** Small areas in the landscape that need some greenery could be enhanced by Hoary Rosemarymint's compact form. Try planting the shrub near walkways, where contact with the foliage will release its fragrance. The needlelike foliage would complement spiky plants such as Soaptree Yucca (*Yucca elata*).

## Honey Mesquite, Texas Mesquite
*Prosopis glandulosa* var. *glandulosa*
FABACEAE [PEA FAMILY]

**Description** Honey Mesquite develops into a large spreading tree 25 feet high and 30 feet wide, with a somewhat weeping form. Under stressful conditions Honey Mesquite remains a shrub. The bright green fernlike leaves are 4 inches long, with individual leaflets ⅛ inch wide by 1 inch long. Among the foliage are thorns, which vary from ¼ inch to 1 inch long. Honey Mesquite is deciduous during the winter. The sweet-smelling flowers are crowded together into fuzzy spikes 2–3 inches long. They bloom predominantly in April and May. Straw-colored leathery pods are about 5 inches long and ½ inch wide.

*Native Distribution* Kansas and Oklahoma, much of Texas, eastern New Mexico, Coahuila, Nuevo León, and Tamaulipas, Mexico, comprise the native distribution of Honey Mesquite. The tree usually grows on desert plains and along washes.

*Culture* Honey Mesquite's deep roots carry it through periods of drought. To encourage faster growth, give supplemental water during the summer. It will tolerate a lawn situation, but give it a heavy soaking every few weeks to encourage deep rooting. Honey Mesquite should be grown in full sun, in well-drained soil. It will accept shallow, rocky soil, but the growth will be somewhat stunted. As you might guess from the northerly extent of its range, this tree is very cold hardy, to 0° F. Prune the lower branches to achieve a distinct tree form and to reveal the sculptural multiple trunks.

*Landscape Use* Honey Mesquite is one of the finest desert shade trees. The spreading canopy casts a moderately dense shade in summer yet allows the sun's warmth to penetrate during winter—an energy-wise strategy. Honey Mesquite's bright green foliage gives a fresh look to the landscape. By planting an informal line of three to seven plants and allowing their lower branches to remain, you'll gain a security hedge and windbreak. An added benefit of a grove of Honey Mesquite is the wildlife it will attract. The seeds feed a variety of desert birds and mammals, while the thorny foliage provides cover.

## Screwbean Mesquite, Tornillo
### *Prosopis pubescens*
FABACEAE [PEA FAMILY]

*Description* Screwbean Mesquite derives its name from the unusually coiled fruits, which are 1–2 inches long and ¼ inch wide, dark tan, and usually in clusters. Fuzzy yellow flower spikes 2 inches long appear from April to June and sometimes in summer. The large shrub to multiple-trunked tree reaches 15 feet in height with a similar spread. Medium green fernlike foliage drops in winter. The compound leaves measure 2 inches long and ½ inch wide, with as many as eighteen tiny leaflets per leaf. Spines to ¾ inch long occur in pairs along the branches. The bark is shaggy.

*Native Distribution* Areas that receive water periodically—flood plains or dry washes—can support Screwbean Mesquite. This Mesquite is found to 4,000 feet in elevation in southeastern California, southern Nevada, southwestern Utah, southern Arizona and New Mexico, and western Texas, as well as in Baja California, Sonora, and Chihuahua, Mexico.

*Culture* Screwbean Mesquite does best in deep, well-drained soil. It accepts ample water, responding with vigorous growth, but also tolerates drought. This tree is cold hardy to 0° F. Provide supplemental irrigation a few times a month through the summer. Full sun is preferred by Screwbean Mesquite. The amount of pruning necessary will depend on what shape you want the plant to have. Let it grow naturally with its branches touching the ground, or create a small tree by exposing the trunk.

*Landscape Use* Summer shade and winter sunlight are possible beneath Screwbean Mesquite. Take advantage of the natural climate control by using this plant near a patio or next to the house. Screwbean Mesquite can create a screen for privacy or wind control. A multiple-trunked specimen could be used as a focal point in the landscape. The fine-textured foliage would also create a good neutral backdrop for other accent plants.

*Plumbago scandens* Plumbago

*Poliomintha incana* Hoary Rosemarymint

*Prosopis glandulosa* var. *glandulosa* Honey Mesquite

*Prosopis pubescens* Screwbean Mesquite

## Velvet Mesquite
### Prosopis velutina
FABACEAE [PEA FAMILY]

**Description** Fine, soft hairs cover the young growth of Velvet Mesquite. The fernlike compound leaves are 3–4 inches long and up to 1 inch wide, divided into sixteen to forty tiny leaflets. The gray-green foliage is deciduous in winter. The spines, usually present at the leaf bases, are ¾ inch long and often paired. The thick trunk with its shaggy bark is nearly hidden by low branches. Velvet Mesquite is a large shrub to tree, depending on growing conditions. Near watercourses it can reach a height of 20 feet with a 30-foot spread. On rocky slopes or dry plains a more typical size is 10 feet high and 15 feet wide. In spring, and sometimes later in the summer, 3-inch-long light yellow fuzzy flowers droop from the branches. Pods 5 inches long by ½ inch wide mature from the flowers, typically tan-colored but sometimes beautifully streaked with red.

**Native Distribution** Velvet Mesquite grows along washes, in valleys, and on desert plains. It ranges from 1,000 to 5,000 feet in elevation. The distribution includes southeastern California, southern Arizona, southern New Mexico, western Texas, and Sonora, Mexico.

**Culture** Deep, regular watering promotes the best growth, though Velvet Mesquite will tolerate drought. It can also be grown in a lawn. Velvet Mesquite should be planted in full sun; the soil type is not critical. Plants will tolerate cold to 5° F. The lower branches can be pruned to encourage a tree form. Minor pruning can be done any time; major work should be done in late winter or early spring.

**Landscape Use** The character shown by Velvet Mesquite's gnarled, shaggy trunk can add interest to the landscape. With some pruning, it can be an attractive shade tree for the patio. The plant's winter-deciduous nature allows sunlight to penetrate when the warmth is most needed. You can encourage wildlife by leaving the plant as an unpruned shrub. Birds seek its shelter for nesting. Many desert animals eat the seedpods, and birds find insects among the leaves and flowers.

## Paperflower
### Psilostrophe cooperi
ASTERACEAE [SUNFLOWER FAMILY]

**Description** Yellow 1-inch flowers absolutely smother the low, rounded form of Paperflower following rain, anytime from March through September. As the flowers age, the petals turn tan and papery and persist for weeks. The leaves are 2 inches long by ⅛ inch wide and light green, due to the white woolly covering. The stems of this semi-woody perennial are also covered with white wool. Paperflower reaches a height of 1 foot with a 1½-foot spread.

**Native Distribution** Paperflower is found in arroyos, on desert plains, and on hillsides, at 2,000–5,000 feet in elevation, in southern Nevada, southwestern Utah, southeastern California, southern Arizona, southwestern New Mexico, and Baja California and Sonora, Mexico.

**Culture** Anything less than full sun causes gangly growth. Well-drained soil is best. Once established, Paperflower tolerates drought, although widely spaced supplemental irrigation in the summer will encourage more flowers. Too much water results in foliage production at the expense of flowers. Paperflower withstands temperatures to at least 15° F.

**Landscape Use** The glowing yellow flowers really add punch to a landscape. Use this plant in flower gardens, patio and poolside plantings, along walkways, or in cactus gardens. For a stunning effect, do a mass planting. Similar flowering periods and complementary colors suggest the combination of Paperflower with blue-flowered Mealycup Sage (*Salvia farinacea*).

---

*Psilostrophe tagetina* closely resembles *Psilostrophe cooperi*, though its distribution differs. It occurs between 4,000 and 7,000 feet in elevation in eastern Arizona, southern New Mexico, western Texas, and northern Mexico.

---

## Indigo Bush
### *Psorothamnus schottii* (syn., *Dalea schottii*)
FABACEAE [PEA FAMILY]

**Description** The deep bluish purple, pealike flowers of Indigo Bush are borne in loose clusters about 3 inches long from April to May. A ¼-inch-long pod dotted with red glands develops from each small flower. The plant's needlelike leaves are ¾ inch long. The new growth of this spiny, many-branched shrub is bright green, turning gray-green with maturity. The plant reaches a height of 5 feet and a width of 6 feet.

**Native Distribution** Indigo Bush is found along washes, on desert plains, and in rocky canyons, below 5,000 feet in elevation. It occurs in southwestern Arizona, southern California, and Baja California, Mexico.

**Culture** Temperatures in the mid- to high 20s F can damage Indigo Bush, so place it in a well-protected location. It prefers well-drained soil and full sun. The foliage of Indigo Bush is typically sparse; you could prune it to encourage denser growth. The trade-off would be compromising the shrub's natural character.

**Landscape Use** Indigo Bush would be appropriate to include in a naturalistic desert landscape, particularly with Smoke Tree (*Psorothamnus spinosus*) and Creosote Bush (*Larrea tridentata*), its usual companions. The shrub could provide erosion control on slopes.

---

## Broom Dalea
### *Psorothamnus scoparia* (syn., *Dalea scoparia*)
FABACEAE [PEA FAMILY]

**Description** The upright gray branches of Broom Dalea form a rounded shrub 3 feet high and 4 feet wide. The needlelike blue-green leaves are ¾ inch long. They are produced following rain or watering. In May and June, and again in August and September, ½-inch clusters of small, fragrant dark blue flowers occur at the tips of branches. The ⅛-inch pods that follow have a dense covering of fine hair.

**Native Distribution** This shrub grows on sand dunes or sandy flats between the elevations of 2,000 and 6,000 feet. Its range includes southeastern Arizona, southern New Mexico, western Texas, and Coahuila and Chihuahua, Mexico.

**Culture** Broom Dalea requires sandy soil and full sun for best growth. Once established, it needs very little water; in fact, it does not tolerate overwatering. A deep soaking about once a month in the summer will keep it looking healthy and encourage heavy flowering. Broom Dalea can withstand cold temperatures to 15° F or lower.

**Landscape Use** Sandy areas prone to erosion from wind or water can be stabilized by Broom Dalea. A mass planting would be not only functional but also very attractive. The gray broomlike branches would combine well with the silvery, medium-textured foliage of Brittlebush (*Encelia farinosa*). Other

Above and insets: *Prosopis velutina* Velvet Mesquite

*Psilostrophe cooperi* Paperflower

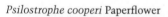

*Psorothamnus schottii* Indigo Bush

*Psorothamnus scoparia* Broom Dalea

plants that can grow in sandy conditions and would look good with Broom Dalea include Soaptree Yucca (*Yucca elata*) and Velvet Mesquite (*Prosopis velutina*).

## Smoke Tree
### *Psorothamnus spinosus* (syn., *Dalea spinosa*)
FABACEAE [PEA FAMILY]

**Description** An intricate network of slender spiny gray branches gives this large shrub or small tree the appearance of a cloud of smoke. It normally reaches a height of 15 feet and a width of about 10 feet. The small leaves are shed soon after they appear each season. Between April and June, deep violet-blue ⅓-inch-long flowers adorn Smoke Tree and perfume the air nearby. The ¼-inch pods, which are dotted with amber-colored glands, contain one or two seeds.

**Native Distribution** Smoke Tree rarely grows anywhere other than gravelly or sandy washes. It occurs below 1,500 feet in elevation in southern California and southwestern Arizona, as well as in northern Sonora and on the Baja California peninsula in Mexico.

**Culture** Two critical factors in growing Smoke Tree are coarse, well-drained soil and mild wintertime temperatures. Cold damage can occur below 25° F. Occasional deep watering through the summer is beneficial. This plant prefers a location in full sun. Pruning shouldn't be necessary other than to remove dead branches.

**Landscape Use** Smoke Tree makes a striking accent plant. It would be best featured against a dark wall or a back-ground of deep green foliage. A scene reminiscent of its natural habitat could be created by planting it along a dry wash. The plant is prickly to brush against, so keep it well back from walkways and patios.

## Scrub Oak
### *Quercus turbinella*
FAGACEAE [BEECH FAMILY]

**Description** Leathery gray-green leaves cover Scrub Oak's rigid branches, forming a rounded shrub 8 feet high and 12 feet wide. The oval evergreen leaves are typically 1 inch long and ½ inch wide, with toothed edges and a pointed tip. Inconspicuous flowers bloom in April and May, followed by light brown acorns ¾ inch long and ¼ inch in diameter.

**Native Distribution** This shrub occurs at the upper edges of the desert and into chaparral and desert grassland. Dry, rocky slopes between 3,500 and 6,000 feet in elevation provide the preferred habitat. Scrub Oak grows in southern Nevada, southern Utah, eastern California, Arizona, southern New Mexico, and western Texas, as well as in northern Baja California, Mexico.

**Culture** Scrub Oak needs full sun for best development, although in the lowest desert areas afternoon shade is beneficial. Supplemental water every two weeks will help plants survive the intense heat of low desert summers. This slow growing shrub accepts most soil types, and it tolerates cold to at least 12° F. Prune only to remove dead wood.

**Landscape Use** An excellent informal hedge can be achieved with Scrub Oak. The dense foliage also provides shelter and nesting sites for birds, and the acorns are eaten by a variety of desert wildlife. The hollylike leaves combine well with spiky plants such as *Yucca* and *Agave* species.

## California Buckthorn
### *Rhamnus californica* ssp. *ursina*
RHAMNACEAE [BUCKTHORN FAMILY]

**Description** The attractive evergreen foliage of California Buckthorn covers a rounded form that is normally a shrub but sometimes a small tree. A typical mature height is 10 feet, with a similar spread. Dark green oval leaves measure about 2 inches long and 1 inch wide. The undersides of the leaves are light green because of a dense covering of short, fine hairs. California Buckthorn produces clusters of greenish white flowers at the ends of the branches in May and June. The black fruit that develops from the flowers is ½ inch in diameter.

*Native Distribution*  California Buckthorn occurs at the upper edges of the desert and into chaparral vegetation, from 3,500 to 6,500 feet in elevation. Its range includes southwestern New Mexico, Arizona, California, southern Nevada, and Baja California, Mexico.

*Culture*  Supplemental irrigation through the summer will benefit California Buckthorn, particularly in the lowest desert areas. A planting site that receives afternoon shade will also ease the stress of summer's heat. This plant's cold hardiness extends to at least 15° F. It will accept a variety of soil types.

*Landscape Use*  California Buckthorn can be used as a hedge or to screen an unattractive view. The deep green foliage would be appropriate around a pool. You might try training it into a small tree for a courtyard or patio garden. The fruits of this plant are eaten by a variety of wildlife.

## Littleleaf Sumac, Desert Sumac
### *Rhus microphylla*
ANACARDIACEAE [SUMAC FAMILY]

*Description*  Littleleaf Sumac's deep green, smooth leaves are divided into five to nine leaflets, usually less than ½ inch long and ¼ inch wide. The plant's rigid branches tend to end in a spine. Tiny whitish flowers bloom in early spring before the winter-deciduous leaves reappear. Through summer and fall, the hairy pea-sized fruits ripen to orange or red. Littleleaf Sumac develops into a large shrub 8 feet high and 12 feet wide.

*Native Distribution*  Littleleaf Sumac grows along washes, on desert flats, and on rocky hillsides, between 2,000 and 6,000 feet in elevation. It occurs in central and western Texas, through New Mexico and Arizona, and into northern Mexico.

*Culture*  Once established, Littleleaf Sumac is very drought tolerant. You might want to give it a few deep waterings during drought to promote fuller growth and better fruit development. It is also quite cold tolerant, hardy to 5° F. It can adapt to sand, loam, clay, or caliche, with good drainage preferred. Provide full sunlight for best growth, although partial shade is okay. This shrub looks great without any shaping, although it can be pruned into a hedge. With fairly drastic pruning you could create a small tree.

*Landscape Use*  Littleleaf Sumac's fruit provides both ornament in the landscape and food for wildlife. The fruit is eaten by ground squirrels and birds. Dense foliage also provides cover. The tart fruits have reportedly been used to make a lemonade-like beverage. You might use Littleleaf Sumac as a foundation planting to provide a visual connection between the house and landscape. It could also function as an informal or formal hedge, depending on how you prune it. Remember that it is deciduous in winter, so consider using it in combination with evergreen plants. The bright green foliage could create a striking contrast with silver-foliaged plants, or simply serve as a backdrop to accent plants.

*Psorothamnus spinosus* Smoke Tree

*Quercus turbinella* Scrub Oak

*Rhamnus californica* ssp. *ursina* California Buckthorn

*Rhus microphylla* Littleleaf Sumac

## Sugar Sumac
### *Rhus ovata*
ANACARDIACEAE [SUMAC FAMILY]

**Description** This dense, rounded shrub has rich, deep green foliage. At maturity, Sugar Sumac can reach 10 feet high and equally wide. The leathery evergreen leaves are generally oval with a pointed tip. They measure 3 inches long by 2 inches wide. From March to May, reddish buds open into white or pinkish flowers borne in dense clusters 1 inch long. The ¼-inch-diameter fruits are reddish and hairy.

**Native Distribution** Sugar Sumac grows on the upper edges of the desert and into the chaparral zone in southern California, central Arizona, and Baja California, Mexico. Its habitat includes washes, canyons, and dry slopes, from 3,000 to 5,000 feet in elevation.

**Culture** Sugar Sumac is cold hardy to 10–15° F but has trouble with the summertime heat in low desert areas unless given supplemental water every two weeks. Afternoon shade also helps reduce heat stress to the plant. In higher-elevation areas, full sun produces the most attractive foliage. The ideal planting site would have well-drained soil. Sugar Sumac's rounded form requires no pruning.

**Landscape Use** The glossy, deep green foliage of Sugar Sumac contrasts with just about all other desert plants. It can lend a tropical feeling to pool areas or courtyards. It also serves well as a screen or informal hedge.

## Evergreen Sumac
### *Rhus virens*
ANACARDIACEAE [SUMAC FAMILY]

**Description** Evergreen Sumac's dark green, glossy compound leaves are divided into five to nine oval leaflets, to 1½ inches long and ¾ inch wide. This large shrub to small tree reaches a mature size of 8 feet high and 10 feet wide. Small white flowers occur in 1½-inch-long clusters in spring and summer. They develop into showy red berries covered with sticky hairs.

**Native Distribution** The natural range of this shrub includes western Texas and northern Mexico. Evergreen Sumac occurs between 2,100 and 5,000 feet in elevation, most often on rocky slopes and in canyons.

**Culture** This plant is quite cold hardy, to 5° F. Full sun is preferred in all but the lowest desert areas, where afternoon shade would be advised. Choose a planting site with well-drained soil. Established plants are drought tolerant; nevertheless, they will appreciate a little extra water through the summer. Evergreen Sumac requires minimal pruning.

**Landscape Use** Plant this shrub as an informal hedge. In addition to serving as a screen, the lushly foliaged plant creates an excellent background for other plants. Those with light green or silvery foliage would stand out best. Evergreen Sumac can be used near swimming pools as well.

## Ruellia
### *Ruellia peninsularis*
ACANTHACEAE [ACANTHUS FAMILY]

**Description** Purple bell-shaped flowers 1 inch across are produced nearly all year on this rounded evergreen shrub. The heaviest bloom is in spring and early summer. The oval leaves are bright green and smooth, 1 inch long by ¾ inch wide, on light gray branches. The foliage may be shiny and varnished-looking. Overall size is typically 4 feet high and a little wider, although plants in frost-prone areas may not get that big.

**Native Distribution** Ruellia's natural range is limited to Baja California and Sonora, Mexico. Dry, gravelly slopes and rocky washes are typical habitats.

**Culture** Choose a warm location for Ruellia. It suffers twig damage at about 26° F, and the entire plant will be blackened by temperatures in the low 20s F. Regrowth is usually rapid once the weather warms up. Wait to prune the frost-damaged foliage until all danger of frost is past. This plant prefers well-drained soil and full sun but tolerates moderate shade. Low light results in sparser foliage and fewer flowers. Once established, Ruellia can survive on rainfall alone, but you'll probably want to give it supplemental water throughout the summer to keep the plant looking more robust.

**Landscape Use** The soft green foliage is suited to poolside and patio plantings. Try a row of Ruellia, unclipped, as an informal hedge. It also works well near buildings for foundation plantings. Because neither the plant's form nor the foliage nor the flowers are particularly showy, it can serve as a backdrop for accent plants and flowers.

---

*Ruellia californica* is very similar in appearance to *Ruellia peninsularis*, except that its leaves are sticky and hairy and have a pungent odor. Like *Ruellia peninsularis*, *Ruellia californica* is found in Baja California and Sonora, Mexico, but generally at lower elevations. *Ruellia californica* is slightly more cold tender.

---

## Paperbag Bush, Bladder-sage
### *Salazaria mexicana*
LAMIACEAE [MINT FAMILY]

**Description** The common names of this plant refer to the fruit that develops into an inflated, light tan pouch ½ to ¾ inch in diameter. This unusual fruit follows a spring bloom of purple and white ½-inch flowers. Paperbag Bush can reach 3 feet high with a similar spread. The wiry branches are sparsely foliated with oblong or oval pointed leaves, ¾ inch long by ¼ inch wide. The foliage is winter deciduous.

**Native Distribution** The range of Paperbag Bush includes southeastern California, southern Nevada, southwestern Utah, Arizona, southern New Mexico, and western Texas, as well as Baja California, Chihuahua, and Coahuila, Mexico. It is usually found from 1,000 to 3,500 feet in elevation in washes and rocky canyons and on desert flats.

**Culture** Paperbag Bush needs good drainage. The best growth will be obtained in full sun, with occasional summer irrigation. The plant's cold tolerance extends to 5° F.

**Landscape Use** You might grow Paperbag Bush as a curiosity, intermingled in a flower garden or perhaps as a low hedge near a patio area. Another potential use is as a groundcover.

---

## White Sage
### *Salvia apiana*
LAMIACEAE [MINT FAMILY]

**Description** White Sage is a rounded shrub with a woody base and herbaceous branches above. It reaches a height of 5 feet and a width of 6 feet. White or pale lavender flower spikes to 3 feet long rise above the evergreen, silvery foliage from March to July. The leaves are oblong, 4 inches long by 1½ inches wide, slightly toothed, wrinkled above, and covered with fine white hairs.

**Native Distribution** Southern California and Baja California, Mexico, are home to

*Rhus ovata* Sugar Sumac

*Rhus virens* Evergreen Sumac

*Ruellia peninsularis* Ruellia; inset *Ruellia californica*

*Salazaria mexicana* Paperbag Bush

*Salvia apiana* White Sage

White Sage. The plant most often grows along sandy washes and rocky hillsides at the upper edges of the desert, to 5,000 feet in elevation.

**Culture** White Sage prefers well-drained soil and full sun. Once established, it requires little supplemental water. Since most of the plant's growth occurs in winter, water just once a month in the summer (the dormant period) to prevent severe drought stress. White Sage is relatively cold hardy, to at least the mid-20s F. It is a moderately fast grower. Cut off the dried flower stalks for a neater appearance. The plant can be kept denser by moderate pruning.

**Landscape Use** Plant White Sage near the back of a flower garden, where the flower stalks can provide height. The silver foliage would look good with red, pink, or blue flowers. Different shades of gray foliage also could be combined for a striking effect. In that scenario, the plants should have contrasting textures, such as the bold leaves of *Agave* species or the delicate, airy foliage of Trailing Indigo Bush (*Dalea greggii*) against White Sage's medium-textured foliage.

# Blue Sage
## Salvia chamaedryoides
LAMIACEAE [MINT FAMILY]

**Description** Cobalt blue flowers and silvery foliage create a striking combination in Blue Sage. The evergreen, herbaceous perennial grows to 1½ feet high and 2 feet wide. It blooms spring through fall, with the ⅜-inch tube-shaped flowers borne in loose, 6-inch-long spikes. The leaves are ½ inch long and ¼ inch wide.

**Native Distribution** Blue Sage grows in Chihuahua, Coahuila, Nuevo León, and Hidalgo, Mexico, between 7,500 and 9,800 feet in elevation.

**Culture** Provide this plant with full sun and well-drained soil. It requires only occasional irrigation after establishment. During the summer, a deep soaking three times a month should be sufficient. Blue Sage is cold hardy to 15° F. Leggy plants can be pruned in the spring to encourage more compact growth.

**Landscape Use** Use Blue Sage as a colorful low-growing border plant along walkways or patios. It also could form an attractive groundcover. Blue Sage can add interest to a desert flower garden. It combines well with the similarly colored but taller Mealycup Sage (*Salvia farinacea*). Try complementing the blues of these two *Salvia* species with the bright yellow flowers of Desert-marigold (*Baileya multiradiata*).

# Desert Sage
## Salvia dorrii var. dorrii
LAMIACEAE [MINT FAMILY]

**Description** The flowering spikes of Desert Sage resemble a miniature topiary, their 1-inch rounded clusters of blue-violet flowers interspersed with bare sections of stem. The plant blooms in late winter and spring. Fine, silvery hairs give the leaves a silver-gray coloration. The leaves are ¾ inch long and ⅜ inch wide at the broad, rounded tip. Desert Sage is a low-growing shrub with mature dimensions of 2 feet high by 2 feet wide.

**Native Distribution** The distribution of Desert Sage includes southern Nevada and northwestern Arizona, as well as the east-central and southeastern portions of California. It occurs at elevations between 2,000 and 7,000 feet.

**Culture** Desert Sage grows best in full sun; however, in the lowest desert areas afternoon shade will ease the stress of summer's heat. Once established, the plant is drought tolerant. Supplemental water every two to three weeks will keep it looking its best. Well-drained soil is preferred. It is cold hardy to 18° F. The dried flower spikes can be clipped off for a neater appearance.

*Landscape Use* Desert Sage could be used as a border plant. Its size allows it to be used in a variety of compact spaces, even in a pot. Another possible landscape use is in a perennial flower garden.

## Mealycup Sage
*Salvia farinacea*
LAMIACEAE [MINT FAMILY]

*Description* Mealycup Sage grows to 2 feet wide and 1½ feet high, including the 6-inch spikes of violet-blue flowers. Mealycup Sage blooms from April to September. The plant is an herbaceous perennial with stems that die back in cold winter areas. The oblong leaves are medium green, 2–3 inches long by ¾ inch wide.

*Native Distribution* Central and western Texas and southern New Mexico make up the natural range of Mealycup Sage. It grows on plains and low hills, often in limestone soils, between 3,500 and 6,000 feet in elevation.

*Culture* Mealycup Sage grows best with supplemental irrigation through the summer. Provide full sun and well-drained soil. The foliage freezes at 28° F, but the roots are quite cold hardy. Trim the spent flower stalks to prolong bloom. If the plant becomes leggy, it can be pruned severely to promote more compact growth.

*Landscape Use* Mealycup Sage makes a good addition to the flower garden and is a good plant for low borders, too. Combine it with evergreen plants to cover its winter bareness.

## Autumn Sage, Texas Red Sage
*Salvia greggii*
LAMIACEAE [MINT FAMILY]

*Description* Don't take the common name Autumn Sage too literally, because the plant's blooming period isn't limited to that season. Autumn Sage typically blooms heavily in March and April and to a lesser extent in summer, and finishes the season with another burst in October or November. The 1-inch tube-shaped magenta flowers are borne in loose spikes. Other color variations include orange, pink, red, and white. Autumn Sage is a rounded evergreen shrub 2–3 feet high and 3 feet wide. The medium green foliage releases a minty fragrance if you brush against it. Individual leaves are 1 inch long and about half as wide, the outer edge rounded but narrowing toward the leaf base.

*Native Distribution* In the wild you'll find Autumn Sage growing on rocky hillsides at elevations between 2,200 and 8,000 feet. It occurs in central, southern, and western Texas, and in northern Mexico to San Luis Potosí.

*Culture* Autumn Sage seems to prefer an eastern exposure, or sunlight filtered through an open tree such as Palo Verde (*Cercidium* species). In full sun, particularly in the hottest desert areas, the plants don't become as lush, nor bloom as abundantly. Good drainage is important, as Autumn Sage is sensitive to over-watering. Once established, it is drought tolerant, although in severe stress it will drop some leaves and cease blooming. Irrigation every few weeks in summer will keep it looking good. Supplemental fertilization with nitrogen during the summer encourages more vigorous plants. Autumn Sage can withstand temperatures to at least 15° F without damage; at 0° F it will die back to the ground. Prune the plant occasionally to keep it dense and compact. Clip off the old flower spikes for

Above left and right: *Salvia chamaedryoides* Blue Sage

*Salvia dorrii* var. *dorrii* Desert Sage

*Salvia farinacea* Mealycup Sage

*Salvia greggii* Autumn Sage; detail above right

a neater appearance and to encourage more flowers.

**Landscape Use** Hummingbirds are attracted to the flowers of Autumn Sage. Locate plants outside a picture window or near a patio, where the tiny birds' antics can be enjoyed. The rich green foliage and magenta flowers are even more vivid when contrasted with silver-leaved plants. Any flower garden would benefit from the addition of a few Autumn Sage plants. It can also be planted as a low hedge or massed as a groundcover.

## Mojave Sage
**Salvia mohavensis**
LAMIACEAE [MINT FAMILY]

**Description** The pale blue to lavender flowers and showy bracts (small leaflike structures that occur just below the flowers) of Mojave Sage appear in solitary ¾-inch clusters at the ends of the flowering stems. The blooming season lasts from April through July. Medium green, wrinkled leaves measure ¾ inch long by ¼ inch wide. Both the upper and lower leaf surfaces are covered with short, stiff hairs. The evergreen foliage is fragrant. At maturity this compact rounded shrub reaches 2 feet high and 2½ feet wide.

**Native Distribution** Mojave Sage is found in southeastern California, southern Nevada, western Arizona, and northwestern Sonora, Mexico. Its habitat includes arroyos, canyons, and rocky slopes, from 1,000 to 5,000 feet in elevation.

**Culture** Full sun is necessary to achieve a compact, mounded form. Once established, the plant requires very little water. Be especially careful not to overwater during the summer, when the plant is mostly dormant. Mojave Sage is cold tolerant to 0° F. The preferred soil type is well drained.

**Landscape Use** The uniquely shaped flowers of Mojave Sage would add interest to a flower garden. This plant's compact form could be utilized for low borders or even for groundcover. Try planting it near a walkway, as the plant releases a minty fragrance anytime someone brushes against the foliage.

## Mexican Jumping-bean
**Sapium biloculare**
EUPHORBIACEAE [SPURGE FAMILY]

**Description** The name of this evergreen shrub or small tree is a little misleading. It isn't really a type of bean; rather, the plant is in the same family as poinsettia. As is typical of plants in the Euphorbiaceae, the stems of Mexican Jumping-bean contain milky juice, which reportedly is poisonous. The dark green leathery leaves are lance-shaped, 2 inches long by ½ inch wide, and finely toothed along the edges. The yellow-green 1-inch spike-shaped flowers, which bloom from March to November, would not be noticeable except for their fragrance. The seed is more or less rounded, with a diameter of ½ inch. Occasionally the seeds will provide a temporary home for the larvae of a moth. The tiny worm's movements can cause the seed to roll over or even jump, like the more famous Mexican Jumping Bean (*Sebastiana pavoniana*), which is sometimes sold as a novelty. At maturity this plant can reach 12 feet in height with a spread of 10 feet.

**Native Distribution** Southwestern Arizona and Sonora and Baja California, Mexico, provide a home for Mexican Jumping-bean. The plants occur widely scattered along washes and on rocky hillsides, between 1,000 and 2,500 feet in elevation.

**Culture** Temperatures below 25° F can damage the foliage. Mexican Jumping-bean does best in full sun and well-drained soil. It is very drought tolerant; however, you can provide supplemental irrigation once or twice a month through the summer.

**Landscape Use** Mexican Jumping-bean would make an excellent hedge for visual screening or wind control. The dark-colored evergreen foliage would be nice around a pool, too. Try combining it with gray-foliaged plants such as Texas Ranger (*Leucophyllum frutescens*).

shade, and is hardy to at least 10° F. Any soil is acceptable. Burro Grass can be cut back when the seedheads begin to look ratty.

**Landscape Use** The dense mat of foliage and roots can be very effective in erosion control. The seedheads of Burro Grass are especially attractive in early morning or late afternoon light; a mass planting would have the most impact. Burro Grass can lend a light texture to the landscape.

## Burro Grass
### *Scleropogon brevifolius*
POACEAE [GRASS FAMILY]

**Description** Burro Grass grows in tufts about 4 inches high and 6 inches across. The light green, sharp-pointed leaf blades measure 1 inch long and $\frac{1}{16}$ inch wide. They are usually somewhat curled. This grass spreads by wiry, creeping stems that root wherever a joint contacts moist soil. Burro Grass blooms from May through October, most heavily in the fall. The 5-inch-long seedheads of the female plants have conspicuous silvery or rose-colored awns (threadlike bristles attached to the seeds).

**Native Distribution** Burro Grass grows on desert plains and in open valleys, below 5,500 feet in elevation. It can become a dominant grass of overgrazed rangeland. The native distribution includes southern Colorado, Utah, Nevada, Arizona, New Mexico, Texas, Mexico, Argentina, and Chile.

**Culture** Because of Burro Grass's ability to spread by stolons (creeping stems), you need to go easy on the water to keep the grass from taking over an area. Well-established plants are very drought tolerant. Supplemental irrigation once a month through the summer should be adequate to keep Burro Grass looking healthy. It can grow in full sun or light

## Threadleaf Groundsel
### *Senecio douglasii* var. *longilobus*
ASTERACEAE [SUNFLOWER FAMILY]

**Description** Daisylike 1-inch flowers with slender yellow petals appear from April through November among Threadleaf Groundsel's silvery foliage. As the common name indicates, this evergreen perennial subshrub has finely divided leaves to 3 inches long, with slender leaflets only $\frac{1}{16}$ inch wide and 1 inch long. Threadleaf Groundsel has an upright form 3 feet high and 2 feet wide.

**Native Distribution** Threadleaf Groundsel grows in sandy washes, along dry, gravelly stream beds, on rocky slopes, and in grasslands. It is poisonous to livestock and is common on overgrazed rangelands and disturbed areas. It occurs between 2,500 and 7,500 feet in elevation in southern Colorado, southern Utah, Arizona, New Mexico, western Texas, and northern Mexico.

**Culture** Threadleaf Groundsel does well in a sunny location with good drainage. The rapidly growing plant needs little water once established; in fact, overwatering produces rangy, weak growth. Cold hardiness extends to near 0° F. The spent flowers can be clipped off for a neater-looking plant. Threadleaf Groundsel reseeds readily and may need to be controlled by thinning.

Above left and right: *Salvia mohavensis* Mojave Sage

*Sapium biloculare* Mexican Jumping-bean

*Scleropogon brevifolius* Burro Grass

Below and above left: *Senecio douglasii* var. *longilobus* Threadleaf Groundsel

**Landscape Use** The silvery foliage and yellow flowers make a handsome combination anywhere in the landscape. Use Threadleaf Groundsel to spice up a flower garden, massed for an accent, or in a planter box. It could also be planted along roadsides and in median strips, and it would look right at home along a wash or scattered throughout a naturalistic landscape.

---

## Spiny Senna
**Senna armata** (syn., **Cassia armata**)
FABACEAE [PEA FAMILY]

**Description** Bright yellow ½-inch flowers borne in loose clusters between March and June soften the spiny appearance of this rounded shrub. At maturity Spiny Senna measures 4 feet high and 6 feet wide. The 2-inch-long leaves, which drop early, are composed of two to eight thick, fleshy leaflets ¼ inch long by ⅛ inch wide. The pale green, usually leafless branches end in a spiny tip. The seedpods are light tan and cylindric, ¼ inch in diameter with a length of about 1½ inches.

**Native Distribution** The usual habitat for this plant includes sandy washes, gravelly plains, and slopes, between 500 and 3,000 feet in elevation. It occurs in southeastern California, southern Nevada, western Arizona, and Baja California, Mexico.

**Culture** Spiny Senna requires well-drained soil. Once established, it is very drought tolerant. Provide full sun for the plant, which tolerates cold to at least 15° F.

**Landscape Use** A mass planting of Spiny Senna would be very attractive, particularly during flowering, when the plants are mounds of yellow. The spiny appearance contrasts well with the round forms of cacti such as Fishhook Barrel (*Ferocactus wislizenii*). A dramatic color contrast could be achieved by planting Spiny Senna against a dark background.

## Bauhin Senna, Two-leaved Senna
**Senna bauhinioides** (syn., **Cassia bauhinioides**)
FABACEAE [PEA FAMILY]

**Description** From April through August, 1-inch yellow flowers with brown veins occur at the ends of Bauhin Senna's branches. The herbaceous stems rise from a woody rootstock to 1 foot high and equally wide. Bauhin Senna's leaves are divided into two oblong leaflets, each 1 inch long by ½ inch wide and rounded at both ends. The grayish green foliage is covered with a soft fuzz. Dark brown pods, 1 inch long and ¼ inch wide, are also fuzzy.

**Native Distribution** Bauhin Senna is found throughout much of Arizona, New Mexico, western Texas, and into Mexico, from Sonora to Hidalgo and Zacatecas. Typical habitat includes gravelly flats and slopes from 2,000 to 5,500 feet in elevation.

**Culture** Full sun promotes the best growth, as does a little extra water every other week or so through the summer. The foliage will freeze in the mid- to low 20s, but Bauhin Senna is root hardy to near 0° F. The preferred soil is well drained, as in the plant's natural habitat.

**Landscape Use** Use Bauhin Senna to provide splashes of color throughout a naturalistic landscape. The colorful perennial can also be used in a more formal situation, such as a flower garden.

Roemer Senna (*Senna roemeriana*) is very similar to Bauhin Senna, but with more elongated leaves (to 1½ inches long). It blooms heavily in March and April and again in September and October, with occasional blooming through the summer. The natural range of Roemer Senna includes central and western Texas, southern New Mexico, and Coahuila, Nuevo León, and Sonora, Mexico.

## Two-flowered Senna
### *Senna biflora* (syn., *Cassia biflora*)
FABACEAE [PEA FAMILY]

*Description* The 1-inch bright yellow flowers of this deciduous shrub usually occur in pairs. The flowering period is from October to April, provided the plant isn't damaged by hard frost. Medium green leaves are divided into oval or elongated leaflets ½ inch long and ¼ inch wide. The flat dark brown pods are 2–4 inches long but only about ¼ inch wide. At maturity the plant can reach 5 feet in height and width.

*Native Distribution* Two-flowered Senna occurs in Baja California, Sonora, and Chihuahua, Mexico, to tropical America. It typically grows along arroyos, on desert plains, and on hillsides.

*Culture* The most prolific flowering will occur on plants in full sun that receive a deep soaking every few weeks through the summer. Two-flowered Senna will accept partial shade. The foliage can be damaged below 15° F, but the roots are quite hardy. Plant this shrub in well-drained soil.

*Landscape Use* The attractive foliage and bright yellow flowers make Two-flowered Senna useful for a colorful accent in flower gardens. It would be just as appropriate used in a naturalistic landscape, intermingled with other desert plants. If you use this shrub in a prominent place, you may wish to interplant it with evergreen shrubs to camouflage its winter bareness.

## Desert Senna
### *Senna covesii* (syn., *Cassia covesii*)
FABACEAE [PEA FAMILY]

*Description* Desert Senna's 1-inch-wide yellow flowers bloom from April to October, followed by slender brown pods 1 inch long. The compound leaves are 2 inches long by 1½ inches wide. A dense covering of short, soft hairs gives the foliage a gray-green cast. This perennial becomes woody at the base with age, and typically reaches a height of 1½ feet with a 2-foot spread.

*Native Distribution* You're most likely to find Desert Senna on desert plains and along washes, between 1,000 and 3,000 feet in elevation. Its range is rather extensive, from southern Nevada to southeastern California and Arizona, plus Baja California, Sonora, and Sinaloa, Mexico.

*Culture* Desert Senna isn't too particular about soil, although good drainage helps. Full sun promotes the most prolific flowers, and you can prolong the blooming season by watering a few times a month through the summer. The plant is hardy to at least the low 20s F. It reseeds readily, and you may want to pull older plants to make room for the seedlings to develop.

*Landscape Use* Mass this long-blooming perennial in a flower garden, or scatter plants throughout the landscape for small bursts of color. Desert Senna can be used near walkways, patios, and pool areas. The plant's low water requirement makes it appropriate for use in cactus gardens where it can help soften the strong forms.

## Lindheimer Senna
### *Senna lindheimeriana* (syn., *Cassia lindheimeriana*)
FABACEAE [PEA FAMILY]

*Description* This plant is mostly herbaceous, though the lower branches can be woody. Lindheimer Senna has an upright form to 3 feet high and 2 feet wide. The dark green divided leaves have a velvety texture. They measure 6 inches long by 3 inches wide overall, with 1½-inch-long oval to oblong leaflets. Clusters of 1-inch

*Senna armata* Spiny Senna

*Senna bauhinioides* Bauhin Senna

*Senna biflora* Two-flowered Senna

Above left and right: *Senna covesii* Desert Senna

Below left and right: *Senna lindheimeriana* Lindheimer Senna

yellow flowers occur at the ends of the branches from June to September. Like the foliage, the pods are velvety, with a width of ¼ inch and a length of 2 inches.

**Native Distribution** Lindheimer Senna is found in southeastern Arizona, southern New Mexico, and western Texas, as well as in Chihuahua and Tamaulipas, Mexico. Gravelly flats and hills between 4,500 and 5,500 feet in elevation are its typical habitat.

**Culture** A little extra water in summer will enhance flowering. Well-drained soil and full sun are recommended for best growth. The plant can die back to the ground below 20° F, but it will recover quickly.

**Landscape Use** The soft, velvety leaves of Lindheimer Senna are nice to touch; try planting it near walkways, patios, or swimming pools. The plant can provide splashes of color throughout a naturalistic desert landscape or in the more formal setting of a flower garden. Birds eat the seeds.

---

### *Senna purpusii* (syn., *Cassia purpusii*)
FABACEAE [PEA FAMILY]

**Description** The foliage of *Senna purpusii* is a distinctive color, dark blue-green, while the bark is gray-black. The compound leaves consist of two to four pairs of broadly oval thick and leathery leaflets, which are ½ inch long. Bright yellow ¾-inch flowers appear from February to April and again from September to November. The fleshy pods are reddish and almost ½ inch wide by 2 inches long. The evergreen shrub's mature size is 5 feet high by 5 feet wide.

**Native Distribution** This shrub is found on coastal mesas and plains and along arroyos in Baja California, Mexico.

**Culture** Full sun will encourage richly colored foliage and bright flowers. Provide *Senna purpusii* with well-drained soil and supplemental irrigation once or twice a month in the summer. Watering should be discontinued in the fall to harden off the foliage for winter. Temperatures below about 28° F can cause damage. This shrub's naturally compact form requires no pruning other than removal of dead wood or frost-damaged foliage.

**Landscape Use** *Senna purpusii* would be a good choice for a foundation planting to link structures with the landscape. This versatile shrub could also be incorporated into poolside plantings, courtyards, or naturalistic desert landscapes. It would make an attractive informal hedge.

---

### Shrubby Senna
### *Senna wislizenii* (syn., *Cassia wislizenii*)
FABACEAE [PEA FAMILY]

**Description** The rounded form of Shrubby Senna is leafless during the winter, exposing slender branches with dark-colored bark. Dark gray-green leaves 1 inch long and ½ inch wide are divided into four to six oval ¼-inch-long leaflets. From June to September, 1-inch bright yellow five-petaled flowers cluster at the ends of rigid branches. The fruit is a flattened, shiny black or dark brown pod, 3–4 inches long and ¼ inch wide. Shrubby Senna averages 6 feet high and 8 feet wide at maturity.

**Native Distribution** Southeastern Arizona, southern New Mexico, western Texas, and Sonora and Chihuahua, Mexico, comprise the natural range of Shrubby Senna. The shrub occurs on dry slopes from 3,000 to 5,000 feet in elevation.

**Culture** Shrubby Senna is quite drought tolerant once established. Occasional deep watering through the summer improves flowering and enhances the naturally slow to moderate growth rate. Although full sun is preferable, Shrubby Senna will grow in partial shade; however, the foliage and flowers will be sparser. This shrub is adaptable to various soil types, including limestone. It is cold hardy to at least 10° F.

***Landscape Use*** When it isn't blooming, Shrubby Senna is somewhat nondescript, especially after it drops its leaves. Combine it with evergreen plants that can help mask its winter dormancy yet allow it to shine during the blooming period. It can be used for a background planting or an informal hedge.

## Plains Bristlegrass
### *Setaria macrostachya*
POACEAE [GRASS FAMILY]

***Description*** From May through October, the narrow, 4-inch-long bristly seedheads that give this bunchgrass its name are borne above the 2-foot-tall plant. Thin, wiry leaves average 10 inches long and ⅓ inch wide. The blades are typically rough and hairy.

***Native Distribution*** Plains Bristlegrass occurs throughout most of Arizona, as well as in Colorado, Texas, New Mexico, and Mexico. It tends to grow on dry plains and rocky slopes and along washes, between 2,000 and 7,000 feet in elevation.

***Culture*** This grass accepts full sun or partial shade. It isn't too particular about soil type; either fine- or coarse-textured will do. Plains Bristlegrass benefits from supplemental irrigation every few weeks during hot weather. It is cold hardy to at least 0° F.

***Landscape Use*** Plains Bristlegrass has attractive seedheads that would be striking silhouetted against a plain background. The fine texture of this plant could be used as a contrast to coarse-textured plants such as Sugar Sumac (*Rhus ovata*). Plains Bristlegrass has functional uses: erosion control and food for wildlife.

## Jojoba, Goat Nut
### *Simmondsia chinensis*
SIMMONDSIACEAE [SIMMONDSIA FAMILY]

***Description*** Mature Jojoba plants develop a rounded form up to 6 feet high and 10 feet wide. Oblong, evergreen leathery leaves are gray-green, 1½ inches long, and ¾ inch wide. Arranged oppositely on rigid branches, the leaves can orient themselves vertically to reduce the amount of leaf surface exposed to summer's intense light. Botanists believe this special adaptation to the extremes of the desert also aids in flower pollination. The leaves form a sort of wind tunnel, channeling the breeze to transport pollen more effectively from the male flowers to the female flowers, which appear on separate plants. Flowering occurs anytime from December to July. Male flowers are yellow-green and form clusters the size of marbles. The solitary female flowers, also yellow-green, develop into 1-inch-long acornlike fruits. Dried scalelike sepals (flower parts that occur below the petals) enclose the dark brown edible seed. Native Americans ate the seeds raw or parched them to reduce the bitter taste, and early white settlers ground and mixed the seeds with boiled egg yolks, sugar, and milk for a coffee substitute.

***Natural Distribution*** Jojoba's natural range is between 1,500 and 5,000 feet in elevation, on gravelly slopes and along washes in southern California, southern Arizona, and Baja California and Sonora, Mexico.

***Culture*** Full sun encourages the most attractive foliage, although plants will tolerate partial shade. Moderate irrigation

Above left and right: *Senna purpusii*

*Senna wislizenii* Shrubby Senna

*Simmondsia chinensis* Jojoba

*Senna wislizenii* detail

*Setaria macrostachya*
Plains Bristlegrass

will help young plants become established; thereafter, periodic deep irrigation should be sufficient to maintain growth. Jojoba can withstand temperatures to about 15° F, though young plants may be damaged at 20° F. Young plants may be somewhat slow to establish, but they will eventually develop at a moderate rate. Soil at the planting site should be well drained. The natural growth form of Jojoba is quite attractive; however, if a more formal effect is desired, plants accept pruning. The warm months are the best time to prune; wait until late summer to prune female plants if the fruit is desired for human consumption or to attract wildlife.

*Landscape Use* Jojoba is one of the workhorse plants of desert landscapes. Tough and undemanding, it has neither flashy flowers nor unusual foliage, yet this very lack of distinction makes it a versatile plant for many landscape situations. The dense foliage is effective for creating visual screens and windbreaks. It is useful around buildings as foundation plantings, and its lack of spines also lends it to planting along walks, around patios, or near children's play areas. The medium-textured foliage sets off bold accent plants such as *Agave* species or cacti. Jojoba's tolerance of adverse conditions also suggests its use for highway medians and roadsides.

---

## Texas Mountain-laurel, Mescal Bean
### Sophora secundiflora
FABACEAE [PEA FAMILY]

*Description* This evergreen shrub grows slowly, in time becoming treelike with multiple trunks. A typical mature size is 15 feet high and 10 feet wide. Glossy dark green leaves to 5 inches long are divided into seven to nine 1-inch rounded leaflets. Large clusters of showy purple flowers hang heavy on the plant in March and April, filling the air with the fragrance of

grape soda. A fine silvery fuzz covers the woody, swollen seed pods, which are 4 inches long and ¾ inch thick. The deep orange seeds inside are poisonous, although it is unlikely that the hard pods could be penetrated.

*Native Distribution* Texas Mountain-laurel occurs in south-central and western Texas, New Mexico, and southward in Mexico to San Luis Potosí. It is typically found on limestone soils in canyons and on slopes, between 1,000 and 5,000 feet in elevation.

*Culture* Texas Mountain-laurel's normally slow growth rate can be increased by a thorough soaking several times a month in summer. However, if you're the patient sort, irrigation can be discontinued after the first or second year of establishment. Texas Mountain-laurel is hardy to near 10° F. It grows well in alkaline soil with good drainage. Choose a site in full sun. Larvae of the Pyralid Moth (*Uresiphita reversalis*) can infest the plant, feeding on young growth and the immature seed pods. *Bacillus thuringiensis*, a biological control commonly used by vegetable gardeners, has proven effective on the caterpillars. Texas Mountain-laurel's naturally shrubby form can be trained into a tree by removing the lower branches. Clip the seedpods off before they mature if you have children or pets who might try to eat the poisonous seeds.

*Landscape Use* Texas Mountain-laurel can be utilized as a small tree for tight spaces such as entry courtyards. The flowers are a very attractive feature, best appreciated at close range, where the fragrance is also most noticeable. Light-colored plants paired with Texas Mountain-laurel will accentuate its rich, deep green foliage. A magnificent informal hedge could be created by planting a row of Texas Mountain-laurel and letting the shrubs develop without shearing. The dense evergreen foliage could also be used to screen an unattractive view.

## Globemallow, Desert-mallow
### *Sphaeralcea ambigua*
MALVACEAE [MALLOW FAMILY]

*Description* Globemallow sends forth many herbaceous stems from a woody central base. The plant's overall size is 3 feet high and about as wide. In springtime, and occasionally throughout the year, 1-inch cup-shaped flowers cover the stems, opening from bottom to top. The most common flower color is orange, although white, pink, peach, lavender, and rose flowers are also seen. Globemallow's leaves are grayish green, their color lightened by whitish to yellowish hairs on the surface. Contact with the hairs can cause an allergic reaction in some people. The leaves are often three-lobed, and they are about 1 inch long and nearly as wide.

*Native Distribution* Globemallow's range extends from southeastern Utah and southern Nevada, through Arizona and southeastern California, to Baja California and Sonora, Mexico. Dry, rocky slopes and washes are preferred habitats for Globemallow. You'll also see it along roadsides. It occurs at elevations below 3,500 feet.

*Culture* Give Globemallow full sun; it will become straggly and flower sparsely in partial shade. Any type of soil is acceptable. A minimal amount of water is needed to keep established plants alive, though supplemental irrigation will promote fuller growth and more flowers. Globemallow is cold hardy. After several years plants can become ratty looking because of dead stems. Either prune away the dead growth, or shear the entire plant back after flowering to about 6 inches high.

*Landscape Use* Flowers are Globemallow's best landscape feature. Combine several plants with other flowering perennials such as *Penstemon* species and Desert-marigold (*Baileya multiradiata*) for a unique desert flower garden. Just as tall plants are used in the back of English perennial borders, Globemallow can serve as a backdrop for shorter plants. It also looks good scattered throughout natural desert plantings. Buy these plants in bloom to ensure a certain flower color, or be adventuresome—buy them anytime, and let the plants surprise you!

## Alkali Sacaton
### *Sporobolus airoides*
POACEAE [GRASS FAMILY]

*Description* Alkali Sacaton's 2- to 3-foot-high stems form dense, tough clumps that can reach a diameter of 1½ feet. The pale green leaf blades are firm and fibrous, 1 foot long by ⅛ inch wide and tapering to a long, slender tip. From May through October the perennial grass bears loose, open seedheads 15 inches long and about half as wide.

*Native Distribution* The typical habitat of Alkali Sacaton consists of flat desert areas with fine-textured, alkaline soil, and sometimes sandy washes, between 2,500 and 6,500 feet in elevation. It is native to the western United States and Mexico.

*Culture* This grass prefers a moderate amount of supplemental irrigation, but it can go for long periods without it. Soils similar to those in Alkali Sacaton's natural habitat—silty or clayey—are preferred in cultivation. Grow it in full sun. The plant's cold tolerance extends to at least -10° F. Older plants can be rejuvenated by pruning to the ground in spring.

*Landscape Use* Alkali Sacaton can grow on heavy, alkaline soils, providing erosion control as well as visual interest. The graceful seedheads are especially attractive when they sway in the breeze. A mass planting could create an interesting textural contrast to coarser-foliaged plants such as Quail Brush (*Atriplex lentiformis*). Birds eat the seeds of Alkali Sacaton.

Above left and right: *Sophora secundiflora* Texas Mountain-laurel

*Sphaeralcea ambigua* Globemallow

Above left and right: *Sporobolus airoides* var. *wrightii* Alkali Sacaton

*Sphaeralcea ambigua* detail

*Sporobolus cryptandrus* Sand Dropseed

## Sand Dropseed
### *Sporobolus cryptandrus*
POACEAE [GRASS FAMILY]

**Description** Sand Dropseed is a perennial bunchgrass to 2 feet high. Rough, blue-green leaves cure to a light straw color. The leaf blades are 4–10 inches long and ¼ inch wide. The purplish seedheads are branched but narrow, and often enclosed by the upper leaves. They average 3 inches wide by 1 foot long, and are borne from July to October.

**Native Distribution** As its name implies, Sand Dropseed often grows in sandy areas, but it also occurs on rocky slopes. The grass is found throughout most of North America, between 200 and 7,000 feet in elevation.

**Culture** A site in full sun with sandy soil is ideal for Sand Dropseed. It is very cold tolerant, to 0° F. After this grass becomes established, it requires only occasional irrigation through the warm season, perhaps every three to four weeks.

**Landscape Use** Sand Dropseed can provide erosion control on slopes. Combine it with other grasses and wildflowers for a meadow effect. Plants scattered randomly through a naturalistic landscape will lighten the overall appearance of the area.

## Tinta
### *Stegnosperma halimifolium*
PHYTOLACCACEAE [POKEBERRY FAMILY]

**Description** The thick, leathery gray-green leaves of Tinta are oval, to 1½ inches long and ¾ inch wide. Small white flowers in elongated 4-inch clusters bloom from October to May, then develop into ¼-inch red berries. These berries can stain, hence the common name Tinta. This rounded evergreen shrub reaches 6 feet in height with an 8-foot spread.

**Native Distribution** Tinta occurs in Baja California and Sonora, Mexico, and south to Central America, at low elevations along washes and on mesas and hillsides.

**Culture** Full sun and well-drained soil are recommended for Tinta. Although drought tolerant, this shrub benefits from once-a-month irrigation through the summer. It is not reliably hardy below 25° F.

**Landscape Use** Tinta can form an attractive informal hedge. The evergreen foliage could also serve as a backdrop to accent plants, particularly those with silvery-gray foliage. The red fruits are an ornamental feature that could be utilized in courtyard gardens. Planting Tinta in such a location also affords it some protection from cold weather.

## Organ Pipe Cactus
### *Stenocereus thurberi*
CACTACEAE [CACTUS FAMILY]

**Description** Many dark olive-green, 6-inch-thick stems rise from the base of Organ Pipe Cactus to a height of 15 feet. A mature plant may be 12 feet wide. Each stem has twelve to nineteen ⅓-inch-high ribs bearing numerous dark brown to black spines that turn gray with age. Three-inch funnel-shaped flowers, tinged with pink or purple, open at night and close by the next morning during April, May, and June. The Organ Pipe Cactus fruit is about the size of a tennis ball. Beneath the spiny exterior is sweet red flesh, said to taste somewhat like watermelon.

**Native Distribution** Southwestern Arizona, Baja California, and Sonora, Mexico, are home to this cactus, which grows on hillsides and desert plains up to 3,000 feet in elevation. Organ Pipe Cactus National Monument, south of Ajo in southern Arizona, has been set aside for the protection of this cactus.

*Culture*  This cactus requires well-drained soil, full sun, and relatively mild temperatures. New growth is damaged in the low 20s F. Like many cacti, Organ Pipe Cactus is slow growing. The plant can survive long periods of drought by relying on moisture in its succulent tissues. Drought stress can be reduced by giving the plant a thorough soaking once a month in summer.

*Landscape Use*  Mature specimens of Organ Pipe Cactus are very costly, if available. All Arizona cacti are protected under the Arizona Native Plant Law, so be sure your source is reputable. A legally obtained plant will have a tag from the Arizona Commission of Agriculture and Horticulture. For less expense, you can buy a younger plant propagated from seed or a cutting and enjoy watching it develop. Give the plant a prominent place in the landscape in anticipation of its eventual beauty. It is especially stunning planted among large boulders. Remember to allow it enough space to develop, and be sure to keep the spiny stems away from pedestrian areas. Organ Pipe Cactus can also be grown in containers.

---

## Yellow Bells, Yellow Trumpet Flower

### *Tecoma stans* var. *angustata*
BIGNONIACEAE [BIGNONIA FAMILY]

*Description*  Bright yellow, trumpet-shaped 2-inch-long flowers in large clusters bloom from April to November. The fruit, a dark tan papery capsule 6 inches long by ⅓ inch wide, splits open when ripe to reveal many flattened seeds with thin white wings. This deciduous shrub reaches a mature size of 5 feet high and about as wide. Yellow Bells has lush-looking bright green foliage borne on upright branches. The compound leaves have seven to thirteen lance-shaped, deeply toothed leaflets measuring 2–3 inches long and ½ inch wide.

*Native Distribution*  Yellow Bells's broad distribution includes southeastern Arizona, southern New Mexico, western Texas, Florida, Mexico, and Central and South America. It occurs at elevations from 2,000 to 5,500 feet, typically on rocky slopes and gravelly plains and along arroyos.

*Culture*  Yellow Bells suffers cold damage at about 28° F and can freeze to the ground when temperatures reach the low 20s F. The plant recovers quickly, however, and the new growth looks better and produces more flowers than before. The frozen branches can be pruned back in late winter after the danger of frost has passed. You can reduce the potential for frost damage by withholding irrigation after late summer. A deep soaking once or twice a month through the warm season keeps the foliage looking good and prolongs blooming. Yellow Bells prefers a site with well-drained soil and full sun.

*Landscape Use*  The lush foliage and showy flowers of Yellow Bells can lend a tropical feeling to poolside plantings. The plant's long blooming season also makes it useful as an accent plant in the landscape. Consider planting it as a backdrop to a bed of flowering perennials. When the plant is used near a patio, the hummingbirds attracted to the yellow flowers can be best enjoyed. Evergreen shrubs such as Desert Broom (*Baccharis sarothroides*) and Creosote Bush (*Larrea tridentata*) make good companions for Yellow Bells during its leafless period.

---

## Turpentine Broom

### *Thamnosma montana*
RUTACEAE [RUE FAMILY]

*Description*  Turpentine Broom is named for its pungent odor. The erect branches also give the shrub a broomlike appearance. It reaches 1½ feet high, with a 2-

Above left and right: *Stegnosperma halimifolium* Tinta
Opposite: *Stenocereus thurberi* Organ Pipe Cactus
*Tecoma stans var. angustata* Yellow Bells          *Thamnosma montana* Turpentine Broom

foot spread. Tiny narrow leaves ¼ inch long drop early in the season, exposing spine-tipped yellow-green branches. The dark purple funnel-shaped flowers are about ⅜ inch long. They appear at the ends of the branches from February to April. The fruit consists of two spheres joined at the base, each part ½ inch in diameter.

**Native Distribution**  Home for Turpentine Broom is southern Utah, southern Nevada, southwestern Arizona, southeastern California, and the Mexican states of Sonora and Baja California. It grows between 2,000 and 4,000 feet in elevation on gravelly slopes and mesas.

**Culture**  In cultivation, as in habitat, Turpentine Broom prefers well-drained soil. It tolerates cold to at least 15° F. Full sun is recommended. Plants will need supplemental water until they are well-established, at which time they can survive on little or no irrigation.

**Landscape Use**  Contrast Turpentine Broom's vertical branches with a low-growing plant such as Dogweed (*Dyssodia pentachaeta*). The purple and yellow flowers would make a nice color combination, too. Other interesting contrasts could be achieved with the rounded forms of Prickly-pear (*Opuntia* species) or the fine-textured foliage of shrubs such as *Acacia* species.

## Plume Tiquilia
### *Tiquilia greggii* (syn., *Coldenia greggii*)
BORAGINACEAE [BORAGE FAMILY]

**Description**  In summertime the compact, rounded form of Plume Tiquilia is smothered with ¾-inch balls of tiny pink to magenta bell-shaped flowers and purplish gray plumed seeds. The deciduous foliage is silvery-gray from a dense covering of short hairs. The leaves measure ⅓ inch long by ¼ inch wide, narrowing to a point at the tip. Plume Tiquilia grows to 2 feet high with a similar spread.

**Native Distribution**  The shrub is common on rocky limestone slopes and desert flats between 2,000 and 4,200 feet in elevation in southern New Mexico and western Texas, and in Chihuahua, Coahuila, Durango, and Zacatecas, Mexico.

**Culture**  Plume Tiquilia prefers limestone-based, well-drained soils. It grows best in full sun, with occasional water through the warm season, and is hardy to 5° F. The compact, rounded form requires no pruning.

**Landscape Use**  It is nearly impossible to resist patting the soft, fuzzy flower heads of Plume Tiquilia, so you may want to plant it in an accessible place, such as in a courtyard garden or at poolside. Another good reason to plant it near outdoor living areas is that it would become lost in a large landscape. A mass planting of Plume Tiquilia would make an excellent groundcover.

## Trixis
### *Trixis californica*
ASTERACEAE [SUNFLOWER FAMILY]

**Description**  Bright green leaves and yellow flowers combine for a striking effect in Trixis. At maturity this evergreen sub-shrub reaches 2 feet high and 2½ feet wide. The leaves are lance-shaped, about 2 inches long and ½ inch broad, with slightly toothed edges. In spring, and sometimes again in fall, clusters of ½-inch bright yellow flowers rise above the foliage. The bristly seedheads are straw-colored and somewhat showy.

**Native Distribution**  Trixis occurs in western Texas, southern New Mexico, Arizona, and southern California, and Baja

California, Sonora, and San Luis Potosí, Mexico. Arroyos, canyons, bajadas, and rocky slopes, between 2,000 and 5,000 feet in elevation, are this plant's habitats.

**Culture** Temperatures in the low 20s F can damage Trixis foliage. Regrowth is rapid, however. Very drought tolerant, but appreciative of supplemental summer irrigation, the plant can grow in the hottest locations. Shade makes it leggy. Well-drained soil is the best for Trixis. If the foliage becomes sparse near the base, prune the plant severely to rejuvenate. Do it after blooming, or anytime during the summer, but not in fall, which would stimulate cold-tender growth.

**Landscape Use** A mass planting of Trixis will create a showy display of color in springtime. The plants can also be scattered among other desert plants such as Creosote Bush (*Larrea tridentata*) and Palo Verde (*Cercidium* species) for a naturalistic landscape. The compact form of Trixis makes it useful for small areas. Its attractive foliage and pretty flowers suggest its use in a flower garden with plants such as Blackfoot Daisy (*Melampodium leucanthum*), Globemallow (*Sphaeralcea ambigua*), or *Penstemon* species.

## Mexican-buckeye
### *Ungnadia speciosa*
SAPINDACEAE [SOAPBERRY FAMILY]

**Description** The fruits of Mexican-buckeye look somewhat like those of the unrelated horsechestnut or buckeye tree (*Aesculus* species), hence the common name. At maturity the fruit is light brown, woody, and three-lobed, to 2 inches across. The black seeds within are poisonous. Mexican-buckeye is winter deciduous, the leaves reappearing just after the clusters of small, fragrant pink flowers bloom in spring. Gray bark is a nice contrast to the rich, deep green leaves. They are about 4 inches long by 3 inches wide, divided into three to seven leaflets. In the fall the leaves often turn yellow. This large shrub or small tree can grow to 15 feet high and about as wide.

**Native Distribution** Mexican-buckeye is usually found on rocky slopes and ridges and in canyons, between 1,000 and 6,500 feet in elevation. Its range includes central, southern, and western Texas, southern New Mexico, and northern Mexico.

**Culture** Full sun to partial shade is acceptable to Mexican-buckeye. It is drought tolerant once established, making summer irrigation optional. It will grow in a wide range of soil types, provided they are well drained. Plants are hardy to about 5° F and fast growing. The lower branches can be pruned to encourage a tree form. Left to develop naturally, Mexican-buckeye becomes an attractive large rounded shrub.

**Landscape Use** Use Mexican-buckeye as a specimen tree in the landscape, highlighting its attractive flowers and foliage, or plant it in a courtyard, patio, or entry area. The winter bareness will be less noticeable if you incorporate some evergreen plants into the design along with Mexican-buckeye. Let the plant retain its natural shrub form, and the dense foliage can shade southern or western walls in summer yet allow the sun's warmth to penetrate in winter.

## Chisos Rosewood, Narrowleaf Vauquelinia
### *Vauquelinia angustifolia*
ROSACEAE [ROSE FAMILY]

**Description** The 4-inch-long, ¼-inch wide finely toothed evergreen leaves of Chisos Rosewood sway gently with the slightest breeze. A color and textural contrast to

Above left and right: *Tiquilia greggii* Plume Tiquilia

Below left and right: *Trixis californica* Trixis

*Ungnadia speciosa* Mexican-buckeye

Below left and right: *Vauquelinia angustifolia* Chisos Rosewood

the deep green, glossy foliage is provided by the chestnut brown rough bark of older branches. Chisos Rosewood can grow to a height of 15 feet and a width of 10 feet. Dense flat-topped clusters of fragrant white flowers perfume the air from June to August. Each flower produces a fuzzy, woody capsule about ¼ inch long.

**Native Distribution**  In southwestern Texas, as well as in Mexico from Coahuila and Chihuahua to Hidalgo, Chisos Rosewood grows on rocky slopes and in canyons. The elevational range is 3,800–6,500 feet.

**Culture**  Chisos Rosewood prefers full sun in all but the hottest low-elevation desert areas, where morning sun only or filtered shade are best. After two to three years of supplemental irrigation to aid establishment, you can decrease the water to one or two deep soakings a month in the summer. Well-drained soil is preferred. Prune only to remove dead wood.

**Landscape Use**  Chisos Rosewood is useful for screening. Its glossy dark green foliage also could be used as a backdrop to plants with contrasting colors or textures such as *Agave* or *Yucca* species. The foliage could lend a tropical feeling to patio or courtyard plantings.

---

## Arizona Rosewood
### *Vauquelinia californica*
ROSACEAE [ROSE FAMILY]

**Description**  Arizona Rosewood derives its name from the color of the heartwood: light brown to red or deep brown. The plant develops into a large erect shrub or small tree, 14 feet high and 10 feet wide. Stiff leathery leaves are dark green, about 2 inches long by ½ inch wide, and edged with tiny teeth. In May and June, 3-inch-wide flat-topped clusters of tiny white flowers adorn Arizona Rosewood. Brown to rust-colored, semi-woody fruits develop from the flowers and sometimes persist into winter.

**Native Distribution**  Canyons and hillsides of the upper desert and lower chaparral, between 2,500 and 5,000 feet in elevation, are typical habitat for Arizona Rosewood. It ranges from southern Arizona to Baja California and Sonora, Mexico.

**Culture**  The growth rate of young plants is somewhat slow, but as the roots become established growth speeds up. Deep watering once a month in summertime will help maintain growth. Arizona Rosewood prefers good drainage, although it is tolerant of poor soil and alkalinity. Full sun is best, but light shade is acceptable. Established plants are cold hardy to 15° F, but tender new growth can be damaged by a hard freeze. Pruning shouldn't be necessary unless you wish to train Arizona Rosewood into a tree, which will require some removal of lower branches. Sometimes spider mites infest the plant; however, damage is usually not significant enough to warrant control.

**Landscape Use**  Arizona Rosewood's dense evergreen growth makes a good hedge for privacy or to control wind and muffle unwanted noise. It is an excellent native alternative to Oleander (*Nerium oleander*). Trained into a tree form, it would work well in a courtyard or near a pool. It can be utilized as an accent plant or play a supporting role, providing background to other accent plants with contrasting foliage color.

---

## Goldeneye
### *Viguiera deltoidea*
ASTERACEAE [SUNFLOWER FAMILY]

**Description**  Yellow daisylike flowers 1 inch or more across brighten the medium green foliage of Goldeneye in springtime. The shrub develops a mounded form 3 feet high and equally wide. Rough hairs cover the 1-inch-long evergreen leaves, making them feel like sandpaper. The leaves are deltoid—broad at the base, narrowing to a point at the tip.

**Native Distribution** Goldeneye occurs in southern Nevada, southeastern California and Arizona, and in Baja California and Sonora, Mexico. It is usually found between elevations of 1,000 and 3,500 feet along arroyos, on dry plains, and on rocky slopes.

**Culture** Young plants can be damaged by temperatures in the range of 25° to 28° F. Established plants are more tolerant of cold and drought. They can survive on natural rainfall, but in a landscape setting irrigation every few weeks through the summer is recommended for a better appearance. Goldeneye needs full sun to develop properly. The preferred soil type is well drained. Lanky plants can be pruned after the spring flowering.

**Landscape Use** The moderate size of Goldeneye makes it useful in a number of landscape situations. You might place it near the house as a foundation planting to link the structure to its site. Along walkways, near patios, or at poolside, the attractive yellow flowers will be most noticeable. Try combining Goldeneye with Brittlebush (*Encelia farinosa*) in a mass planting; the similarity in size and form makes the plants visually compatible, yet the contrast between the green and gray foliage creates interest. Goldeneye can also stand on its own as an accent plant. Non-residential landscape applications could include highway medians or parking lot planting strips.

---

## Skeletonleaf Goldeneye
### *Viguiera stenoloba*
ASTERACEAE [SUNFLOWER FAMILY]

**Description** Bright green threadlike foliage is a beautiful backdrop for the 1-inch

yellow daisylike flowers that Skeletonleaf Goldeneye produces throughout warm weather. The many-branched evergreen shrub typically reaches a height and spread of 3 feet.

**Native Distribution** Southwestern Texas and southern New Mexico, Chihuahua, Coahuila, Durango, Nuevo León, and Tamaulipas, Mexico, are home to Skeletonleaf Goldeneye. The elevational range is 2,000–6,200 feet, while the topography varies from plains to dry, rocky slopes.

**Culture** Skeletonleaf Goldeneye prefers full sun. It will accept partial shade, with a slight reduction in flowering and sparser foliage. Plants are very drought tolerant once established, and summer irrigation is optional; excessive watering can result in rangy growth. A wide range of soil types is acceptable, though good drainage is important. Skeletonleaf Goldeneye is hardy to around 10° F. For a neater appearance, you may want to trim the flower stalks after they bloom. A compact growth form can be maintained by cutting the plant back severely once or twice a year during the warm season.

**Landscape Use** Skeletonleaf Goldeneye's foliage differs both in color and texture from most other desert plants, so a number of contrasting combinations could be achieved. Patio, courtyard, or poolside plantings of Skeletonleaf Goldeneye would allow its attractive features to be appreciated at close range. You can use the shrub individually as an accent or mass several plants for a dramatic display. The soft green foliage and pretty flowers would be right at home in a flower garden with other drought-tolerant plants such as *Penstemon* species or *Salvia* species. Because of its moderate size, Skeletonleaf Goldeneye can be utilized in medians, parking lot planting strips, and even planter boxes.

Above left and right: *Vauquelinia californica* Arizona Rosewood

*Viguiera deltoidea* Goldeneye

## Mojave Aster

### *Xylorhiza tortifolia* (syn., *Machaeranthera tortifolia*)
ASTERACEAE [SUNFLOWER]

**Description** The lance-shaped leaves of Mojave Aster are 2 inches long and ½ inch wide. Their rough, leathery texture and toothed edges make the pale lavender flowers seem fragile in contrast. Fifty or more long, slender petals surround a yellow center; 4 inches is an average diameter of the flower heads. Mojave Aster blooms from March to May, and sometimes again in October, depending on rainfall. The grayish, leafy stems are herbaceous, but the base is usually woody. At maturity, Mojave Aster reaches a height of 1–2 feet, with a similar spread.

**Native Distribution** Mojave Aster grows in southern Nevada, southwestern Utah, western Arizona, and southeastern California, on rocky slopes and desert flats, between 2,000 and 5,500 feet in elevation.

**Culture** A site with full sun and well-drained soil is ideal for Mojave Aster. It tolerates cold to 20° F. A deep soaking twice a month through the summer will promote flowering in the fall.

**Landscape Use** This predominantly spring-flowering plant can brighten a flower garden or wildflower meadow. At other times of the year, the distinctive leaves can create interest. An interesting effect could be achieved by mingling Mojave Aster's sharply toothed foliage with cacti and other succulents.

spectacular white bell-shaped flowers are borne in large clusters. The flower cluster can be 2 feet tall and is often partially enclosed within the rosette of leaves. Banana Yucca blooms between April and June for about two weeks. The leaves are stiff and bluish green, 1½ to 2 inches wide and 2 feet long. They usually end in a spine and often have coarse, curling fibers along the edges. Banana Yucca can be single-stemmed or form multiple-headed clumps reaching 4 feet high and 6 feet across.

**Native Distribution** Banana Yucca grows on grasslands and dry, rocky slopes, between 2,000 and 7,000 feet in elevation. It has a wide distribution, from southeastern California, southern Utah, and southern Nevada, to southwestern Colorado, Texas, Arizona, and New Mexico. In Mexico, it occurs from Coahuila to Tamaulipas, and south to Querétaro.

**Culture** One of the toughest native plants used in landscaping, Banana Yucca is very drought-tolerant and cold hardy. Soil at the planting site should be coarse and well drained. Full sun is necessary for best growth.

**Landscape Use** Banana Yucca can lend a distinct Southwestern flavor to the landscape. Its coarse, spiky appearance contrasts well with fine-textured trees and shrubs. It could also be used on its own as an accent plant. Beneath a window, the plant's intimidating appearance can discourage intruders. On the other hand, be sure to keep the pointed leaves away from walkways, patios, or play areas.

## Banana Yucca

### *Yucca baccata*
LILIACEAE [LILY FAMILY]

**Description** Banana Yucca's fruits look like short green bananas, about 5 inches long and 2 inches in diameter. The

## Joshua Tree

### *Yucca brevifolia*
LILIACEAE [LILY FAMILY]

**Description** One of the most distinctive plants of the Mojave Desert, Joshua Tree was so named by early Mormon settlers

274

*Viguiera stenoloba* Skeletonleaf Goldeneye

*Yucca baccata* Banana Yucca

*Xylorhiza tortifolia* Mojave Aster

*Yucca brevifolia* Joshua Tree

because its branches brought to mind the prophet Joshua with his arms outstretched to the heavens. Joshua Tree is a massive treelike plant, reaching a height of 30 feet. The trunk can be 2 feet in diameter, branching 4–10 feet above ground. Stout stems are thickly covered with rigid light green leaves. Joshua Tree differs from other yuccas in having tiny teeth along its leaf edges. The leaves, ½ inch broad and up to 12 inches long, end in a sharp point. Older, dried leaves cling to the branches, creating a thatch, and eventually drop to reveal gray corky bark. Beginning in March and continuing through April, Joshua Tree's branches are crowned with dense, heavy 1-foot-long clusters of cream to pale green flowers. Following the bloom, black seeds develop within 3-inch-long capsules.

**Native Distribution** Joshua Tree's range includes southwestern Utah, southern Nevada, northwestern Arizona, and southeastern California. It grows on dry mesas and gravelly slopes, from 2,000 to 5,000 feet in elevation.

**Culture** Slow growing and extremely drought tolerant, Joshua Tree withstands cold to 10° F but has trouble with the summer temperatures in the low desert areas. Supplemental water can help make the heat more tolerable. Well-drained soil is preferred, along with full sun. Insect pests and diseases are generally not a problem, although one insect plays a key role in Joshua Tree's life cycle. The female yucca moth (*Pronuba yuccasella*) gathers pollen from one flower, then deposits her eggs and the pollen in a flower on another plant. This arrangement benefits both plant and moth; the flowers are pollinated, and the yucca moth larvae are ensured a steady food supply by eating some, but not all, of the developing seeds.

**Landscape Use** Joshua Tree creates a striking silhouette in any landscape. The contrast in form between this plant and broad-canopied trees, spreading shrubs, and cacti such as Prickly-pear (*Opuntia* species) or Barrel Cactus (*Ferocactus* species) can be very effective. Be careful when locating Joshua Tree in the landscape; keep its sharp-pointed leaves away from pedestrian or play areas. And remember, although it is a slow grower, eventually it will become a sizeable plant, so leave ample room for growth.

## Soaptree Yucca
### Yucca elata
LILIACEAE [LILY FAMILY]

**Description** A single- or multiple-branched trunk to 15 feet high bears grasslike leaves, with fibers curling from the white margins. Soaptree Yucca can reach a width of 8–10 feet. The blue-green leaves are about 24 inches long and less than 1 inch wide, terminating in a sharp point. Old leaves hang on the trunk as a straw-colored thatch. A tall, slender flower stalk emerges from the foliage in late spring and eventually opens into a magnificent cluster of white bell-shaped flowers. Dry, woody capsules 2–3 inches long and 1–2 inches in diameter develop from the flowers.

**Native Distribution** Soaptree Yucca occurs from Arizona and southern Utah to New Mexico and western Texas, and also in Sonora, Chihuahua, and Coahuila, Mexico. At elevations from 1,500 to 6,000 feet, this plant is most abundant on desert plains, hills, and grasslands.

**Culture** Good drainage is an important element in successfully growing Soaptree Yucca. Once established, it is very drought tolerant, although several deep soakings during the summer will help maintain a moderate growth rate. Too much water, particularly in winter, can be fatal. The plant does best in full sun; light shade is tolerable. It is very cold hardy. Resist the urge to "tidy-up" Soaptree Yucca by pulling off the dead leaves. The thatch provides protection from sunburn, cold, and insect infestation.

*Landscape Use* Soaptree Yucca is a dramatic accent plant, its graceful form somewhat reminiscent of a palm. A plain background emphasizes the plant's silhouette. You might use Soaptree Yucca as the focal point of a desert planting, surrounded by low-growing plants and shrubs with contrasting colors and textures. Keep the sharp-pointed leaves a safe distance from pedestrians. Soaptree Yucca is the state flower of New Mexico.

## Faxon Yucca, Spanish Bayonet
### *Yucca faxoniana* (syn., *Yucca carnerosana*)
LILIACEAE [LILY FAMILY]

*Description* A large cluster of 2½-foot-long, 2-inch-wide leaves tops the 15-foot-high, 8-foot-wide form of Faxon Yucca. The trunk is usually unbranched, 1 foot wide or more, and covered with a thatch of dead leaves. Faxon Yucca's showy flower cluster is carried just above the foliage anytime between March and July. The 3- to 4-foot-high cluster is composed of many 3-inch white flowers. A reddish brown to black capsule, 3 inches long by 1½ inches wide, develops from the flowers.

*Native Distribution* Faxon Yucca occurs between 2,700 and 6,700 feet in elevation on plains or rocky slopes in western Texas and in Coahuila, San Luis Potosí, Zacatecas, and Chihuahua, Mexico.

*Culture* Drought and cold tolerance are among the attributes of Faxon Yucca. It can withstand temperatures to at least 10° F. Provide a planting site with full sun and well-drained soil. Allow the dried leaves to remain, as the thatch provides some protection from climatic extremes and pests.

*Landscape Use* This yucca would be a stunning focal point in a large-scale landscape but would overpower small areas. A strong contrast in forms could be achieved by combining Faxon Yucca and Prickly-pear (*Opuntia* species), or you can plant fine-textured shrubs and groundcovers nearby to emphasize the bold form of the yucca. Faxon Yucca adorns some highways in western Texas, a landscape use that is effective because the plant's large size creates an impact even when viewed from a fast-moving car.

## Blue Yucca
### *Yucca rigida*
LILIACEAE [LILY FAMILY]

*Description* Mature specimens of Blue Yucca are usually branched in the upper portion, spreading to 5 feet and reaching 12 feet in height. The powder blue leaves are stiff and sharp-tipped, to 2 feet long and 1 inch wide. As the plant grows, the lower leaves dry and remain on the trunk, forming a thatch. In early summer, 2-foot-high, 1-foot-wide clusters of white flowers emerge from the spiky rosette of leaves. Woody capsules about 2 inches long and an inch wide develop from the flowers.

*Native Distribution* Blue Yucca grows between 3,300 and 5,500 feet in elevation on rocky hillsides in Chihuahua, Coahuila, Durango, and Zacatecas, Mexico.

*Culture* This yucca is very cold hardy, to at least 10° F. It tolerates a wide range of soils, provided they are well drained. Once established, Blue Yucca can survive on minimal water. Full sun is recommended. The thatch of dried leaves is not detrimental to the plant's health, and should be left on for the most natural appearance.

*Landscape Use* Blue Yucca's striking coloration makes it an outstanding accent plant. Low shrubs such as Bur-sage

*Yucca elata* Soaptree Yucca

*Yucca rigida* Blue Yucca

Opposite: *Y. rostrata* Beaked Yucca

Below left and right: *Yucca faxoniana* Faxon Yucca

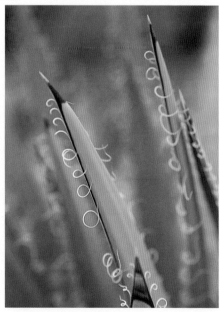

(*Ambrosia deltoidea*) or Fairy Duster (*Calliandra eriophylla*) could be used at the base of the plant to counterbalance its vertical form. A background of dark foliage, such as Velvet Mesquite (*Prosopis velutina*), would best showcase the blue leaves. Keep the plant a safe distance from walkways and patios.

## Beaked Yucca
### *Yucca rostrata* (syn., *Yucca thompsoniana*)
LILIACEAE [LILY FAMILY]

**Description**  The 2-foot-long, ½-inch-wide blue-green leaves of Beaked Yucca radiate outward to a symmetrical, elongated sphere. The trunk may or may not branch near the top. Ultimately, Beaked Yucca reaches about 12 feet high, with a spread of 2½ feet. The dried leaves persist as a thatch, sometimes to the ground. March and April bring the 2-foot-long, 1-foot-wide clusters of white flowers, which rise above the foliage on 2-foot stalks. The common name refers to the beaked capsule, which is 2 inches long and 1 inch wide.

**Native Distribution**  Beaked Yucca is found in canyons and on rocky slopes in southwestern Texas and the Mexican states of Coahuila and Chihuahua.

**Culture**  Beaked Yucca grows best in well-drained soil with full sun. It is very drought tolerant once established. You could give it supplemental water during prolonged drought; otherwise, rainfall will suffice. This slow-growing yucca is cold hardy to 10° F or lower. Some plants sold in nurseries have the dried leaves clipped back to the trunk. This creates an entirely different look, and it doesn't really do harm, but you'll achieve a much more natural appearance by letting the leaves remain as a thatch.

**Landscape Use**  Year-round sculptural interest can be provided in the landscape by Beaked Yucca. The springtime display of large flower clusters adds to the drama. This yucca could be utilized in a cactus and succulent garden or in a mixed desert planting. If you use it near patios, walkways, or swimming pools, keep the sharp leaves a safe distance from people.

## Mojave Yucca
### *Yucca schidigera*
LILIACEAE [LILY FAMILY]

**Description**  Mojave Yucca develops a woody trunk, either single- or multiple-branched. Mature size is 10–12 feet high and 6 feet wide. The tough gray-green leaves have curling fibers along the edges and end in a sharp point; they measure 3 feet long and 1½ inches wide. Large clusters of purple-tinged white 1½-inch-long flowers appear on a stalk just above the foliage in March and April. The fleshy green fruits are 3 inches long and 1½ inches thick.

**Native Distribution**  Mojave Yucca is widespread throughout the Mojave Desert, in other parts of southern California nearly to the coast, and in Baja California, Mexico. It grows along washes, on dry, rocky slopes, and on mesas, below 5,000 feet in elevation.

**Culture**  Provide Mojave Yucca with well-drained soil and full sunlight. It is hardy to at least 12° F. Once established, this yucca is drought tolerant. An occasional watering will help it through the summers of the hottest desert areas.

**Landscape Use**  You can feature Mojave Yucca as an accent plant, surrounded by low-growing, fine-textured shrubs for contrast, or you can use it in a cactus and succulent garden. The plant's pointed leaves can be useful in security barriers;

just be sure that attribute doesn't become a hazard near walkways or patios. Birds and small mammals like the fleshy fruits and the seeds within.

## Torrey Yucca, Shag Yucca
*Yucca treculeana* (syn., *Yucca torreyi*)
LILIACEAE [LILY FAMILY]

*Description* Torrey Yucca forms a trunk to 12 feet high with 3-foot-long, 1½-inch-wide leaves in a cluster as large as 8 feet across. The leaves have a sharp point and tough fibers along the margins. A large cluster of white bell-shaped flowers is produced between March and May, followed by fruits 3 inches long and 1 inch thick.

*Native Distribution* This yucca is common in western Texas, southern New Mexico, and northern Texas, at elevations from 3,500 to 5,000 feet. It grows on plains, slopes, and mesas.

*Culture* Torrey Yucca requires well-drained soil and full sun for best growth. It is very drought tolerant once established, with a slow to moderate growth rate. Temperatures to at least 15° F pose no threat to this plant. The dried lower leaves can look shaggy, but they provide protection from sunburn, cold, and insect pests, so it's best to leave them.

*Landscape Use* Desert birds such as Scott's Orioles sometimes nest in this yucca. The coarse, spiky foliage can be used to contrast with finer-textured plants, or you can silhouette Torrey Yucca against a plain background. It can be grouped with other succulents and cacti to create a focal point with real desert flavor. A cluster of plants along property lines could discourage trespassers.

## Tree Yucca, Datilillo
*Yucca valida*
LILIACEAE [LILY FAMILY]

*Description* The treelike form of this yucca can be single- or multiple-trunked, to a height of 15 feet and a spread of 5–10 feet. Yellowish green leaves average 10 inches long and ¾ inch wide. The rigid, sharp-tipped leaves are softened by whitish threads along the margins. A thatch of dead leaves typically persists for about 5 feet below the living foliage. In March and April, Tree Yucca's creamy white bell-shaped flowers appear in 1-foot-long clusters atop the branches. They have a faint fragrance similar to dill.

*Native Distribution* Tree Yucca occurs only in southern Baja California, Mexico, where it grows on slopes and sandy to rocky plains.

*Culture* Tree Yucca's ability to thrive in a landscape setting is determined in part by the cold it must endure. Generally, temperatures as low as 25° F pose no problem. Well-drained soil and full sun are preferred. This yucca, like most of the other species, is very drought tolerant. Once established, it requires water only during extended drought.

*Landscape Use* The distinctive form of Tree Yucca could serve as a focal point in a mixed desert planting or in a cactus and succulent garden. Silhouetting the plant against a plain background would show it off most effectively. Keep in mind the plant's mature size and sharp leaves when choosing a location.

*Yucca schidigera* Mojave Yucca

*Yucca treculeana* Torrey Yucca

*Yucca valida* Tree Yucca

*Yucca whipplei* Our Lord's Candle

*Zinnia acerosa* Desert Zinnia

*Zinnia grandiflora* Prairie Zinnia

*Zizyphus obtusifolia* Gray Thorn

## Our Lord's Candle
### *Yucca whipplei*
LILIACEAE [LILY FAMILY]

*Description* Slender, stiff gray-green leaves 1½ feet long and ¾ inch wide radiate from a central base into a handsome rosette 2 feet high and 3 feet across. Our Lord's Candle sends up an 8-foot-high flower stalk, laden with 1- to 2-inch-long fragrant white bell-shaped flowers, from April to June. The ripening of 1½-inch fruiting capsules begins the plant's decline. Like the genus *Agave*, this species of yucca dies after flowering. New plants can develop from seed or sometimes from offsets.

*Native Distribution* Our Lord's Candle is found mostly in chaparral vegetation, though it does occur in the desert at elevations from 1,000 to 4,000 feet. It grows on hillsides in northwestern Arizona, southern California, and adjacent Baja California, Mexico.

*Culture* Full sun to partial shade (especially in the hottest desert areas) is recommended for this yucca. It is very drought tolerant, and it can withstand cold temperatures to about 10° F. Well-drained soil is preferred. The growth rate is slow to moderate.

*Landscape Use* Our Lord's Candle is stunning in bloom, and the foliage also is attractive. It could be used as an accent plant, complemented by small-leaved shrubs. The plant would add interest to a cactus and succulent garden. Allow plenty of space between the sharp-tipped foliage and pedestrian areas.

---

## Desert Zinnia, Spinyleaf Zinnia
### *Zinnia acerosa*
ASTERACEAE [SUNFLOWER FAMILY]

*Description* White flowers an inch across bloom profusely in the spring, and to a lesser extent through summer and fall.

The petals persist, becoming papery and light tan. Desert Zinnia's base and taproot (main root that grows straight down) are woody, while the herbaceous branches are covered with gray-green, needlelike ½-inch leaves. This plant is typically 6 inches high with a spread of 10 inches.

*Native Distribution* Desert Zinnia occurs in southern Arizona, southern New Mexico, and western Texas, and in Sonora, Chihuahua, Coahuila, Durango, Nuevo León, Zacatecas, and San Luis Potosí, Mexico. Preferred habitat includes desert plains, rocky slopes, and grasslands, between 2,000 and 5,000 feet in elevation.

*Culture* This attractive plant prefers full sun, supplemental irrigation every two weeks or so through the summer, and well-drained soil. Desert Zinnia is relatively cold hardy, to about 10° F.

*Landscape Use* Desert Zinnia's low mounded form can be used along walkways, near a pool, in courtyard or flower gardens, and throughout naturalistic plantings. The light-colored foliage and white flowers can get lost against a light background, so combine it with dark-foliaged plants or colorful flowers, or let the plant spill over a dark paved surface such as brick.

---

## Prairie Zinnia
### *Zinnia grandiflora*
ASTERACEAE [SUNFLOWER FAMILY]

*Description* Prairie Zinnia blooms from May through October with daisylike, yellow-orange 1-inch flowers. The green needlelike leaves, 1 inch long and ⅛ inch wide, cover the low mounded form of Prairie Zinnia. The subshrub spreads by rhizomes (creeping underground stems) to 10 inches wide and 6–8 inches high.

**Native Distribution**  The natural range of Prairie Zinnia includes Kansas, Colorado, Texas, New Mexico, and Arizona, and Chihuahua, Coahuila, Durango, and Zacatecas, Mexico. It prefers dry slopes and mesas from 2,600 to 6,000 feet in elevation.

**Culture**  Provide Prairie Zinnia with full sun, well-drained soil, and supplemental water twice a month in the summer to extend the blooming period. It withstands temperatures to 0° F without damage.

**Landscape Use**  Prairie Zinnia makes a nice addition to a flower garden. Its compact form could be used for borders along walkways, or simply tucked into small spaces. The plant's spreading habit makes it useful for planting on slopes for erosion control.

Texas, New Mexico, and Arizona, and southward in Mexico to San Luis Potosí and Veracruz.

**Culture**  Give plants full sun and well-drained soil. Gray Thorn is cold hardy to 15° F. The growth rate will vary from slow to moderate, depending on soil conditions and water availability. After becoming established, the plant can survive on rainfall.

**Landscape Use**  Gray Thorn's primary value in the landscape is for attracting wildlife. The fruits are a favorite food of birds and small mammals, while the thorny branches provide good shelter for nesting. Gray Thorn could be used in a naturalistic landscape, intermingled in a random way with other desert shrubs and trees. The plant's thorniness could be used to advantage for a security barrier.

## Gray Thorn
### *Zizyphus obtusifolia*
RHAMNACEAE [BUCKTHORN FAMILY]

**Description**  Gray Thorn is a rather descriptive common name for this rigidly branched deciduous shrub. The green stems are covered with a grayish waxlike coating and usually end in a stout thorn. Grayish green leaves are oval to linear, about ½ inch long and ¼ inch wide. The flowers are tiny and inconspicuous, while the fruit is blue-black and oval-shaped, ¼ inch long and ⅛ inch wide. Flowering and fruiting both occur in summer. A mature plant can reach 6 feet in height with an 8-foot spread.

**Native Distribution**  Gray Thorn grows on dry plains, mesas, and slopes between 1,000 and 5,000 feet in elevation. *Zizyphus obtusifolia* variety *canescens* occurs in Arizona, Nevada, and California, plus Sonora and Baja California, Mexico, while *Zizyphus obtusifolia* variety *obtusifolia* occurs in Oklahoma, much of

# Appendix A. Plant Selection Guide

CONSULT CHAPTER 5 FOR DETAILED PLANT
DESCRIPTIONS.

### EVERGREEN TREES

*Acacia farnesiana* Sweet Acacia
*Cercidium praecox* Palo Brea
*Lysiloma candida* White Bark Acacia
*Olneya tesota* Ironwood

### DECIDUOUS TREES

*Acacia schaffneri* Twisted Acacia
*Acacia willardiana* Palo Blanco
*Bursera microphylla* Elephant Tree
*Canotia holacantha* Crucifixion Thorn
*Cercidium floridum* Blue Palo Verde
*Cercidium microphyllum* Littleleaf Palo Verde
*Chilopsis linearis* Desert-willow
*Leucaena retusa* Golden Ball Lead Tree
*Pithecellobium mexicanum* Mexican-ebony
*Prosopis glandulosa* var. *glandulosa* Honey Mesquite
*Prosopis pubescens* Screwbean Mesquite
*Prosopis velutina* Velvet Mesquite

### EVERGREEN SHRUBS

*Acacia berlandieri* Guajillo
*Ambrosia ambrosioides* Giant Bur-sage
*Ambrosia deltoidea* Bur-sage
*Ambrosia dumosa* White Bur-sage
*Artemisia filifolia* Sand Sagebrush
*Asclepias linaria* Pineleaf Milkweed
*Atriplex acanthocarpa* Tubercled Saltbush
*Atriplex canescens* Fourwing Saltbush
*Atriplex hymenelytra* Desert-holly
*Atriplex obovata* Obovateleaf Saltbush
*Baccharis sarothroides* Desert Broom
*Berberis haematocarpa* Red Barberry
*Berberis trifoliolata* Agarita
*Buddleia marrubifolia* Woolly Butterfly Bush
*Calliandra californica* Baja Fairy Duster

*Calliandra eriophylla* Fairy Duster
*Celtis pallida* Desert Hackberry
*Chrysothamnus nauseosus* Rabbitbrush
*Condalia globosa* Bitter Condalia
*Condalia warnockii* Warnock Condalia
*Dalea bicolor* var. *argyraea* Silver Dalea
*Dalea bicolor* var. *orcuttiana* Baja Dalea
*Dalea pulchra* Bush Dalea
*Dalea versicolor* var. *sessilis* Wislizenus Dalea
*Diospyros texana* Texas Persimmon
*Dodonaea viscosa* Hopbush
*Encelia farinosa* Brittlebush
*Encelia frutescens* Green Brittlebush
*Ephedra antisyphilitica* Joint-fir
*Ephedra aspera* Joint-fir
*Ephedra californica* Joint-fir
*Ephedra nevadensis* Joint-fir
*Ephedra trifurca* Joint-fir
*Ephedra viridis* Joint-fir
*Ericameria laricifolia* Turpentine Bush
*Eriogonum fasciculatum* var. *poliofolium* Flattop Buckwheat
*Eriogonum wrightii* Wright Buckwheat
*Fallugia paradoxa* Apache Plume
*Flourensia cernua* Tarbush
*Fraxinus greggii* Gregg Ash
*Garrya wrightii* Wright Silktassel
*Guaiacum angustifolium* Guayacan
*Guaiacum coulteri* Guayacan
*Gutierrezia sarothrae* Snakeweed
*Hyptis emoryi* Desert-lavender
*Isomeris arborea* Bladderpod
*Jatropha cuneata* Leatherplant
*Justicia candicans* Red Justicia
*Larrea tridentata* Creosote Bush
*Leucophyllum candidum* Violet Silverleaf
*Leucophyllum candidum* 'Silver Cloud'
*Leucophyllum frutescens* Texas Ranger
*Leucophyllum frutescens* 'Green Cloud'
*Leucophyllum frutescens* 'White Cloud'
*Leucophyllum frutescens* var. *compactum*
*Leucophyllum laevigatum* Chihuahuan-sage

*Leucophyllum minus* Big Bend Silverleaf
*Leucophyllum zygophyllum* Blue Ranger
*Lysiloma microphylla* var. *thornberi* Desert-fern
*Mortonia scabrella* Rough Mortonia
*Parthenium argentatum* Guayule
*Parthenium incanum* Mariola
*Peucephyllum schottii* Desert-fir
*Quercus turbinella* Scrub Oak
*Rhamnus californica* ssp. *ursina* California Buckthorn
*Rhus ovata* Sugar Sumac
*Rhus virens* Evergreen Sumac
*Ruellia peninsularis* Ruellia
*Ruellia californica* Ruellia
*Salvia greggii* Autumn Sage
*Salvia mohavensis* Mojave Sage
*Sapium biloculare* Mexican Jumping-bean
*Senna purpusii*
*Simmondsia chinensis* Jojoba
*Sophora secundiflora* Texas Mountain-laurel
*Stegnosperma halimifolium* Tinta
*Vauquelinia angustifolia* Chisos Rosewood
*Vauquelinia californica* Arizona Rosewood
*Viguiera deltoidea* Goldeneye
*Viguiera stenoloba* Skeletonleaf Goldeneye

### DECIDUOUS SHRUBS

*Acacia constricta* Whitethorn Acacia
*Acacia greggii* Catclaw Acacia
*Acacia millefolia* Santa Rita Acacia
*Acacia neovernicosa* Viscid Acacia
*Acacia rigidula* Blackbrush Acacia
*Acacia roemeriana* Roemer Acacia
*Acacia schottii* Schott Acacia
*Acacia wrightii* Wright Acacia
*Aloysia gratissima* Whitebrush
*Aloysia wrightii* Oreganillo
*Anisacanthus quadrifidus* var. *wrightii* Flame Anisacanthus
*Anisacanthus thurberi* Desert-honeysuckle
*Asclepias subulata* Desert Milkweed
*Atriplex lentiformis* Quail Brush
*Atriplex polycarpa* Desert Saltbush
*Cordia parvifolia* Littleleaf Cordia
*Coursetia glandulosa* Coursetia
*Dalea formosa* Feather Dalea
*Dalea frutescens* Black Dalea

*Erythrina flabelliformis* Southwest Coral Bean
*Forestiera neomexicana* Desert-olive
*Fouquieria macdougalii* Mexican Tree Ocotillo
*Fouquieria splendens* Ocotillo
*Hymenoclea monogyra* Burrobrush
*Hymenoclea salsola* Burrobrush
*Jatropha cardiophylla* Limber Bush
*Jatropha dioica* Leatherstem
*Justicia californica* Chuparosa
*Koeberlinia spinosa* Allthorn
*Lycium andersonii* Anderson Thornbush
*Lycium berlandieri* Berlandier Wolfberry
*Lycium exsertum* Thornbush
*Lycium fremontii* Fremont Thornbush
*Lycium pallidum* Pale Wolfberry
*Lycium torreyi* Torrey Thornbush
*Mimosa biuncifera* Catclaw Mimosa
*Mimosa borealis* Fragrant Mimosa
*Mimosa dysocarpa* Velvetpod Mimosa
*Poliomintha incana* Hoary Rosemarymint
*Psorothamnus schottii* Indigo Bush
*Psorothamnus scoparia* Broom Dalea
*Psorothamnus spinosus* Smoke Tree
*Rhus microphylla* Littleleaf Sumac
*Senna armata* Spiny Senna
*Senna biflora* Two-flowered Senna
*Senna wislizenii* Shrubby Senna
*Tecoma stans* var. *angustata* Yellow Bells
*Thamnosma montana* Turpentine Broom
*Tiquilia greggii* Plume Tiquilia
*Ungnadia speciosa* Mexican-buckeye
*Zizyphus obtusifolia* Gray Thorn

### GROUNDCOVERS

*Ambrosia deltoidea* Bur-sage
*Ambrosia dumosa* White Bur-sage
*Atriplex obovata* Obovateleaf Saltbush
*Bahia absinthifolia* Bahia
*Cissus trifoliata* Arizona Grape Ivy
*Dalea bicolor* var. *argyraea* Silver Dalea
*Dalea formosa* Feather Dalea
*Dalea greggii* Trailing Indigo Bush
*Dyssodia acerosa* Shrubby Dogweed
*Dyssodia pentachaeta* Dogweed
*Eriogonum wrightii* Wright Buckwheat

*Gutierrezia sarothrae* Snakeweed
*Salazaria mexicana* Paperbag Bush
*Tiquilia greggii* Plume Tiquilia
*Zinnia acerosa* Desert Zinnia
*Zinnia grandiflora* Prairie Zinnia

## VINES

*Antigonon leptopus* Queen's Wreath
*Callaeum macroptera* Yellow Orchid-vine
*Cissus trifoliata* Arizona Grape Ivy
*Clematis drummondii* Old Man's Beard
*Janusia gracilis* Slender Janusia
*Marah gilensis* Wild-cucumber
*Mascagnia lilacina* Purple Mascagnia
*Maurandya antirrhiniflora* Snapdragon-vine
*Merremia aurea* Yellow Morning Glory–vine

## GRASSES

*Andropogon barbinodis* Cane Beardgrass
*Aristida purpurea* Purple Threeawn
*Bouteloua curtipendula* Sideoats Grama
*Bouteloua gracilis* Blue Grama
*Diplachne dubia* Green Sprangletop
*Eragrostis intermedia* Plains Lovegrass
*Hilaria rigida* Big Galleta
*Muhlenbergia dumosa* Bamboo-muhly
*Muhlenbergia rigens* Deer Grass
*Oryzopsis hymenoides* Indian Ricegrass
*Scleropogon brevifolius* Burro Grass
*Setaria macrostachya* Plains Bristlegrass
*Sporobolus airoides* Alkali Sacaton
*Sporobolus cryptandrus* Sand Dropseed

## ACCENT PLANTS

*Acacia schaffneri* Twisted Acacia
*Acacia willardiana* White Bark Acacia
*Agave chrysantha* Golden-flowered Agave
*Agave deserti* ssp. *deserti* Desert Agave
*Agave deserti* ssp. *simplex* Desert Agave
*Agave havardiana* Havard Agave
*Agave lechuguilla* Lechuguilla
*Agave neomexicana* New Mexico Agave
*Agave ocahui*
*Agave palmeri* Palmer Agave

*Agave toumeyana* Toumey Agave
*Agave utahensis* Utah Agave
*Agave victoriae-reginae* Queen Victoria
   Agave
*Asclepias subulata* Desert Milkweed
*Carnegiea gigantea* Saguaro
*Ceratoides lanata* Winterfat
*Dasylirion acrotriche* Green Desert Spoon
*Dasylirion leiophyllum* Sotol
*Dasylirion longissimum*
*Dasylirion texanum* Texas Sotol
*Dasylirion wheeleri* Desert Spoon
*Echinocereus engelmannii* Hedgehog Cactus
*Echinocereus stramineus* Spiny Strawberry
   Hedgehog
*Euphorbia antisyphilitica* Candelilla
*Ferocactus cylindraceus* Compass Barrel
*Ferocactus emoryi* Coville Barrel
*Ferocactus wislizenii* Fishhook Barrel
*Fouquieria macdougalii* Mexican Tree
   Ocotillo
*Fouquieria splendens* Ocotillo
*Hechtia texensis* Texas False-agave
*Hesperaloe funifera* Coahuilan Hesperaloe
*Hesperaloe parviflora* Red Hesperaloe
*Lophocereus schottii* Senita
*Lophocereus schottii* forma *monstrosus*
   Totem Pole Cactus
*Nolina bigelovii* Bigelow Nolina
*Nolina erumpens* Beargrass
*Nolina microcarpa* Sacahuista
*Nolina texana* Texas Sacahuista
*Opuntia acanthocarpa* Buckhorn Cholla
*Opuntia basilaris* Beavertail Prickly-pear
*Opuntia bigelovii* Teddy Bear Cholla
*Opuntia chlorotica* Pancake Prickly-pear
*Opuntia echinocarpa* Silver Cholla
*Opuntia engelmannii* Engelmann's Prickly-
   pear
*Opuntia fulgida* Chainfruit Cholla
*Opuntia imbricata* Tree Cholla
*Opuntia leptocaulis* Desert Christmas
   Cholla
*Opuntia macrocentra* Purple Prickly-pear
*Opuntia ramosissima* Diamond Cholla
*Opuntia rufida* Blind Prickly-pear
*Opuntia santa-rita* Santa Rita Prickly-pear
*Opuntia spinosior* Cane Cholla
*Pedilanthus macrocarpus* Slipper Plant

*Psorothamnus spinosus* Smoke Tree
*Stenocereus thurberi* Organ Pipe Cactus
*Yucca baccata* Banana Yucca
*Yucca brevifolia* Joshua Tree
*Yucca elata* Soaptree Yucca
*Yucca faxoniana* Faxon Yucca
*Yucca rigida* Blue Yucca
*Yucca rostrata* Beaked Yucca
*Yucca schidigera* Mojave Yucca
*Yucca treculeana* Torrey Yucca
*Yucca valida* Tree Yucca
*Yucca whipplei* Our Lord's Candle


PLANTS FOR SEASONAL COLOR

*Acacia farnesiana* Sweet Acacia
*Antigonon leptopus* Queen's Wreath
*Argemone platyceras* Prickly-poppy
*Bahia absinthifolia* Bahia
*Baileya multiradiata* Desert-marigold
*Calliandra californica* Baja Fairy Duster
*Calliandra eriophylla* Fairy Duster
*Cercidium floridum* Blue Palo Verde
*Cercidium microphyllum* Littleleaf Palo
  Verde
*Cercidium praecox* Palo Brea
*Chrysactinia mexicana* Damianita
*Chrysothamnus nauseosus* Rabbitbrush
*Dalea frutescens* Black Dalea
*Dalea pulchra* Bush Dalea
*Dalea versicolor* var. *sessilis* Wislizenus
  Dalea
*Datura wrightii* Sacred Datura
*Dyssodia acerosa* Shrubby Dogweed
*Dyssodia pentachaeta* Dogweed
*Echinocereus engelmannii* Hedgehog Cactus
*Echinocereus stramineus* Spiny Strawberry
  Hedgehog
*Encelia farinosa* Brittlebush
*Ericameria laricifolia* Turpentine Bush
*Fouquieria splendens* Ocotillo
*Glandularia gooddingii* Goodding-verbena
*Glandularia wrightii* Wright-verbena
*Guaiacum coulteri* Guayacan
*Gutierrezia sarothrae* Snakeweed
*Hesperaloe parviflora* Red Hesperaloe
*Hibiscus coulteri* Desert Rose-mallow
*Hibiscus denudatus* Paleface Rose-mallow
*Isomeris arborea* Bladderpod

*Justicia californica* Chuparosa
*Leucaena retusa* Golden Ball Lead Tree
*Leucophyllum frutescens* Texas Ranger
*Leucophyllum frutescens* 'Green Cloud'
*Leucophyllum frutescens* var. *compactum*
*Leucophyllum laevigatum* Chihuahuan-sage
*Melampodium leucanthum* Blackfoot Daisy
*Merremia aurea* Yellow Morning Glory–vine
*Oenothera caespitosa* Tufted Evening-
  primrose
*Opuntia basilaris* Beavertail Prickly-pear
*Opuntia engelmannii* Engelmann's Prickly-
  pear
*Opuntia macrocentra* Purple Prickly-pear
*Opuntia santa-rita* Santa Rita Prickly-pear
*Penstemon ambiguus* Bush Penstemon
*Penstemon baccharifolius* Baccharisleaf
  Penstemon
*Penstemon eatonii* Firecracker Penstemon
*Penstemon fendleri* Fendler Penstemon
*Penstemon havardii* Havard Penstemon
*Penstemon palmeri* Palmer Penstemon
*Penstemon parryi* Parry Penstemon
*Penstemon pseudospectabilis* Canyon
  Penstemon
*Penstemon superbus* Superb Penstemon
*Penstemon thurberi* Thurber Penstemon
*Phlox tenuifolia* Desert Phlox
*Psilostrophe cooperi* Paperflower
*Psilostrophe tagetina* Paperflower
*Salvia chamaedryoides* Blue Sage
*Salvia farinacea* Mealycup Sage
*Salvia greggii* Autumn Sage
*Senecio douglasii* var. *longilobus* Threadleaf
  Groundsel
*Senna armata* Spiny Senna
*Senna bauhinioides* Bauhin Senna
*Senna biflora* Two-flowered Senna
*Senna purpusii*
*Senna roemeriana* Roemer Senna
*Senna wislizenii* Shrubby Senna
*Sophora secundiflora* Texas Mountain-laurel
*Sphaeralcea ambigua* Globemallow
*Tecoma stans* var. *angustata* Yellow Bells
*Trixis californica* Trixis
*Viguiera deltoidea* Goldeneye
*Viguiera stenoloba* Skeletonleaf Goldeneye
*Xylorhiza tortifolia* Mojave Aster
*Zinnia grandiflora* Prairie Zinnia

PLANTS WITH FRAGRANT FLOWERS
OR FOLIAGE

*Acacia constricta* Whitethorn Acacia
*Acacia farnesiana* Sweet Acacia
*Aloysia gratissima* Whitebrush
*Aloysia wrightii* Oreganillo
*Bursera microphylla* Elephant Tree
*Chrysactinia mexicana* Damianita
*Condalia globosa* Bitter Condalia
*Condalia warnockii* Warnock Condalia
*Diospyros texana* Texas Persimmon
*Dyssodia acerosa* Shrubby Dogweed
*Dyssodia pentachaeta* Dogweed
*Hyptis emoryi* Desert-lavender
*Larrea tridentata* Creosote Bush
*Leucophyllum laevigatum* Chihuahuan-sage
*Peucephyllum schottii* Desert-fir
*Poliomintha incana* Hoary Rosemarymint
*Psorothamnus scoparia* Broom Dalea
*Salvia greggii* Autumn Sage
*Salvia mohavensis* Mojave Sage
*Sapium biloculare* Mexican Jumping-bean
*Sophora secundiflora* Texas Mountain-laurel
*Ungnadia speciosa* Mexican-buckeye
*Vauquelinia angustifolia* Chisos Rosewood


SHADE-TOLERANT PLANTS

*Acacia millefolia* Santa Rita Acacia
*Aloysia gratissima* Whitebrush
*Aloysia wrightii* Oreganillo
*Ambrosia ambrosioides* Giant Bur-sage
*Andropogon barbinodis* Cane Beardgrass
*Anisacanthus quadrifidus* var. *wrightii*
    Flame Anisacanthus
*Anisacanthus thurberi* Desert-honeysuckle
*Artemisia ludoviciana* Western Mugwort
*Berberis haematocarpa* Red Barberry
*Berberis trifoliolata* Agarita
*Calliandra eriophylla* Fairy Duster
*Cissus trifoliata* Arizona Grape Ivy
*Clematis drummondii* Old Man's Beard
*Dalea bicolor* var. *orcuttiana* Baja Dalea
*Dalea frutescens* Black Dalea
*Dalea greggii* Trailing Indigo Bush
*Dalea versicolor* var. *sessilis* Wislizenus
    Dalea
*Datura wrightii* Sacred Datura

*Dicliptera resupinata* Dicliptera
*Diospyros texana* Texas Persimmon
*Dodonaea viscosa* Hopbush
*Guaiacum angustifolium* Guayacan
*Hechtia texensis* Texas False-agave
*Hesperaloe parviflora* Red Hesperaloe
*Hyptis emoryi* Desert-lavender
*Janusia gracilis* Slender Janusia
*Justicia candicans* Red Justicia
*Leucophyllum candidum* Violet Silverleaf
*Leucophyllum candidum* 'Silver Cloud'
*Leucophyllum laevigatum* Chihuahuan-sage
*Lycium andersonii* Anderson Thornbush
*Lycium berlandieri* Berlandier Wolfberry
*Lycium exsertum* Thornbush
*Lycium fremontii* Fremont Thornbush
*Lycium pallidum* Pale Wolfberry
*Lycium torreyi* Torrey Thornbush
*Lysiloma microphylla* var. *thornberi* Desert-
    fern
*Marah gilensis* Wild-cucumber
*Maurandya antirrhiniflora* Snapdragon-vine
*Melampodium leucanthum* Blackfoot Daisy
*Muhlenbergia dumosa* Bamboo-muhly
*Oryzopsis hymenoides* Indian Ricegrass
*Penstemon baccharifolius* Baccharisleaf
    Penstemon
*Penstemon eatonii* Firecracker Penstemon
*Penstemon fendleri* Fendler Penstemon
*Penstemon havardii* Havard Penstemon
*Penstemon palmeri* Palmer Penstemon
*Penstemon parryi* Parry Penstemon
*Penstemon pseudospectabilis* Canyon
    Penstemon
*Penstemon superbus* Superb Penstemon
*Penstemon thurberi* Thurber Penstemon
*Plumbago scandens* Plumbago
*Rhus microphylla* Littleleaf Sumac
*Ruellia peninsularis* Ruellia
*Salvia greggii* Autumn Sage
*Senna biflora* Two-flowered Senna
*Simmondsia chinensis* Jojoba
*Viguiera stenoloba* Skeletonleaf Goldeneye


PLANTS FOR POOLSIDE

*Acacia berlandieri* Guajillo
*Artemisia filifolia* Sand Sagebrush
*Artemisia ludoviciana* Western Mugwort

*Asclepias linaria* Pineleaf Milkweed
*Asclepias subulata* Desert Milkweed
*Baccharis sarothroides* Desert Broom
*Bahia absinthifolia* Bahia
*Baileya multiradiata* Desert-marigold
*Buddleia marrubifolia* Woolly Butterfly Bush
*Callaeum macroptera* Yellow Orchid-vine
*Calliandra californica* Baja Fairy Duster
*Chrysactinia mexicana* Damianita
*Cissus trifoliata* Arizona Grape Ivy
*Cordia parvifolia* Littleleaf Cordia
*Dalea bicolor* var. *argyraea* Silver Dalea
*Dalea bicolor* var. *orcuttiana* Baja Dalea
*Dalea greggii* Trailing Indigo Bush
*Dalea pulchra* Bush Dalea
*Dalea versicolor* var. *sessilis* Wislizenus Dalea
*Dicliptera resupinata* Dicliptera
*Diospyros texana* Texas Persimmon
*Dodonaea viscosa* Hopbush
*Dyssodia acerosa* Shrubby Dogweed
*Dyssodia pentachaeta* Dogweed
*Encelia farinosa* Brittlebush
*Ericameria laricifolia* Turpentine Bush
*Erythrina flabelliformis* Southwest Coral Bean
*Gossypium harknessii* San Marcos–hibiscus
*Guaiacum angustifolium* Guayacan
*Guaiacum coulteri* Guayacan
*Hesperaloe parviflora* Red Hesperaloe
*Jatropha cuneata* Leatherplant
*Justicia candicans* Red Justicia
*Leucophyllum candidum* Violet Silverleaf
*Leucophyllum candidum* 'Silver Cloud'
*Leucophyllum frutescens* 'Green Cloud'
*Leucophyllum frutescens* var. *compactum*
*Leucophyllum laevigatum* Chihuahuan-sage
*Lysiloma microphylla* var. *thornberi* Desert-fern
*Melampodium leucanthum* Blackfoot Daisy
*Merremia aurea* Yellow Morning Glory–vine
*Muhlenbergia dumosa* Bamboo-muhly
*Nolina erumpens* Beargrass
*Nolina microcarpa* Sacahuista
*Nolina texana* Texas Sacahuista
*Oenothera caespitosa* Tufted Evening-primrose
*Olneya tesota* Ironwood
*Penstemon baccharifolius* Baccharisleaf Penstemon

*Penstemon eatonii* Firecracker Penstemon
*Penstemon fendleri* Fendler Penstemon
*Penstemon havardii* Havard Penstemon
*Penstemon palmeri* Palmer Penstemon
*Penstemon parryi* Parry Penstemon
*Penstemon pseudospectabilis* Canyon Penstemon
*Penstemon superbus* Superb Penstemon
*Penstemon thurberi* Thurber Penstemon
*Phlox tenuifolia* Desert Phlox
*Psilostrophe cooperi* Paperflower
*Psilostrophe tagetina*
*Rhamnus californica* ssp. *ursina* California Buckthorn
*Rhus ovata* Sugar Sumac
*Rhus virens* Evergreen Sumac
*Ruellia peninsularis* Ruellia
*Ruellia californica* Ruellia
*Salvia greggii* Autumn Sage
*Sapium biloculare* Mexican Jumping-bean
*Senecio douglasii* var. *longilobus* Threadleaf Groundsel
*Senna biflora* Two-flowered Senna
*Senna covesii* Desert Senna
*Senna lindheimeriana* Lindheimer Senna
*Senna purpusii*
*Simmondsia chinensis* Jojoba
*Sophora secundiflora* Texas Mountain-laurel
*Stegnosperma halimifolium* Tinta
*Tiquilia greggii* Plume Tiquilia
*Vauquelinia angustifolia* Chisos Rosewood
*Vauquelinia californica* Arizona Rosewood
*Viguiera stenoloba* Skeletonleaf Goldeneye
*Zinnia acerosa* Desert Zinnia
*Zinnia grandiflora* Prairie Zinnia

SPINELESS PLANTS

*Acacia millefolia* Santa Rita Acacia
*Acacia willardiana* White Bark Acacia
*Aloysia wrightii* Oreganillo
*Ambrosia ambrosioides* Giant Bur-sage
*Ambrosia deltoidea* Bur-sage
*Andropogon barbinodis* Cane Beardgrass
*Anisacanthus quadrifidus* var. *wrightii* Flame Anisacanthus
*Anisacanthus thurberi* Desert-honeysuckle
*Antigonon leptopus* Queen's Wreath
*Aristida purpurea* Purple Threeawn

*Artemisia filifolia* Sand Sagebrush
*Artemisia ludoviciana* Western Mugwort
*Asclepias linaria* Pineleaf Milkweed
*Asclepias subulata* Desert Milkweed
*Atriplex acanthocarpa* Tubercled Saltbush
*Atriplex canescens* Fourwing Saltbush
*Atriplex lentiformis* Quail Brush
*Atriplex obovata* Obovateleaf Saltbush
*Baccharis sarothroides* Desert Broom
*Bahia absinthifolia* Bahia
*Baileya multiradiata* Desert-marigold
*Bouteloua curtipendula* Sideoats Grama
*Bouteloua gracilis* Blue Grama
*Buddleia marrubifolia* Woolly Butterfly Bush
*Bursera microphylla* Elephant Tree
*Callaeum macroptera* Yellow Orchid-vine
*Calliandra californica* Baja Fairy Duster
*Calliandra eriophylla* Fairy Duster
*Ceratoides lanata* Winterfat
*Chilopsis linearis* Desert-willow
*Chrysactinia mexicana* Damianita
*Chrysothamnus nauseosus* Rabbitbrush
*Cissus trifoliata* Arizona Grape Ivy
*Clematis drummondii* Old Man's Beard
*Cordia parvifolia* Littleleaf Cordia
*Coursetia glandulosa* Coursetia
*Dalea bicolor* var. *argyraea* Silver Dalea
*Dalea bicolor* var. *orcuttiana* Baja Dalea
*Dalea formosa* Feather Dalea
*Dalea frutescens* Black Dalea
*Dalea greggii* Trailing Indigo Bush
*Dalea pulchra* Bush Dalea
*Dalea versicolor* var. *sessilis* Wislizenus
  Dalea
*Datura wrightii* Sacred Datura
*Dicliptera resupinata* Dicliptera
*Diospyros texana* Texas Persimmon
*Diplachne dubia* Green Sprangletop
*Dodonaea viscosa* Hopbush
*Dyssodia acerosa* Shrubby Dogweed
*Dyssodia pentachaeta* Dogweed
*Encelia farinosa* Brittlebush
*Encelia frutescens* Green Brittlebush
*Ephedra antisyphilitica* Joint-fir
*Ephedra aspera* Joint-fir
*Ephedra californica* Joint-fir
*Ephedra nevadensis* Joint-fir
*Ephedra trifurca* Joint-fir
*Ephedra viridis* Joint-fir

*Eragrostis intermedia* Plains Lovegrass
*Ericameria laricifolia* Turpentine Bush
*Eriogonum fasciculatum* var. *poliofolium*
  Flattop Buckwheat
*Eriogonum wrightii* Wright Buckwheat
*Euphorbia antisyphilitica* Candelilla
*Fallugia paradoxa* Apache Plume
*Flourensia cernua* Tarbush
*Forestiera neomexicana* Desert-olive
*Fraxinus greggii* Gregg Ash
*Garrya wrightii* Wright Silktassel
*Glandularia gooddingii* Goodding-verbena
*Glandularia wrightii* Wright-verbena
*Gossypium harknessii* San Marcos–hibiscus
*Guaiacum angustifolium* Guayacan
*Guaiacum coulteri* Guayacan
*Gutierrezia sarothrae* Snakeweed
*Hesperaloe parviflora* Red Hesperaloe
*Hilaria rigida* Big Galleta
*Hymenoclea monogyra* Burrobrush
*Hymenoclea salsola* Burrobrush
*Hyptis emoryi* Desert-lavender
*Isomeris arborea* Bladderpod
*Janusia gracilis* Slender Janusia
*Jatropha cardiophylla* Limber Bush
*Jatropha cuneata* Leatherplant
*Jatropha dioica* Leatherstem
*Justicia californica* Chuparosa
*Justicia candicans* Red Justicia
*Larrea tridentata* Creosote Bush
*Leucaena retusa* Golden Ball Lead Tree
*Leucophyllum candidum* Violet Silverleaf
*Leucophyllum candidum* 'Silver Cloud'
*Leucophyllum frutescens* Texas Ranger
*Leucophyllum frutescens* 'Green Cloud'
*Leucophyllum frutescens* 'White Cloud'
*Leucophyllum frutescens* var. *compactum*
*Leucophyllum laevigatum* Chihuahuan-sage
*Leucophyllum minus* Big Bend Silverleaf
*Leucophyllum zygophyllum* Blue Ranger
*Lophocereus schottii* forma *monstrosus*
  Totem Pole Cactus
*Lotus rigidus* Deer-vetch
*Lysiloma candida* Palo Blanco
*Lysiloma microphylla* var. *thornberi* Desert-
  fern
*Marah gilensis* Wild-cucumber
*Mascagnia lilacina* Purple Mascagnia
*Maurandya antirrhiniflora* Snapdragon-vine

*Melampodium leucanthum* Blackfoot Daisy
*Menodora scabra* Rough Menodora
*Merremia aurea* Yellow Morning Glory – vine
*Mortonia scabrella* Rough Mortonia
*Muhlenbergia dumosa* Bamboo-muhly
*Muhlenbergia rigens* Deer Grass
*Nolina erumpens* Beargrass
*Nolina microcarpa* Sacahuista
*Nolina texana* Texas Sacahuista
*Oenothera caespitosa* Tufted Evening-
primrose
*Oryzopsis hymenoides* Indian Ricegrass
*Parthenium argentatum* Guayule
*Parthenium incanum* Mariola
*Pedilanthus macrocarpus* Slipper Plant
*Penstemon ambiguus* Bush Penstemon
*Penstemon baccharifolius* Baccharisleaf
Penstemon
*Penstemon eatonii* Firecracker Penstemon
*Penstemon fendleri* Fendler Penstemon
*Penstemon havardii* Havard Penstemon
*Penstemon palmeri* Palmer Penstemon
*Penstemon parryi* Parry Penstemon
*Penstemon pseudospectabilis* Canyon
Penstemon
*Penstemon superbus* Superb Penstemon
*Penstemon thurberi* Thurber Penstemon
*Peucephyllum schottii* Desert-fir
*Phlox tenuifolia* Desert Phlox
*Plumbago scandens* Plumbago
*Poliomintha incana* Hoary Rosemarymint
*Psilostrophe cooperi* Paperflower
*Psilostrophe tagetina* Paperflower
*Psorothamnus scoparia* Broom Dalea
*Rhamnus californica* ssp. *ursina* California
Buckthorn
*Rhus ovata* Sugar Sumac
*Rhus virens* Evergreen Sumac
*Ruellia peninsularis* Ruellia
*Ruellia californica* Ruellia
*Salazaria mexicana* Paperbag Bush
*Salvia apiana* White Sage
*Salvia chamaedryoides* Blue Sage
*Salvia dorrii* var. *dorrii* Desert Sage
*Salvia farinacea* Mealycup Sage
*Salvia greggii* Autumn Sage
*Salvia mohavensis* Mojave Sage
*Sapium biloculare* Mexican Jumping-bean
*Scleropogon brevifolius* Burro Grass

*Senecio douglasii* var. *longilobus* Threadleaf
Groundsel
*Senna bauhinioides* Bauhin Senna
*Senna biflora* Two-flowered Senna
*Senna covesii* Desert Senna
*Senna lindheimeriana* Lindheimer Senna
*Senna purpusii*
*Senna roemeriana* Roemer Senna
*Senna wislizenii* Shrubby Senna
*Setaria macrostachya* Plains Bristlegrass
*Simmondsia chinensis* Jojoba
*Sophora secundiflora* Texas Mountain-laurel
*Sphaeralcea ambigua* Globemallow
*Sporobolus airoides* Alkali Sacaton
*Sporobolus cryptandrus* Sand Dropseed
*Stegnosperma halimifolium* Tinta
*Tecoma stans* var. *angustata* Yellow Bells
*Tiquilia greggii* Plume Tiquilia
*Trixis californica* Trixis
*Ungnadia speciosa* Mexican-buckeye
*Vauquelinia angustifolia* Chisos Rosewood
*Vauquelinia californica* Arizona Rosewood
*Viguiera deltoidea* Goldeneye
*Zinnia acerosa* Desert Zinnia
*Zinnia grandiflora* Prairie Zinnia

## PLANTS FOR SCREENING

*Acacia berlandieri* Guajillo
*Acacia farnesiana* Sweet Acacia
*Acacia wrightii* Wright Acacia
*Berberis trifoliolata* Agarita
*Canotia holacantha* Crucifixion Thorn
*Celtis pallida* Desert Hackberry
*Cercidium floridum* Blue Palo Verde
*Cercidium microphyllum* Littleleaf Palo
Verde
*Condalia globosa* Bitter Condalia
*Condalia warnockii* Warnock Condalia
*Diospyros texana* Texas Persimmon
*Dodonaea viscosa* Hopbush
*Fallugia paradoxa* Apache Plume
*Fraxinus greggii* Gregg Ash
*Garrya wrightii* Wright Silktassel
*Guaiacum angustifolium* Guayacan
*Hyptis emoryi* Desert-lavender
*Leucophyllum frutescens* Texas Ranger
*Leucophyllum frutescens* 'Green Cloud'
*Leucophyllum frutescens* 'White Cloud'

*Lysiloma microphylla* var. *thornberi* Desert-fern
*Mortonia scabrella* Rough Mortonia
*Olneya tesota* Ironwood
*Quercus turbinella* Scrub Oak
*Rhamnus californica* ssp. *ursina* California Buckthorn
*Rhus ovata* Sugar Sumac
*Rhus virens* Evergreen Sumac
*Sapium biloculare* Mexican Jumping-bean
*Simmondsia chinensis* Jojoba
*Sophora secundiflora* Texas Mountain-laurel
*Stegnosperma halimifolium* Tinta
*Vauquelinia angustifolia* Chisos Rosewood
*Vauquelinia californica* Arizona Rosewood

## PLANTS FOR ATTRACTING WILDLIFE

*Acacia constricta* Whitethorn Acacia
*Acacia greggii* Catclaw Acacia
*Acacia wrightii* Wright Acacia
*Anisacanthus quadrifidus* var. *wrightii* Flame Anisacanthus
*Anisacanthus thurberi* Desert-honeysuckle
*Asclepias linaria* Pineleaf Milkweed
*Asclepias subulata* Desert Milkweed
*Atriplex canescens* Fourwing Saltbush
*Atriplex lentiformis* Quail Brush
*Atriplex polycarpa* Desert Saltbush
*Berberis haematocarpa* Red Barberry
*Berberis trifoliolata* Agarita
*Bouteloua curtipendula* Sideoats Grama
*Bouteloua gracilis* Blue Grama
*Buddleia marrubifolia* Woolly Butterfly Bush
*Bursera microphylla* Elephant Tree
*Calliandra californica* Baja Fairy Duster
*Calliandra eriophylla* Fairy Duster
*Carnegiea gigantea* Saguaro
*Celtis pallida* Desert Hackberry
*Cercidium floridum* Blue Palo Verde
*Cercidium microphyllum* Littleleaf Palo Verde
*Cercidium praecox* Palo Brea
*Chilopsis linearis* Desert-willow
*Condalia globosa* Bitter Condalia
*Condalia warnockii* Warnock Condalia
*Diospyros texana* Texas Persimmon
*Dodonaea viscosa* Hopbush
*Encelia farinosa* Brittlebush

*Encelia frutescens* Green Brittlebush
*Eriogonum fasciculatum* var. *poliofolium* Flattop Buckwheat
*Erythrina flabelliformis* Southwest Coral Bean
*Fallugia paradoxa* Apache Plume
*Ferocactus cylindraceus* Compass Barrel
*Ferocactus wislizenii* Fishhook Barrel
*Forestiera neomexicana* Desert-olive
*Fouquieria splendens* Ocotillo
*Garrya wrightii* Wright Silktassel
*Glandularia gooddingii* Goodding-verbena
*Glandularia wrightii* Wright-verbena
*Hesperaloe parviflora* Red Hesperaloe
*Hyptis emoryi* Desert-lavender
*Justicia californica* Chuparosa
*Justicia candicans* Red Justicia
*Koeberlinia spinosa* Allthorn
*Lycium andersonii* Anderson Thornbush
*Lycium berlandieri* Berlandier Wolfberry
*Lycium exsertum* Thornbush
*Lycium fremontii* Fremont Thornbush
*Lycium pallidum* Pale Wolfberry
*Lycium torreyi* Torrey Thornbush
*Mimosa biuncifera* Catclaw Mimosa
*Opuntia engelmannii* Engelmann's Prickly-pear
*Opuntia fulgida* Chainfruit Cholla
*Opuntia imbricata* Tree Cholla
*Opuntia spinosior* Cane Cholla
*Oryzopsis hymenoides* Indian Ricegrass
*Penstemon baccharifolius* Baccharisleaf Penstemon
*Penstemon eatonii* Firecracker Penstemon
*Penstemon fendleri* Fendler Penstemon
*Penstemon havardii* Havard Penstemon
*Penstemon palmeri* Palmer Penstemon
*Penstemon parryi* Parry Penstemon
*Penstemon pseudospectabilis* Canyon Penstemon
*Penstemon superbus* Superb Penstemon
*Penstemon thurberi* Thurber Penstemon
*Prosopis glandulosa* var. *glandulosa* Honey Mesquite
*Prosopis velutina* Velvet Mesquite
*Quercus turbinella* Scrub Oak
*Rhamnus californica* ssp. *ursina* California Buckthorn
*Rhus microphylla* Littleleaf Sumac
*Salvia greggii* Autumn Sage
*Senna lindheimeriana* Lindheimer Senna
*Zizyphus obtusifolia* Gray Thorn

# *Appendix B. Resources*

NATIONAL

National Wildflower Research Center
2600 FM 973 North
Austin, TX 78725
(512) 929-3600
*The National Wildflower Research Center is
a non-profit research and educational
organization committed to the preservation
and reestablishment of native wildflowers,
grasses, shrubs, and trees.*

ARIZONA

Arizona Native Plant Society
P.O. Box 41206, Sun Station
Tucson, AZ 85717

Arizona-Sonora Desert Museum
2021 North Kinney Road
Tucson, AZ 85743
(602) 883-2702 (information recording)
(602) 883-1380

Boyce Thompson Southwestern Arboretum
P.O. Box AB
Superior, AZ 85273
*Located 1 mile west of Superior on Hwy. 60*
(602) 689-2811 (information recording)
(602) 689-2723

Desert Botanical Garden
1201 North Galvin Parkway
Phoenix, AZ 85008
(602) 941-1217 (information recording)
(602) 941-1225

Xeriscape Demonstration Garden at Mesa
Community College
1833 West Southern Avenue
Mesa, AZ 85202
(602) 461-7107

Superstition Springs Center
6555 East Southern Avenue
Mesa, AZ 85206
(602) 832-0212

Tohono Chul Park
7366 North Paseo Del Norte
Tucson, AZ 85704
(602) 575-8468 (information recording)
(602) 742-6455

Tucson Botanical Gardens
2150 North Alvernon Way
Tucson, AZ 85712
(602) 326-9255 (information recording)
(602) 326-9686

CALIFORNIA

California Native Plant Society
909 12th Street, Suite 116
Sacramento, CA 95814
(916) 447-2677

The Living Desert
47900 South Portola Avenue
Palm Desert, CA 92260
(619) 346-5694

Anza-Borrego Desert State Park
P.O. Box 299
Borrego Springs, CA 92004
(619) 767-4684 (information recording)
(619) 767-4205 (visitor center)
(619) 767-5311 (administration office)

Moorten Botanical Garden
1702 South Palm Canyon Drive
Palm Springs, CA 92264
(619) 327-6555

NEVADA

Ethel M. Chocolates Botanic Garden
2 Cactus Garden Drive
Henderson, NV 89014
(702) 435-2641

University of Nevada, Las Vegas Arboretum
4505 Maryland Parkway
Las Vegas, NV 89154
(702) 739-3392

Desert Demonstration Gardens
3701 Alta Drive
3700 W. Charleston (mailing address)
Las Vegas, NV 89153
(702) 258-3205

NEW MEXICO

Native Plant Society of New Mexico
1302 Canyon Road
Alamogordo, NM 88310
(505) 434-3041

Living Desert State Park
1504 Skyline Drive
Carlsbad, NM 88220
(505) 887-5516

New Mexico State University Botanical
Garden
Department of Agronomy & Horticulture
Box 3Q
Las Cruces, NM 88003
*Located at the corner of Hwy. 85 and
University*
(505) 646-3638

TEXAS

Chihuahuan Desert Research Institute
P.O. Box 1334
Alpine, TX 79831
(915) 837-8370

Texas A & M Research Center
1380 A & M Circle
El Paso, TX 79927
(915) 859-9111

Barton Warnock Environmental Education
Center
Highway Contract 70, Box 475
Terlingua, TX 79852
*Located 1 mile east of Lajitas on Farm
Road 170*
(915) 424-3327

El Paso Native Plant Society
c/o James F. George
6804 Tolvea
El Paso, TX 79912
(915) 541-5588

Native Plant Society of Texas
P.O. Box 891
Georgetown, TX 78627
(512) 863-9685

UTAH

Utah Native Plant Society
P.O. Box 520041
Salt Lake City, UT 84152
(801) 581-3744

# Bibliography

Ajilvsgi, Geyata. *Wildflowers of Texas.* Bryan, TX: Shearer Publishing, 1984.

Arizona Native Plant Society, Urban Landscape Committee. *Desert Ground Covers and Vines.* Tucson: Arizona Native Plant Society, 1989.

———. *Desert Shrubs.* Tucson: Arizona Native Plant Society, Trees for Tucson/ Global ReLeaf, 1990.

———. *Desert Trees.* Tucson: Arizona Native Plant Society, 1991.

———. *Desert Wildflowers.* Tucson: Arizona Native Plant Society, 1991.

Backeberg, Curt. *Cactus Lexicon.* Poole, England: Blandford Press Ltd., 1976.

Benson, Lyman, and Robert A. Darrow. *Trees and Shrubs of the Southwestern Deserts.* Tucson: University of Arizona Press, 1981.

Bowden, Laura. "Native Plant Revegetation." *Wildflower* 4, no. 3 (1991): 62–67.

Bowers, Janice E. "Catastrophic Freezes in the Sonoran Desert." *Desert Plants* 2, no. 4 (1980–1981): 232–236.

Bowers, Janice Emily. *100 Desert Wild-flowers of the Southwest.* Tucson: Southwest Parks And Monuments Association, 1989.

Brown, David E. "Chihuahuan Desertscrub." *Desert Plants* 4, nos. 1–4 (1982): 169–178.

Correll, Donovan Stewart, Marshall Conring Johnston, and collaborators. *Manual of the Vascular Plants of Texas.* Renner: Texas Research Foundation, 1970. Reprint: University of Texas at Dallas, 1979.

Coyle, Jeanette, and Norman C. Roberts. *A Field Guide to the Common and Inter-esting Plants of Baja California.* La Jolla, CA: Natural History Publishing Co., 1975.

Crampton, Beecher. *Grasses in California.* Berkeley: University of California Press, 1974.

Crosswhite, C. D., and C. Randall. "Damage to Mescal Bean (*Sophora secundiflora*) by a Pyralid Moth (*Uresiphita reversalis*)." *Desert Plants* 7, no. 1 (1985): 32.

Daniel, Thomas F. "The Acanthaceae of the Southwestern United States." *Desert Plants* 5, no. 4 (1984): 162–179.

Desert Botanical Garden Staff. *Arizona Highways Presents Desert Wildflowers.* Phoenix: Arizona Department of Transportation, State of Arizona, 1988.

Desert Plants Editorial Staff. "The Severe Freeze of 1978–79 in the Southwestern United States." *Desert Plants* 1, no. 1 (1979): 37–39.

Dinchak, Ronald K. *An Illustrated Guide to Landscape Shrubs of Southern Arizona.* Mesa, AZ: 3D Publishers, 1981.

———. *An Illustrated Guide to Landscape Trees of Southern Arizona.* Mesa, AZ: 3D Publishers, 1981.

Dodge, Natt N. *100 Desert Wildflowers in Natural Color.* Globe, AZ: Southwestern Monuments Association, 1963.

Dodge, Natt N., and Jeanne R. Janish. *Flowers of the Southwest Deserts.* Tucson: Southwest Parks and Monuments Association, 1985.

Duffield, Mary Rose, and Warren Jones. *Plants for Dry Climates.* Tucson: H.P. Books, 1981.

Felger, Richard S. "Vegetation and Flora of the Gran Desierto, Sonora, Mexico." *Desert Plants* 2, no. 2 (1980): 87–114.

Fischer, Pierre C. *70 Common Cacti of the Southwest.* Tucson: Southwest Parks and Monuments Association, 1989.

Gass, Ron. "Mojave and Sonoran Desert Plants for Landscaping." *Wildflower* 4, no. 3 (1991): 40–43.

Gates, Howard E. "Interesting Things in Lower California." *Cactus and Succulent Journal* 3, no. 2 (August 1931): 38.

Gentry, Howard Scott. *Agaves of Conti-nental North America.* Tucson: University of Arizona Press, 1982.

Gould, Frank W. *Grasses of the Southwestern United States.* University of Arizona Biological Sciences Bulletin #7. Tucson: University of Arizona Press, 1951.

Haustein, Eric. *The Cactus Handbook.* Secaucus, NJ: Chartwell Books, Inc., 1988.

Henrickson, James, and L. David Flyr. "Systematics of *Leucophyllum* and *Eremogeton* (Scrophulariaceae)." *SIDA, Contributions to Botany* II, no. 2 (December 1985): 107–167.

Humphrey, Robert R. *Arizona Range Grasses.* Tucson: University of Arizona Press, 1970.

Jaeger, Edmund C. *Desert Wild Flowers.* Stanford: Stanford University Press, 1941.

James, Dan. "Native Grasses in Desert Revegetation." *Wildflower* 4, no. 3 (1991): 44–46.

Johnson, Matthew B. "Summer Salvage of Native Shrubby Composites in Arizona." *Plant Press* 13, no. 2 (1989): 4–5.

Jones, Warren D. "Effects of the 1978 Freeze on Native Plants of Sonora, Mexico." *Desert Plants* 1, no. 1 (1979): 33–36.

———. "New Ground Cover Releases." *Desert Plants* 2, no. 2 (1980): 127–130.

Kearney, Thomas Henry, Robert H. Peebles, and collaborators. *Arizona Flora.* Berkeley: University of California Press, 1951.

Kinnison, William A. "Preliminary Evaluation of Cold-hardiness in Desert Landscaping Plants at Central Arizona College." *Desert Plants* 1, no. 1 (1979): 29–32.

Lamb, Samuel H. *Woody Plants of the Southwest.* Santa Fe: Sunstone Press, 1975.

Lampe, Kenneth F. "Contact Dermatitis from Sonoran Desert Plants." *Desert Plants* 8, no. 1 (1986): 32–37.

Larson, Peggy. *The Deserts of the Southwest.* San Francisco: Sierra Club Books, 1977.

Lehr, J. Harry. *A Catalogue of the Flora of Arizona.* Phoenix: Desert Botanical Garden, 1978.

Lenz, Lee W., and John Dourley. *California Native Trees & Shrubs.* Claremont, CA: Rancho Santa Ana Botanic Garden, 1981.

Loughmiller, Campbell, and Lynn Loughmiller. *Texas Wildflowers.* Austin: University of Texas Press, 1984.

MacMahon, James A. *Deserts.* New York: Alfred A. Knopf, 1985.

Martin, William C., and Charles R. Hutchins. *A Flora of New Mexico.* 2 vols. Vaduz, Germany: J. Cramer, 1980–1981.

McAuliffe, Joseph R. "Desert Environments." *Wildflower* 4, no. 3 (1991): 6–14.

McGinnies, William G. *Flowering Periods for Common Desert Plants.* Tucson: Office of Arid Lands Studies, College of Agriculture, University of Arizona, n.d.

McPherson, E. Gregory, and Charles Sacamano. *Southwestern Landscaping That Saves Energy and Water.* Tucson: Cooperative Extension, College of Agriculture, University of Arizona, 1989.

Mockel, Henry R., and Beverly Mockel. *Mockel's Desert Flower Notebook.* Twentynine Palms, CA: Henry R. Mockel and Beverly Mockel, 1971.

Miller, George O. *Landscaping with Native Plants of Texas and the Southwest.* Stillwater, OK: Voyageur Press, 1991.

Miller, James D. *Design and the Desert Environment: Landscape Architecture and the American Southwest.* Tucson: Office of Arid Lands Studies, University of Arizona, 1978.

Munz, Philip A. *California Desert Wildflowers.* Berkeley: University of California Press, 1974.

———. *A Flora of Southern California.* Berkeley: University of California Press, 1962.

National Wildflower Research Center. *The National Wildflower Research Center's Wildflower Handbook.* Austin: Texas Monthly Press, 1989.

New Mexico State University Cooperative Extension Service. "Native Plants for New Mexico Landscapes." *Circular* 513 (1984): 13.

Niehaus, Theodore F., Charles L. Ripper, and Virginia Savage. *A Field Guide to Southwestern and Texas Wildflowers.* Boston: Houghton Mifflin, 1984.

Nokes, Jill. *How to Grow Native Plants of Texas and the Southwest*. Austin: Texas Monthly Press, 1986.

Ottesen, Carole. *Ornamental Grasses: The Amber Wave*. New York: McGraw-Hill Publishing Co., 1989.

Pearce, E. A., and C. G. Smith. *The Times Books World Weather Guide*. New York: New York Times Book Co., Inc., 1984.

Perry, Bob. *Trees and Shrubs for Dry California Landscapes*. San Dimas, CA: Land Design Publishing, 1987.

Phillips, Judith. *Southwestern Landscaping with Native Plants*. Santa Fe: Museum of New Mexico Press, 1987.

Pilz, Erma, and Jean Heflin. *The Beautiful Beardtongues of New Mexico*. Albuquerque: Jack Rabbit Press, 1990.

*Plants of the Southwest. 1991 Catalog*. Santa Fe: Plants of the Southwest, 1991.

Powell, A. Michael. *Trees and Shrubs of Trans-Pecos Texas*. Big Bend National Park: Big Bend Natural History Association, Inc., 1988.

Rand McNally & Company. *Rand McNally Road Atlas*. Chicago: Rand McNally & Co., 1982.

Ricketts, Harold William. *Wildflowers of the United States*, vol. 4, *The Southwestern States*. New York: McGraw-Hill Publishing Co., 1966.

Roberts, Norman C. *Baja California Plant Field Guide*. La Jolla, CA: Natural History Publishing Co., 1989.

Ruffner, James A., and Frank E. Blair, eds. *Weather of U.S. Cities*, vols. 1–2. Michigan: Gale Research Co., 1987.

Sacamano, Charles M., and Warren D. Jones. *Native Trees and Shrubs for Landscape Use in the Desert Southwest*. Tucson: College of Agriculture, Cooperative Extension Service, University of Arizona, 1976.

"The Severe Freeze of 1978–79 in the Southwestern United States." *Desert Plants* 1, no. 1 (1979): 37–39.

Shreve, Forrest, and Ira L. Wiggins. *Vegetation and Flora of the Sonoran Desert*. Stanford: Stanford University Press, 1964.

Spellenberg, Richard. *The Audubon Society Field Guide to North American Wildflowers, Western Region*. New York: Alfred A. Knopf, 1979.

Staff of the Liberty Hyde Bailey Hortorium. *Hortus Third*. New York: Macmillan Publishing Co., 1976.

Standley, Paul Carpenter. *Trees and Shrubs of Mexico*. Washington: Smithsonian Institution, 1961.

Starr, Greg. "Dalea—Horticulturally Promising Legumes for Desert Landscapes." *The Plant Press* 15, nos. 3–4 (1991): 3.

———. "Introductions of Little Known and Seldom Grown Species." *Desert Plants* 9, no. 1 (1988): 3–5, 28–31.

———. "New World Salvias for Cultivation in Southern Arizona." *Desert Plants* 7, no. 4 (1985): 167–171, 184–189, 204–207.

Sunset Editorial Staff. "The Unthirsty 100." *Sunset* (October 1988): 74–83.

Tipton, Jimmy L. "Chihuahuan Desert Landscape Plants." *Wildflower* 4, no. 3 (1991): 54–61.

———. *Desert Trees and Shrubs: Sources and Cultural Practices*. Alpine, TX: Chihuahuan Desert Research Institute, n.d.

Tucson Citizen. *Southern Arizona Wild Flower Guide*. Tucson: Tucson Citizen, 1972.

Turner, Raymond M. "Mohave Desertscrub." *Desert Plants* 4, nos. 1–4 (1982): 157–162.

Turner, Raymond M., and David E. Brown. "Sonoran Desertscrub." *Desert Plants* 4, nos. 1–4 (1982): 182–189.

United States Bureau of the Census. *Statistical Abstract of the United States, 1990*.

Vines, Robert A. *Trees, Shrubs, and Woody Vines of the Southwest*. Austin: University of Texas Press, 1960.

Ward, Grace B., and Onas M. Ward. *Desert Wildflowers*. Palm Desert, CA: Living Desert Association, 1978.

Waring, Gwen. "Creosote Bush: The Ultimate Desert Survivor." *Agave* 2, no. 1 (Summer 1986): 13.

Warnock, Barton H. *Wildflowers of the Big Bend Country, Texas*. Alpine, TX: Sul Ross State University, 1970.

———. *Wildflowers of the Guadalupe Mountains and the Sand Dune Country, Texas*. Alpine, TX: Sul Ross State University, 1974.

Wasowski, Sally, and Andy Wasowski. *Native Texas Plants*. Austin: Texas Monthly Press, 1988.

Wiggins, Ira Loren. *Flora of Baja California*. Stanford: Stanford University Press, 1980.

Williamson, Joseph F., et al., eds. *Sunset Western Garden Book*. Menlo Park, CA: Lane Publishing Co., 1988.

# Index

Bold type indicates an illustration or
photograph.